GENIUSES ◆ OF ◆ ART

SOROLLA

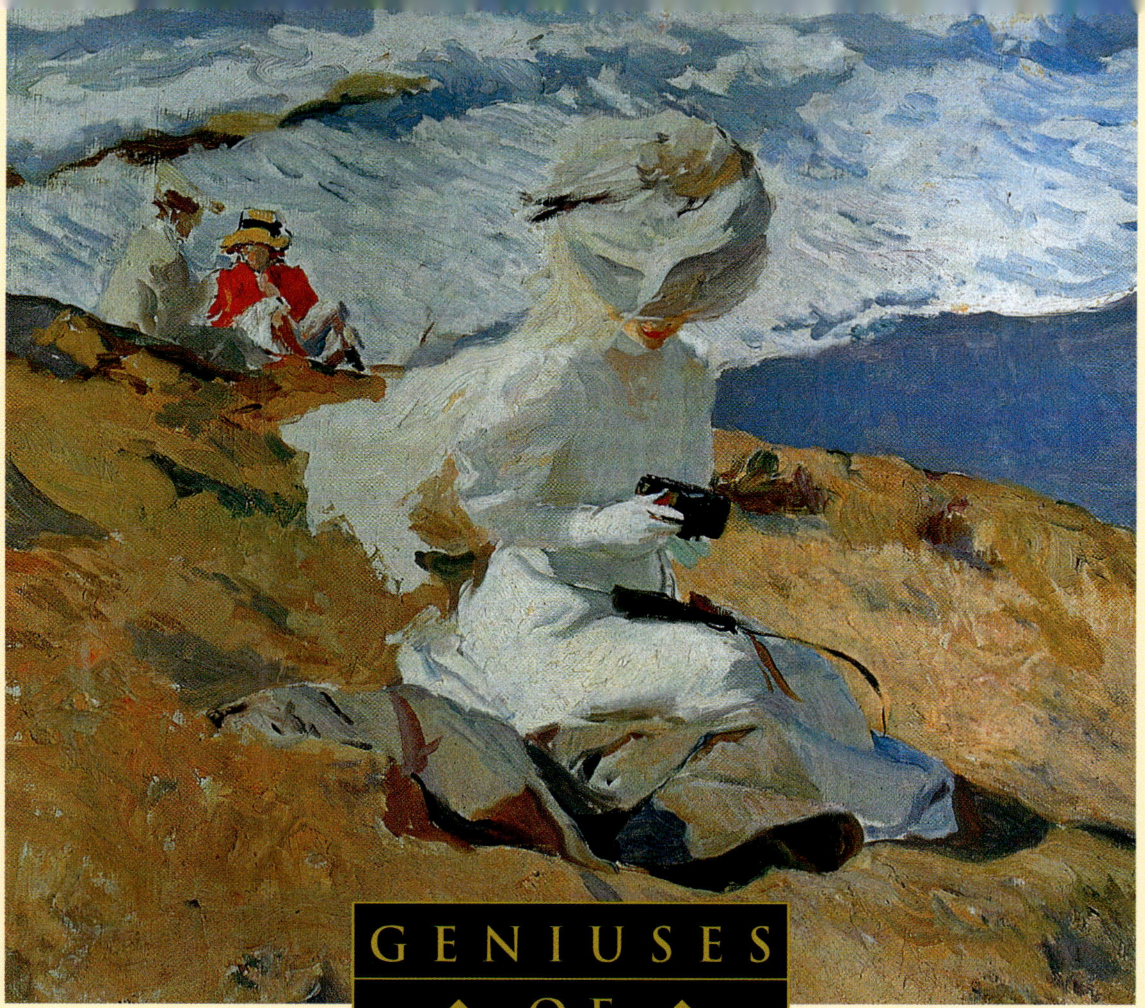

GENIUSES
◆ OF ◆
ART

SOROLLA

susaeta

Scientific Co-ordination:
Juan-Ramón Triadó Tur
Titular Professor of History of Art
at the University of Barcelona

Text:
Laura García Sánchez
Doctor in History of Art

Translated by:
Carole Patton

Cover Design:
Paniagua & Calleja

The Editors wish to thank
the **Museo Sorolla** and the **Fundación Museo Sorolla**
for their collaboration and cooperation in making this book.

CONTENTS

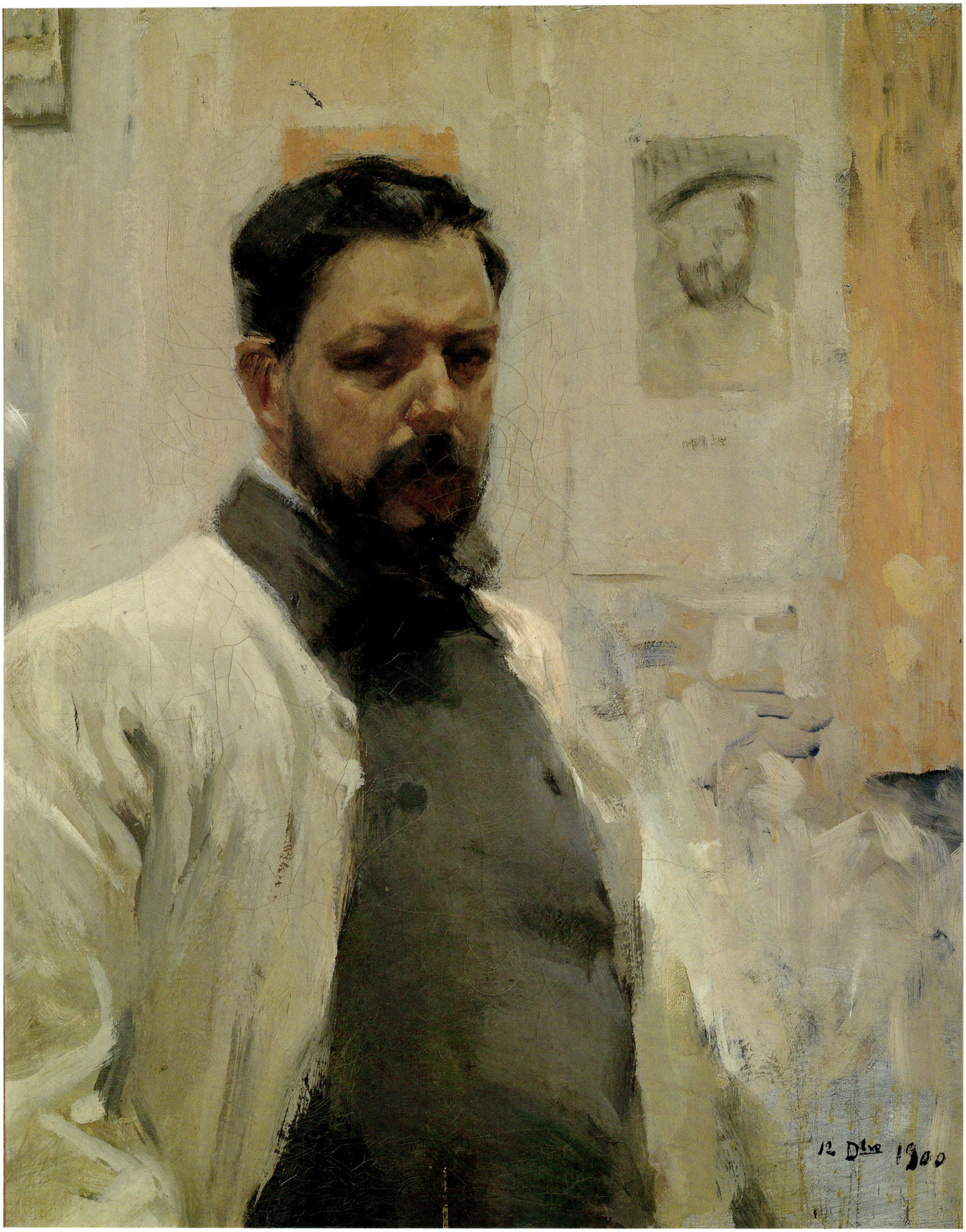

The heir to Spanish realism

Considered as being one of the most outstanding painters of the late nineteenth/early twentieth century art scene, not only in Spain but also abroad, the exceptional vision of Joaquin Sorolla y Bastida's artistic work allowed him to lead a brilliant international career that gave him not only prestige, economic standing and an endless number of disciples and followers, but also, within the wide range of styles going from the birth of impressionism to the first "-isms" of avant-garde painting, his life and work carry their own weight through the vibrating light of his paintings.

Sorolla was born into a humble family on 27th February 1863, in Valencia, Calle Nueva, in the old fishing quarters. His father, also called Joaquín, was a tradesman from Cantavieja (Teruel), and his mother, María Concepción, was from Valencia. His only sibling was his sister, Concha, who was born one year later. However, it wasn't long before they were orphaned, since in August 1865 their mother died, apparently from the outbreak of cholera that swept through the city that year, their father following her to the grave only three days later. And so Joaquín and his sister were adopted by their aunt on their mother's side, Isabel Bastida, and her husband, José Piqueres, a locksmith by trade, who were childless.

Around 1874, *Chimet,* as he had now become known, enrolled in the Escuela Normal Superior de la Provincia de Valencia, where the headmaster soon noticed the new student's passion for drawing and extraordinary skill for painting, to the detriment of a wider education, which would be made up for in the future by his relationships with artists and intellectuals. He advised the boy's guardian to encourage his nephew's talent, and enrol him in evening drawing classes given by the sculptor Cayetano Capuz at the Escuela de Artesanos, later know as Escuela de Artesanos y Artes y Oficios de Valencia. There are several drawings on decorative subjects and machines made at this Art & Crafts School, in 1877, the year he probably entered. Here, just like it would also occur later on at the Academia de Bellas Artes de San Carlos, where he enrolled in 1878, he made exceptionally rapid progress, being praised by all his teachers. During that period, it seems that he received only academic training, since the usual instruction received at that type of institutions was the copying of plasters and engravings.

Naturally, young Joaquín was awarded all the main prizes granted at this School. The best of them was a box of paints bearing an inscription in silver, apart from the corresponding diploma, which said "... for his constant application in the drawing of figures, so that at all times it may be seen as public testimony."

Soon more distinctions would come, this time from the Escuela de San Carlos, where he received prizes for Natural Drawing, Perspective and Colour.

Autorretrato
(Self Portrait)
1900, oil on canvas, 91.5 × 72.5 cm
Madrid: Museo Sorolla

Joaquín Sorolla y Bastida represents the triumph of Mediterranean painting of bright blues and whites. Although he is better known for his beach scenes than for his portraits, here we can see how he expertly depicts a character moving away from the academicism prevailing at the turn of the century, anticipating the new European vanguards.

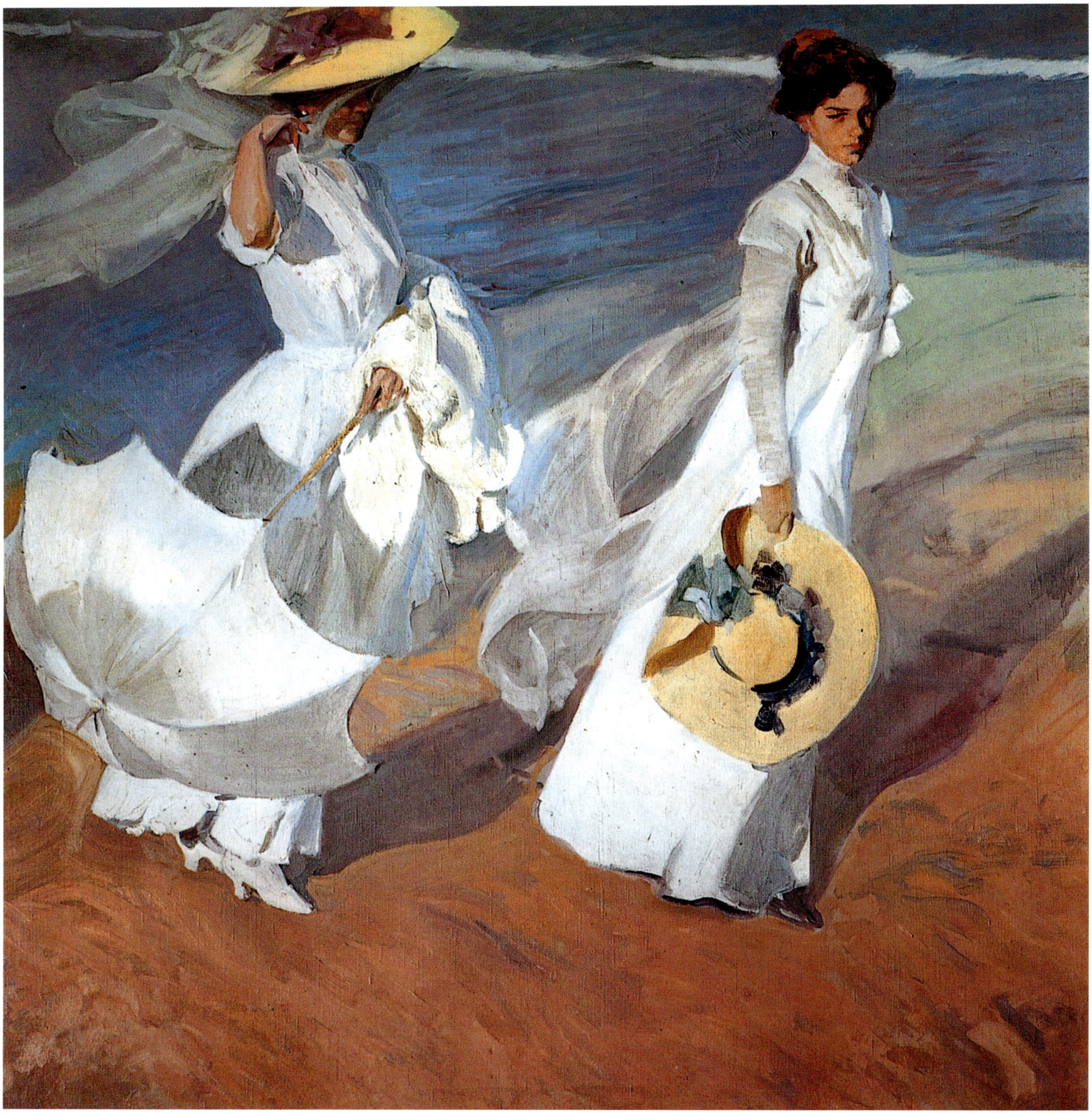

Paseo a orillas del mar
(A Walk Upon the Beach)
1909, oil on canvas, 205 × 200 cm
Madrid: Fundación Museo Sorolla

Sorolla uses an everyday scene to paint a family portrait of his wife Clotilde and eldest daughter María walking along the shore. The artist knows superbly how to capture the atmosphere, allowing us to feel the sea breeze through the movement of the clothes and the gesture of Clotilde holding onto her hat.

During this period Sorolla received some lessons from José Estruch, a not-very-well-known painter from Valencia, 25 years his senior. Soon both Estuch and Capuz looked on in admiration at how their young pupil progressed, showing how life was light, a pure and luminous experience that he discovered through observation of the sea, the reflection of the sky and the daily work of the fishermen, a synthesis of his whole work and a stimulus for his life.

While he continued with his studies, and to help out with the fragile economy of his protectors, he worked at his uncle's forge. The latter wanted him to learn the trade well just in case he would not be able to earn a living in the difficult world of painting. In 1879 he obtained his first success and, with it, an opportune incentive to continue studying. One of his watercolours, *El patio del Instituto,* presented at the Exposición Regional de Valencia that year, was awarded a Copper Medal, as Manuel Ossorio y Bernard tells us in his well-known work *Galería biográfica de artistas españoles* (1844). One year later, he took part in the exhibition held by the Sociedad Recreativa El Iris, winning his first Silver Medal, with the painting *Moro acechando la ocasión de su venganza.*

During this period he met Antonio, the father of Juan Antonio García, a fellow student at the Escuela de San Carlos, who was a renowned photographer and designer and very fond of art. It didn't take long for him to realize the young artist's talent, and he took him on as an illuminator of photographs and so he managed to earn a decent wage to help his uncle out. It was at Antonio's house where Joaquín met Clotilde, the second of four children, whom

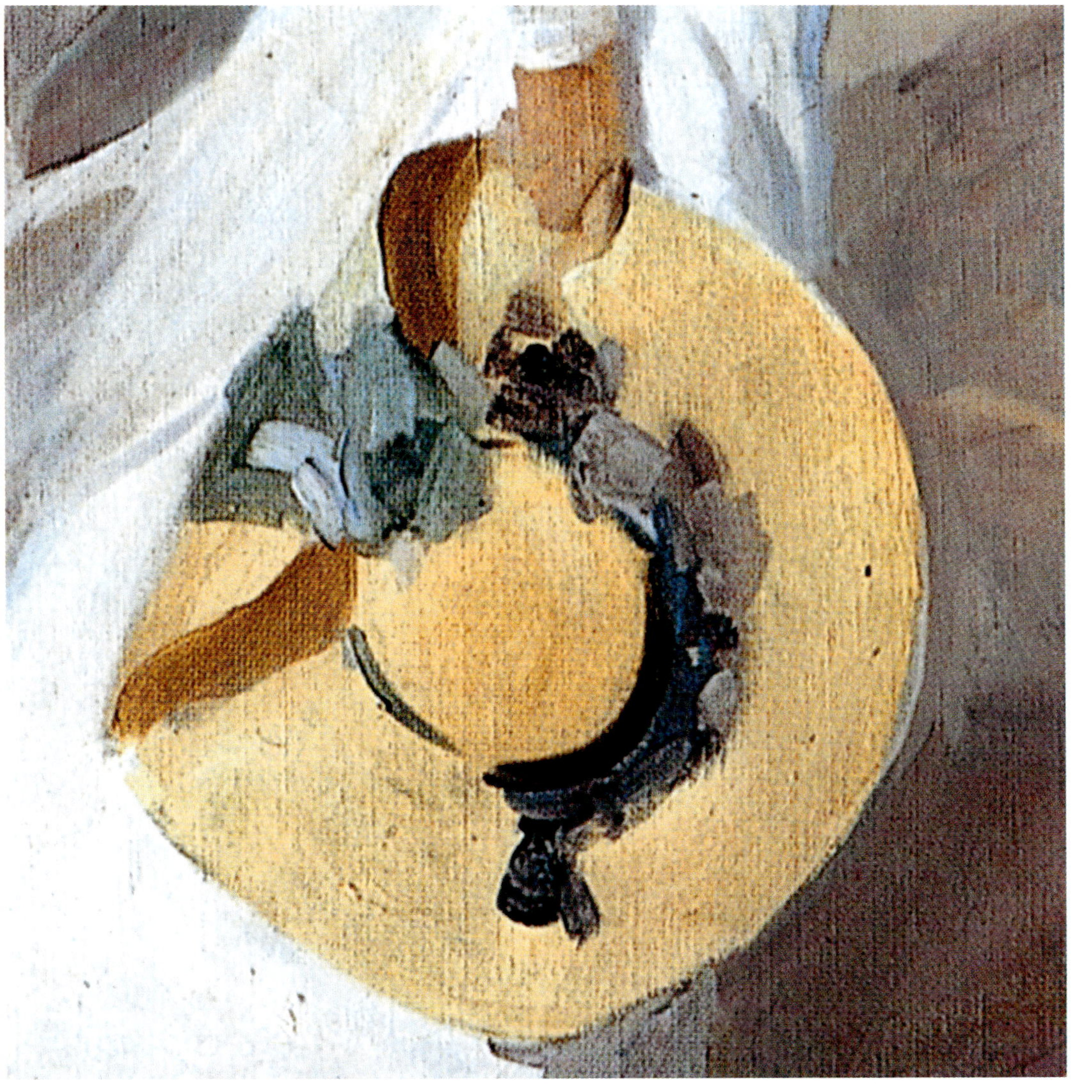

Paseo a orillas del mar
(A Walk Upon the Beach)
Detail

María holding her hat in her right hand, which stands out against the intense white of her dress and her shadow on the sand.

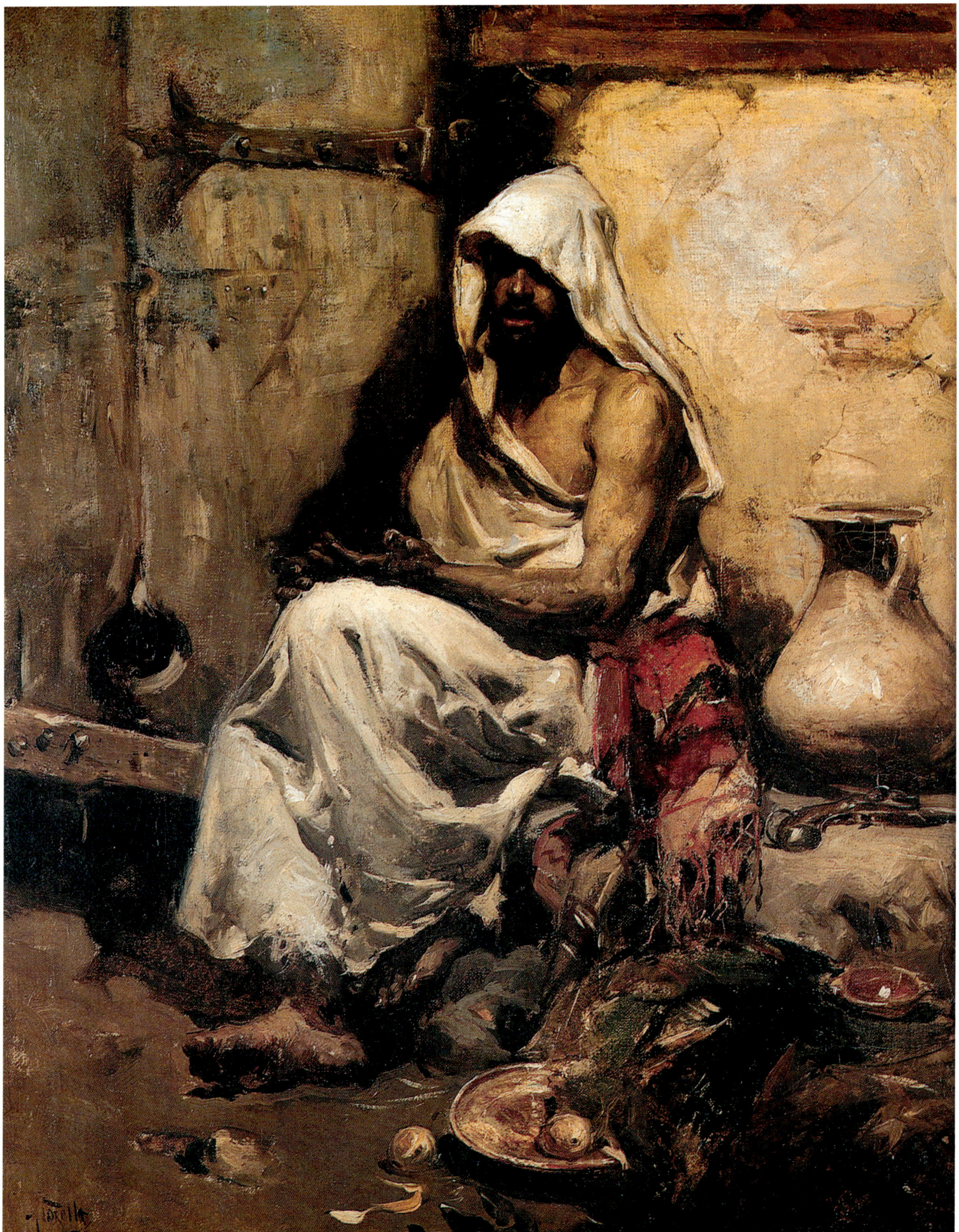

Un árabe examinando una pistola
(An Arab Examining a Pistol)
1881, oil on canvas, 85 × 60 cm
Museo de la Abadía de Montserrat

Painted when the artist was only 18, this canvas belongs to the orientalist trend that became fashionable at the end of the 19th century following the proposals on the part of Eugène Delacroix, followed in Spain by Mariano Fortuny and José Villegas. The relationship between Spain and the protectorate of Morocco, frequently a warring one, is not totally indifferent to this theme.

he would marry on 8th September 1888, so becoming part of his protector's family.

A few years before the wedding, Sorolla had taken part in the X Exposición Nacional de Bellas Artes, held in Madrid in the spring of 1881. These national exhibitions were at the time almost the only way for an artist to show their paintings and sculptures to the public, and the obtaining of a medal helped to achieve an official category as well as meaning an incipient career towards fame.

Sorolla decided to try his luck presenting three seascapes, but they went practically unnoticed, as neither the jury nor the critics hardly paid any attention to them. The reason for such a decision could be: either their low pictorial quality, or that a genre such as seascapes at that time could not compete with other more consolidated ones like historic paintings, where crude topics such as death, war and the taste for desolation prevailed. The subject matter of nearly all the paintings winning prizes at these competitions before the year 1881 was of a tragic nature.

The Prado Museum and Pinazo

Sorolla's stay in the capital meant that he could come into contact with Spanish realism, something with which he was not very well acquainted in his hometown. He was mainly interested in the Prado Museum and the works of El Greco, Ribera, Velázquez and Goya, as well as those of John Constable. And so, once he had finished his studies at the Escuela de San Carlos de Valencia, he decided to return to the capital the following year, to imbue himself once again with the museum's visual discipline. And so, for several months he was just another of those many art students who would stand in front of Ribera, Ribalta, Velázquez and Goya, seeking inspiration, art techniques and ideas.

Velázquez really impressed him, and he made several copies of his paintings, which we still have today together with one of Ribera. The impact received by Velázquez' s work underlies throughout his entire production, since, being the exceptional student he was, he knew how to make the most of the lesson learned regarding the study and treatment of light on the part of the latter, as well as the composition technique and treatment of light in portraits.

Just as important as the discovery of Velázquez, or maybe more, was his relationship with Ignacio Pinazo (1849-1916), which started in 1881 when the latter came to Valencia after having been in Rome where he had been studying thanks to a scholarship. Pinazo was, together with other fellow townsmen, for example Antonio Muñoz Degrain (1841-1924) and Emilio Sala (1850-1910), an important point of reference for Sorolla's painting. His bond with that artist was very significant, since Sorolla found in this artist's painting a different way of approaching his work, more in line with his own concerns and aims. Pinazo, unacquainted as he was with the artistic proposals of the School of Fontainebleau, did however defend a very similar style of painting, based on open-air painting. His style, sketchy and nervous, in which colour prevails over line, made him the Valencian painter closest to French impressionism, although his production is of an unequal quality. In favour of a solid construction of the work based on drawing, Pinazo always reproached Sorolla for the instantaneous and improvised nature of his pro-

Clotilde sentada en un sofá
(Clotilde Seated on the Sofa)
1910, oil on canvas,
180 × 110 cm
Madrid: Museo Sorolla

In this elegant portrait of the painter's wife wearing a white evening dress, Clotilde stands out against a dark background in which various objects can be faintly made out (a book and a sculpture by Troubezkoy), this vagueness enhancing her figure.

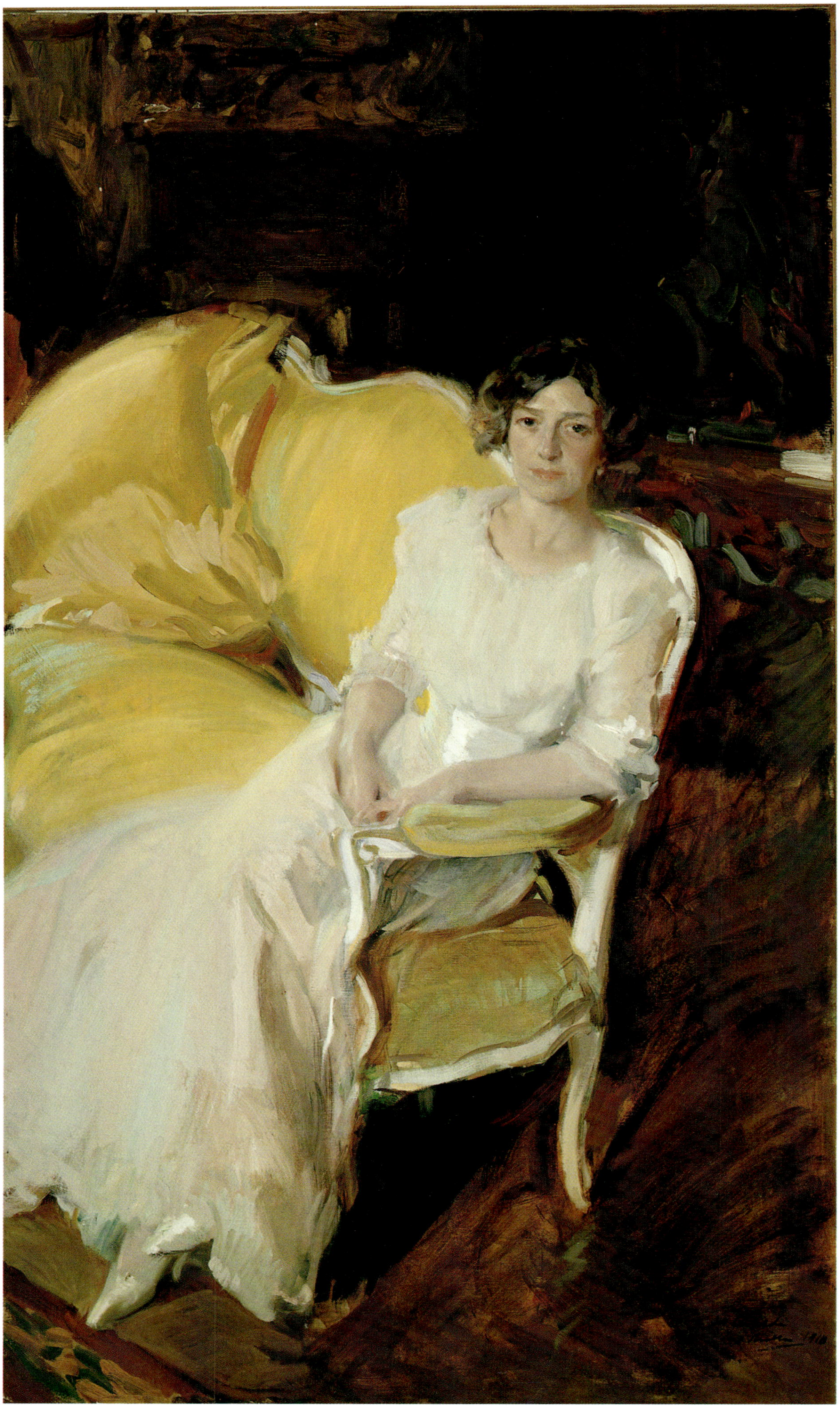

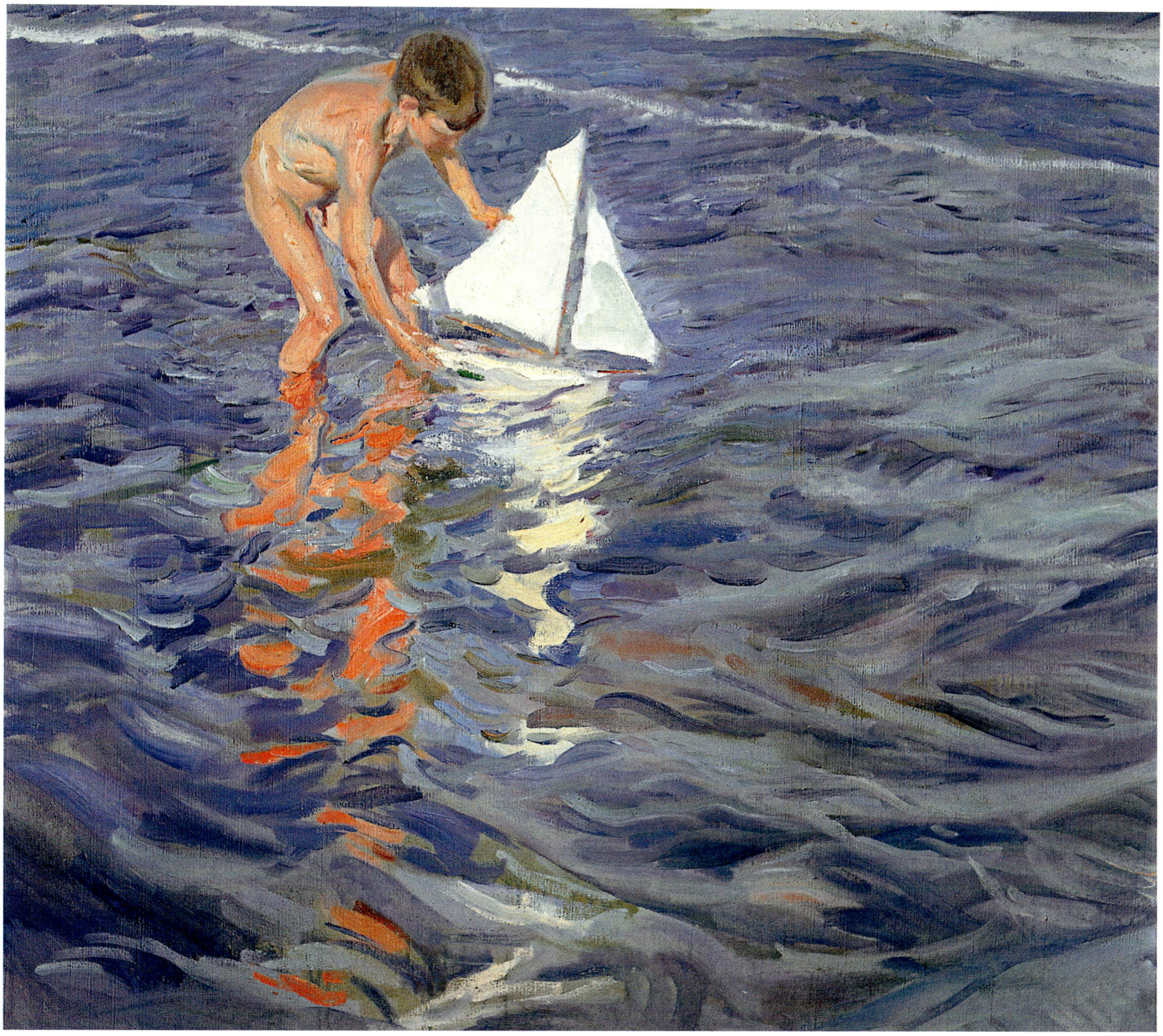

duction, something, on the other hand, that the latter could not avoid due to his artistic skill.

Pinazo's influence can easily be seen in Sorolla's works, especially those of the early years. The realist approach and the importance of *plein air* in the works of the former had its impact on Sorolla's first history painting, *El Dos de Mayo* ["The Second of May"], painted in the Valencia bullring. Maybe this was why this work caused such a sensation at the Exposición Nacional de Madrid in 1884, where the artist received one of the 15 second-prize medals awarded at the competition.

A year earlier he had taken part in the Exposición Regional de Valencia with three works: *Monja en oración* (for which he got a Gold Medal), a head study and two nudes. This work reminds us of the painting *Santa Clara* by Francisco Domingo (1842-1920), a professor of the Escuela de Bellas Artes de San Carlos, a colourist artist in favour of free-style painting. He also carried on the line of Spanish painting studied on his visits to the Prado Museum.

El balandrito
(The Young Yachtsman)
1909, oil on canvas, 100 × 109 cm
Madrid: Museo Sorolla

The brown skin of the naked boy is set off against the white boat, thus becoming a chromatic counterpoint of the blues produced by the water and the sunlight.

El grito de Palleter
(The Cry of Palleter)
1884, oil on canvas, 152 × 202 cm
Valencia: Diputación Provincial

This work marks the end of Sorolla's history paintings, just before he set off for Rome with his scholarship. Bernardino de Pantorba, his first biographer, speaks to us of its realism: "See all his effort … in the search for the 'natural', free from any conventionalism; see the love of the open air and, above all, the 'pieces' of painting 'wrenched' from the natural, which give the canvas a certain air and aspect of 'being alive'."

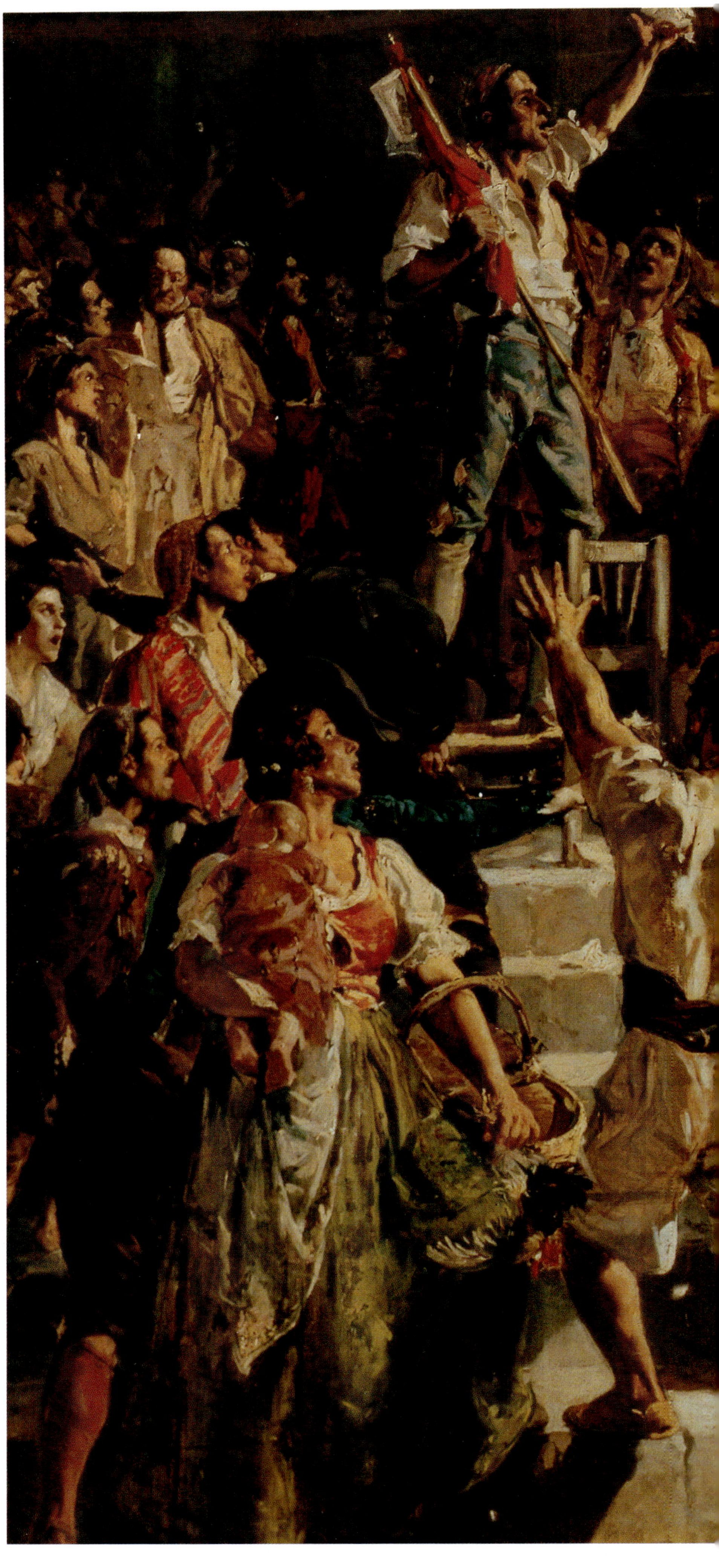

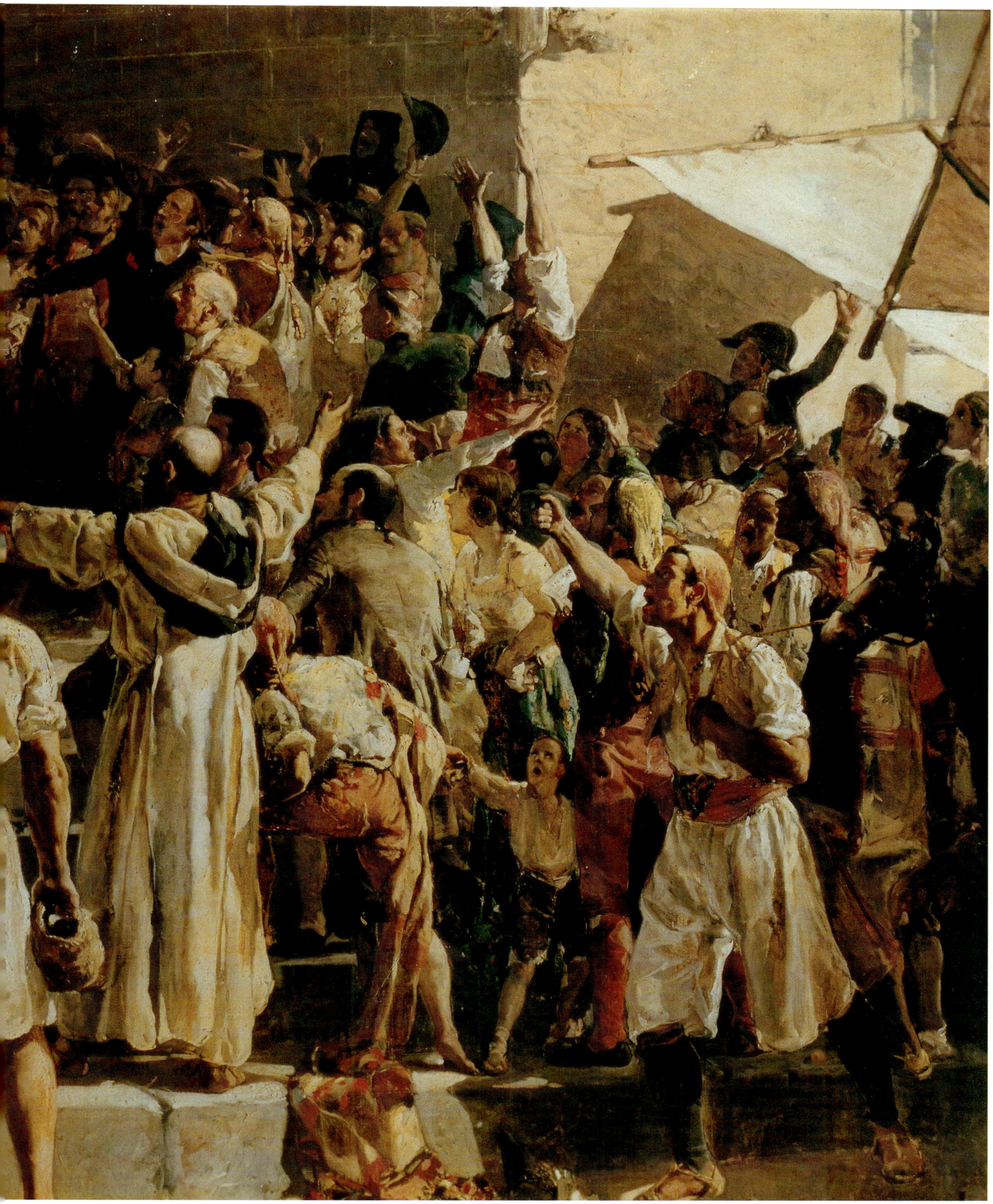

In the meantime, his solid modelling and partially obscure palette are influenced by Ribera who he studied in Madrid and Ribalta, studied in Valencia.

In *El Dos de Mayo* Sorolla portrayed the heroic defence of the people of Madrid in the Parque de Artillería during the bloody battle against Napoleon's soldiers. A history theme painted on a canvas of a great size was what Sorolla needed to adapt his real possibilities to the tastes of those competitions. And although the young artist's composition, clearly revealing his scarce professional experience, depicts affected attitudes, careless drawing and many of the figures have been drawn following a common model, it is true to say that the expressiveness of form and the splendour of colour stand out well; he also tried to represent the intense light of the real scene as faithfully as possible, since the usual thing to do in history paintings was to respond chromatically to the premeditated light of the studio. In this work we can see what would be the supports of his painting, that is, the open-air study in the sunlight. And so he made the most of the occasion to make his third trip to Madrid and then return to Valencia with a certain consolidated prestige.

Beruete
1902, oil on canvas, 115 × 102 cm
Madrid: Museo del Prado

Of the many portraits painted of Aureliano de Beruete, the artist who became young Sorolla's critic, model and friend, this is one of the most freely painted, a fair tribute to someone who supported and influenced him following the 1906 exhibition in Paris. Six years later, with grateful admiration, Sorolla left Beruete his studio so that he could prepare his last exhibition in Paris.

Artistic opportunity in Rome and Paris

Following the Exposición Nacional, it wasn't long before Sorolla had another chance to paint a similar type of scene. On 11th June of the same year, the Diputación Provincial de Valencia called a public competition, just as it had been doing since 1863, for granting a painting scholarship in Rome. Sorolla finally won with the compulsory theme *El grito del Palleter* ["The Cry of Palleter"], a history painting very similar to *El Dos de Mayo* and with which the artist was now taken as being an experienced painter. Once his military service was over, he set off for Italy at the beginning of 1885.

When he arrived in the city, Sorolla had to introduce himself to the Aragonese painter Francisco Pradilla y Ortiz (1848-1921), at the time Director of the Spanish Academy. As Sorolla himself said, Pradilla had "a blind love for the beauty of the line, a love that he knew how to inculcate in me, and I had to make the most of it. As a restless and revolutionary spirit burned inside me, I needed a regulator, a sense of quietude, a reasoning for equilibrium, and I found it all in Pradilla, who knew how to calm and restrain my rebellious impetuosity."

As Sorolla was a scholarship holder, the director of the Academy enforced the strict study of drawing on him, but nothing was more contrary to the naturalistic tendency than the art of that lover of history painting, genre themes, portraits and eighteenth-century scenes. The loose and wide brushstrokes and the vibrating clarity of the colour that would soon characterize Sorolla's works were also quite the opposite to the patient and detailed painting of the Aragonese teacher. There he met Pedro Gil, another scholarship holder who had settled in France, and who for a great part of his life was a faithful collaborator and advisor on his trips outside Spain.

In the three months that Sorolla stayed in Rome, he would probably visit monuments, academies and museums, but we do not have many works left from that period: a few quill drawings of catacombs and some small panels of architectural elements. As the days went by, he became more and more disappointed, since the painting done there was completely unmotivating. He spent his days there drawing and painting nudes, that is, the usual activities of the first stage of instruction of any scholarship holder in a new city.

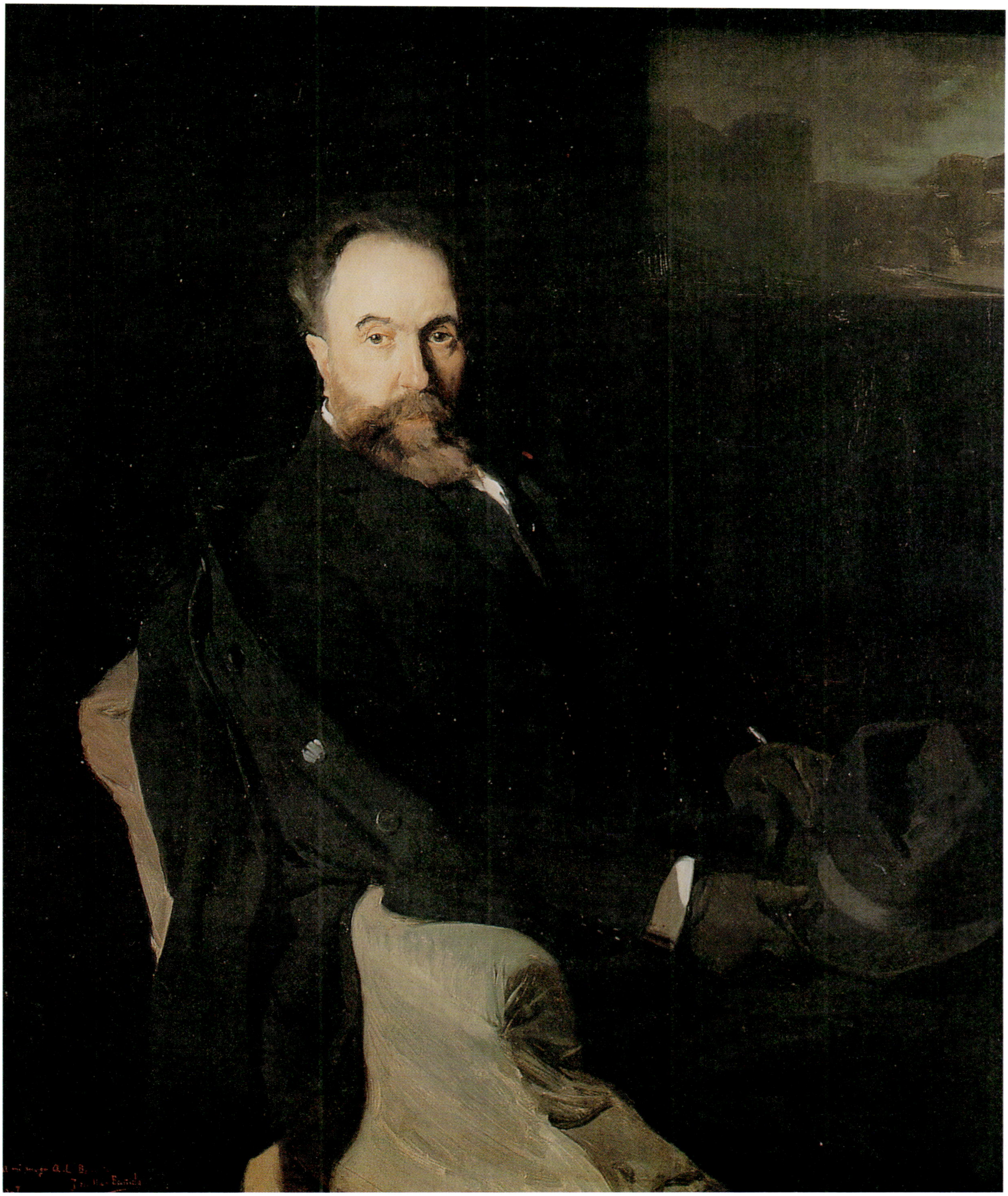

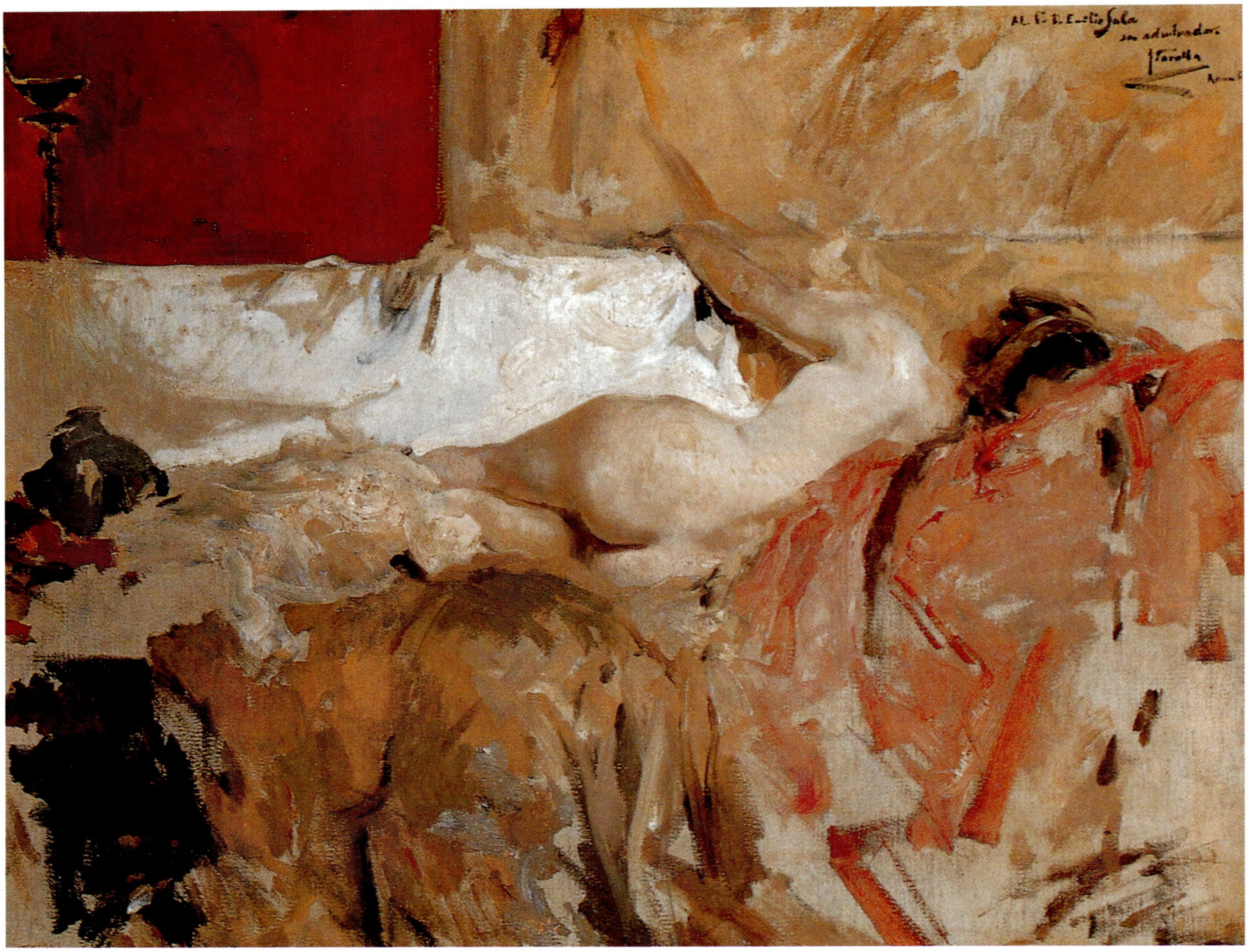

Bacante
(Bacchante)
1886, oil on canvas, 60 × 75 cm
Puerto Rico: Museo de Arte de Ponce

Dedicated in the top, right-hand corner to the painter Emilio Sala, this canvas sketched in Rome shows the young artist's mastery, in a display of boldness against the mediocre academic and preciosist art of the late 19th century.

In the spring, Sorolla travelled to Paris with Gil, where he stayed for six months, working a lot. According to the artist Aureliano de Beruete (1845-1912), a good friend of his as well as a reliable biographer of his early years: "During his stay in Paris, Sorolla saw the new modern painting movement for the first time, and he would work non-stop; by day making serious studies in his studio, by night making pencil sketches of everything that drew his attention in the street, on the omnibus and in the bustling boulevard cafés, well into the early hours of the morning." And this is how he came to master the paintbrush and pencil.

During this period he came into contact with the School of Fontainebleau at the retrospective exhibition on a French artist who had died only a few months earlier at the early age of 36, Jules Bastien-Lepage (1848-1884), held at the Hôtel de Chimay, whose works impressed him greatly. This is easy to understand, since Sorolla, now aged 22, like so many other artists of his generation, felt unhappy about the academic instruction received and somewhat disorientated regarding which was the alternative. Together with Édouard Manet (1832-1883), Bastien-Lepage offered many of those young artists a new option based on the observation of reality. Under the influence of the impressionists, not only had the French painter advocated the recovery of rural themes, but, above all, the excuse for using those arguments to reproduce nature in a truthful way.

He also visited the exhibition held in the Tulleries, on the German artist Adolf Menzel (1815-1905), then in his seventies, admiring the intensity of his palette. Menzel was considered by his contemporaries as the first German painter of the nineteenth century, and had founded his prestige on what was precisely appreciated as a careful reproduction of reality.

This exhibition, like the previous one, in spite of the disparity of opinions of some critics, for example Rafael Doménech and Manuel Abril, regarding the influence on Sorolla's painting, also profoundly affected his sensibility.

He went to see other exhibitions, such as that year's Salon, getting to know French realism and all its alternatives. There is no documentation showing he observed impressionist painting, so much in vogue since the first Salon had been held in 1874. Until 1885 he had received an academic training, with a certain tendency toward the realism developed by Domingo Marqués, Pinazo and Sala, amongst others, experienced very intensely in Valencia and which increased when he became acquainted with Spanish realism after visiting the Prado Museum and

Cabeza de italiana
(Head of an Italian Girl)
1886, oil on canvas, 59 × 41 cm
Private collection

When staying in Rome as a scholarship holder, Sorolla followed the advice of its director at the time, Francisco Pradilla. Apart from painting nudes with an academicism of his own, he knew how to capture daily and human reality, as we can see in this beautiful head of this Italian girl.

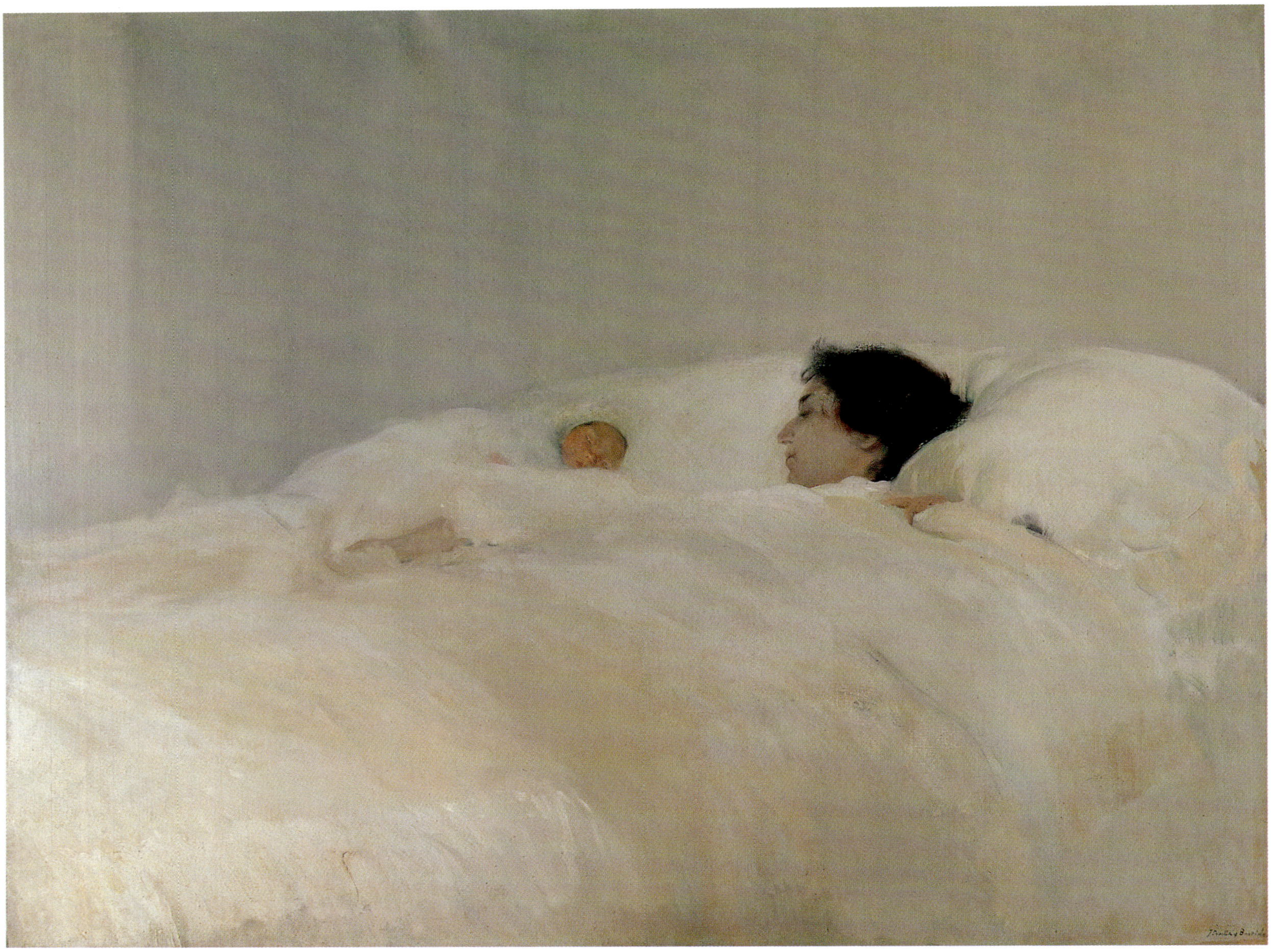

Madre
(Mother)
1895, oil on canvas, 123 × 168 cm
Madrid: Museo Sorolla

There are only nine years between this peaceful and luminous canvas commemorating the birth of his daughter Elena and the one on the previous page. However, Sorolla's aesthetic ideal has evolved towards a simplification in which the luminosity of whites and pale greys is a prelude of his plein-air works on the sunny beaches of Valencia.

the Museo de Valencia, to which we could also add the new artistic trends recently studied in Paris. After this experience, Sorolla could live and feel how, apart from the conventional history canvas and genre panel, a desire for renovation did exist, Paris being at that time the visible head of this movement, while Rome got lost in its splendid past. For an artist of his calibre, whose intention was not merely the simplicity of a work well done or an easy work, but who had other aspirations related with the market tendency, it is clear that Paris was livelier and had a lot more to offer than Rome.

Menzel and Bastien-Lepage clearly did not unveil anything essential to the eyes of a Spaniard who had spent countless hours making studies in the Prado Museum, but they were significant with regard to directing the conception and the execution of the work of art toward the natural. At that time Sorolla was not a naturalistic painter, but an artist submerged in the inevitable period of uncertainties, indecision and trial and error, although he had already conveyed in some of his works that realism was the tendency which made him feel more at ease.

Although at that time the artistic atmosphere of Paris was, on the whole, much richer than that of Italy, in autumn 1885 Sorolla was obliged to join the group of Spanish scholarship holders in Rome. Once there again, he probably travelled around a good part of Italy during what was left of that year and the next. The numerous panels we conserve from that period show landscapes of Naples,

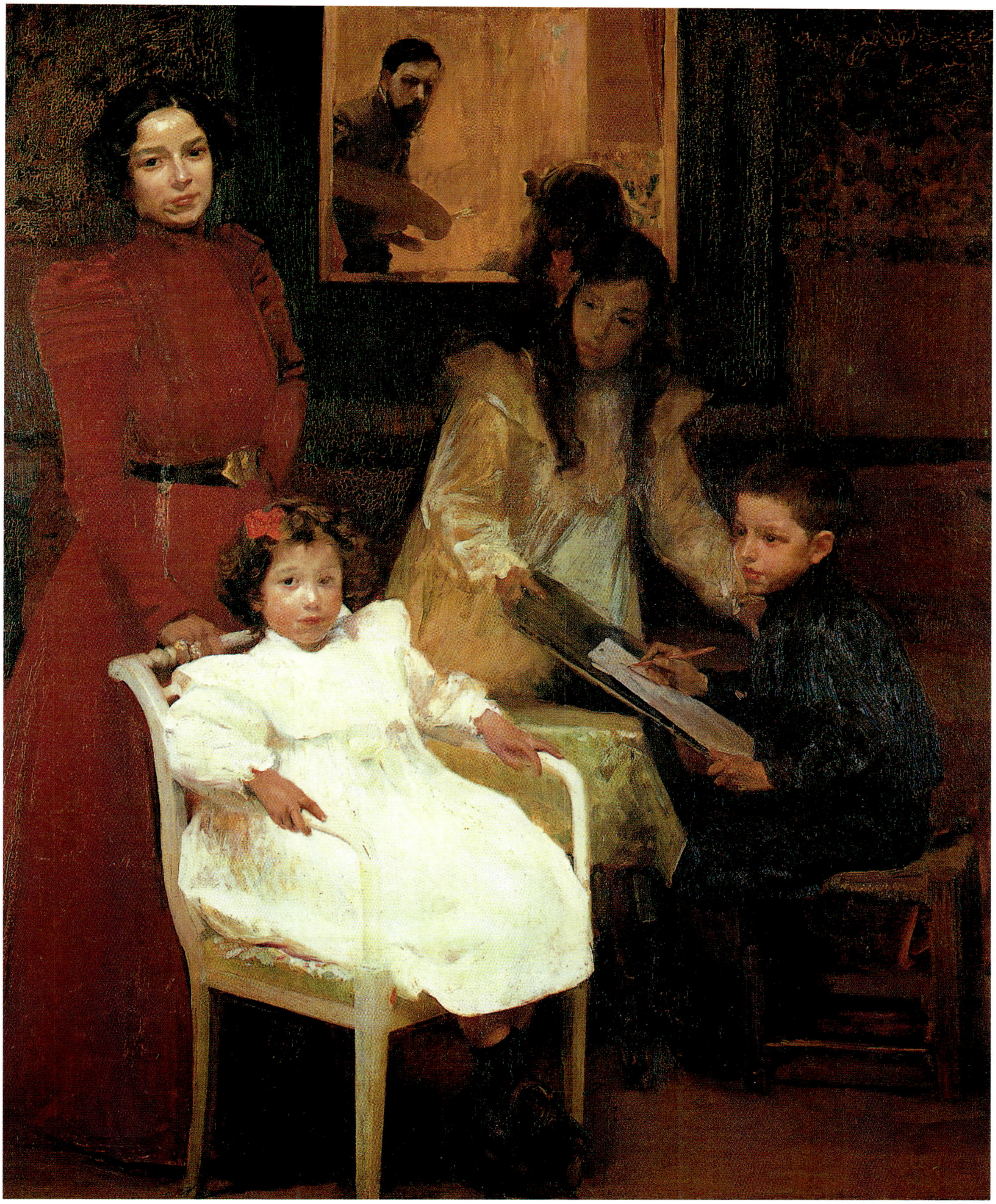

Mi familia
(My Family)
1901, oil on canvas, 185 × 159 cm
Valencia: City Council

In spite of being a cosmopolitan artist, he was a great family man, painting many portraits of his family, both individually and together. In contrast to Las Meninas, *the famous painting by Velazquéz, here it is the painter who is reflected in the mirror, and not the canvas that is being painted.*

Florence or Venice. But once again, he began to feel unhappy about his surroundings, with their discouraging limitations. He prepared his first regulatory consignment of works as a scholarship holder to the Valencia Regional Council, consisting of six drawings and two oil paintings, which, in the opinion of the San Carlos Academy members did not comply with their regulations, in spite of which they acknowledged a certain merit, although, according to them, "they lacked the conclusion, sobriety and constancy required", since "they are not true academy works, but just amusing sketches very worthy of an artist's portfolio, but in no way can be seriously taken as coming from a scholarship holder." He made pencil or ink sketches of several historic and religious themes until he opted for *El entierro de Cristo* ["The Burial of Christ"], a huge painting measuring nearly 7 m long by more than 4 m high, with the intention of taking part in the Exposición Nacional of 1887 and on which he worked for nearly a year and half. He didn't paint it outdoors, but in his studio in Rome, which is why the final canvas, on which he had pinned his hopes of getting first prize and that turned out to be a complete failure due to its continuous retouching in the artist's persistent search for the best style, showed some of his first signs of luminism. The critic Isidoro Fernández-Flórez is famous for having reproached Sorolla for not having painted the *burial* of Christ, but the *tim*e at which he was buried, saying, amongst other things: "I think *El entierro de Cristo* is praiseworthy as a huge draft, as a happy note of a landscape painter, but very ill-fated in its composition and posture of the figures; those of the Virgin and the Disciple, with less life in them than the divine corpse, and who manage to stand up thanks to a miracle of balance... There is nothing in the painting ... but a marvellous display of style and a note of sure effect for its only too evident poetic tones."

If that was the prevailing opinion amongst the comments at that year's Exposición, it was not the one shared by all the artists attending the competition. Finally, Sorolla's painting, together with those of Joaquín Araujo, Juan Antonio Benlliure, Sebastián Gessa, Joaquín Agrasot and Mariano García y Mas, received an honorary certificate. It can be said that Sorolla, with his skill and palette, turned a classical theme into a modern representation of an open-air scene. This approach led to the rejection of those critics who were less inclined to accept novelties, but allowed Sorolla to direct his painting in what he believed to be the right direction, even in the case of a work that was going to be judged at an Exposición Nacional. Some critics have seen in this work reminiscences of the Neapolitan artist Domenico Morelli (1823-1901), whose paintings, highly idealized and very colourful, were very popular in Italy during the last three decades of the nineteenth century.

Sorolla now suffered a period of crisis. Pinazo's teachings had aroused his interest, even more so when he came into contact with Bastien-Lepage and Menzel's works. However, in Rome, and indirectly in Valencia, through the works he was instructed to carry out by the commission as a scholarship holder, he was also required to carry out another type of painting, more in line with the artistic spirit of the institution that was in charge of his studies. During that period, at the same time as he painted his scholarship holder works, he also did oil paintings and watercolours for art dealers, which allowed him to supplement his monthly allowance of 250 pesetas.

Sorolla's experience in Assisi

After the exhibition, and back in Italy, he worked intensely in Rome and in Assisi, at that time just a village, seeking the tranquillity and solitude of a peace-

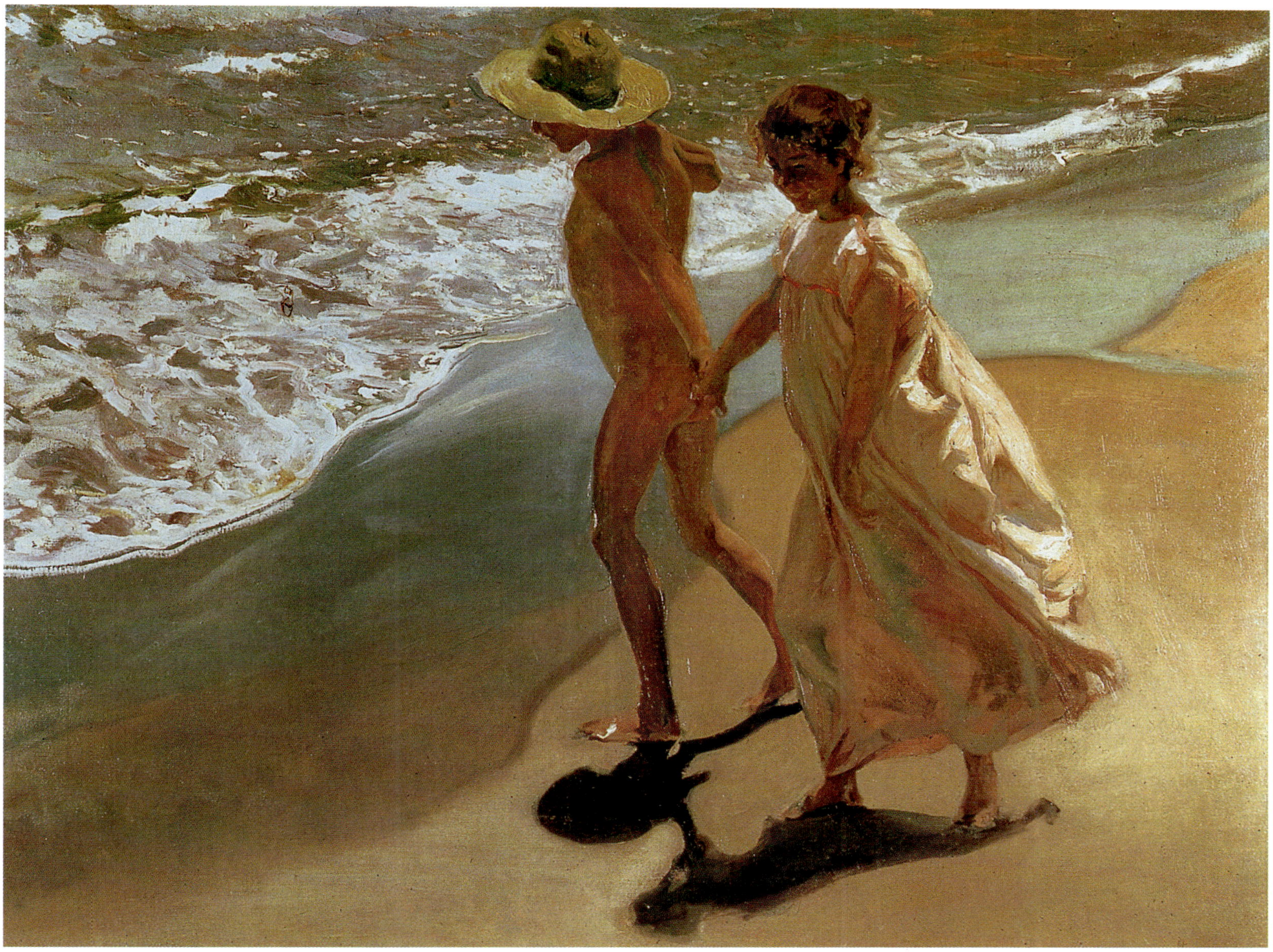

ful place where he could paint more and with more serenity. Without any doubt, Sorolla must have had some contact with the Spanish colony during his stay in the Eternal City, where there were many artists. Some of his closest acquaintances were the Valencian José Benlliure y Gil (1855-1937), the Sevillian José Villegas y Cordero (1848-1922) and Emilio Sala. The three, as the artist himself admitted over the years, had their influence on his painting. His relationship with Emilio Sala probably began in Valencia or Madrid, where they must have met, bearing in mind that Emilio Sala was a fellow student and close friend of Pinazo's, who was almost certainly the person that introduced them. Therefore, if in Sorolla's early works we can find Pinazo's influence, after 1890 Sala was the artist with whom he felt more identified. His unceasing concern for the treatment of light and the mutual admiration for Velázquez joined them for a lifetime. With his advice and friendship, Sala was the only person who could say he had actually contributed to the artistic education of a painter who it was clear, before the end of the century, was going to be one of the most outstanding Spanish artists of his time.

During that stage Sorolla was devoted to the study of the human figure, to copying *trecento* century paintings and to painting numerous watercolours with local themes, an inheritance received, without any doubt, from the Valencian artist Bernardo Ferrándiz (1835-1885). At the end of 1887 he finished *El Padre*

Al agua
(To the Water)
1908, oil on canvas, 81 × 106 cm
Private collection

Instantaneousness, light, white and blue are terms that sum up Sorolla's work, which explain his world. The artist turns daily actions into a subject for painting; without abandoning realism, he creates a new plastic realism.

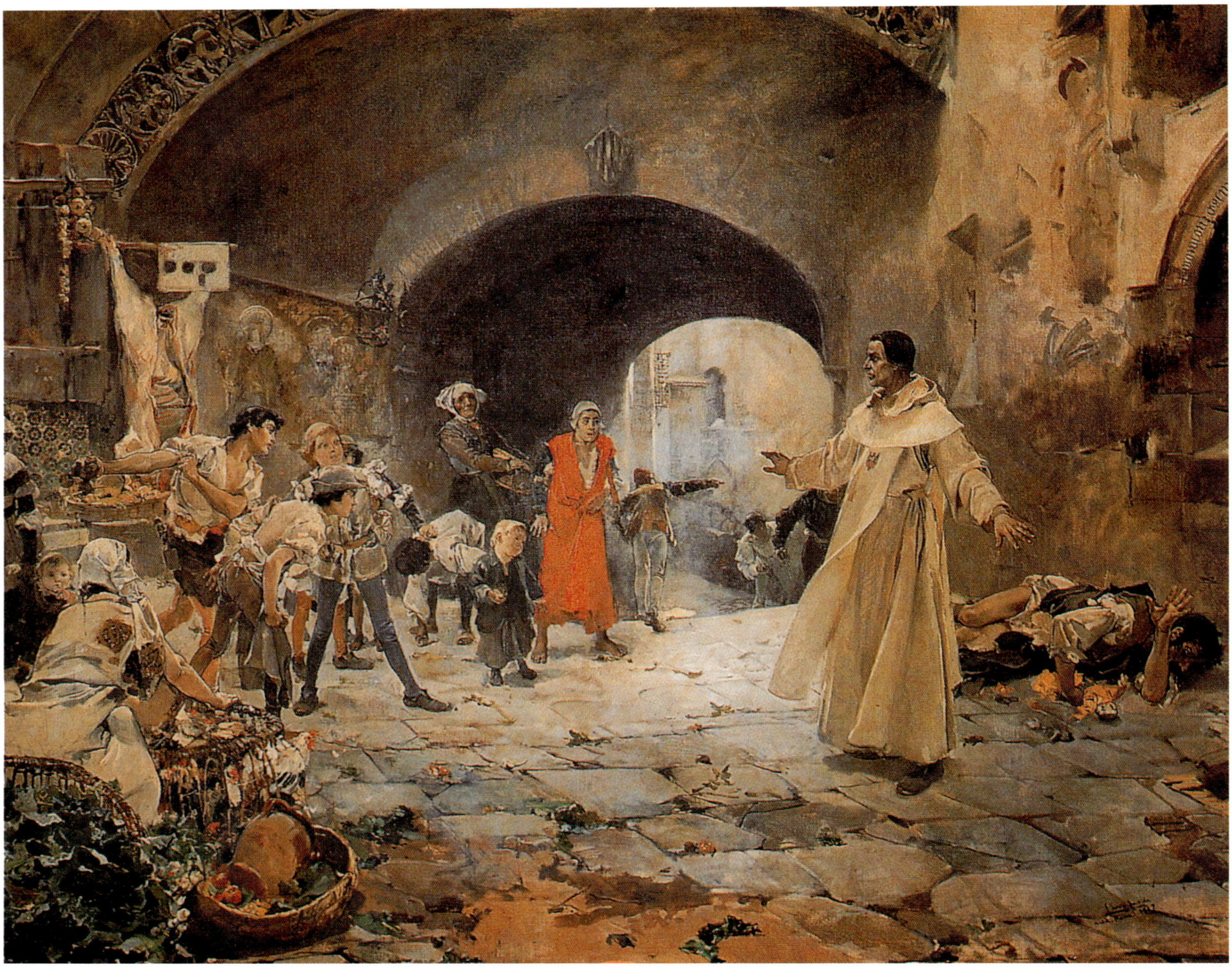

El Padre Jofré protegiendo a un loco
(Father Jofré Protecting a Madman)
1887, oil on canvas, 154 × 205 cm
Valencia: Diputación Provincial

This scene describes the true story of Father Juan Gilabert Jofré preventing a mad crowd from stoning a mentally deranged man. Father Jofré was a Mercedarian friar who founded the "Espital dels Folls" in 1419, which today is the Hospital Provincial de Valencia.

Jofré protegiendo a un loco ["Father Jofré Protecting a Madman"], as the last and most important of his scholarship works, a canvas that clearly denotes the influence of Emilio Sala in the range of colours used. The subject had been imposed since he had been awarded the grant and, for its similarity with history paintings like *El Dos de Mayo* and *El grito del Palleter*, Sorolla proved his progresses in technique and studies to his protectors and followers, at the same time as he announced the brilliant future concealed in the skilful use of his palette. In May the following year the Academia de San Carlos, on the Regional Council's request, established that the canvas, although not excessively praised, be granted the regulatory extra time with full liberty regarding the artist's work and stay.

In the summer of 1888, the fourth year of the scholarship not yet over, Sorolla moved to Valencia to marry his fiancée Clotilde. The same day of the wedding they left for Italy and, after a few days in Rome, settled in Assisi, the painter strongly attracted by the well-known air of peacefulness and tranquillity of the place and where he could carry on enjoying the friendship of Benlliure. They stayed there for more than eight months, until June 1889, now without the economic support of the scholarship, which would have come in so handy at the home of the newly-weds. Everyday needs led Sorolla to painting easy-to-sell pictures, such as the simple genre paintings so much in vogue in those days, without forgetting about his more artistically committed work.

Therefore he painted many watercolours of a more or less trivial content, although he also made a series of very useful studies to practice his command of drawing, in order to achieve a greater strength of composition. In spite of his broadmindedness, and even in those years in which the *preciosist* style was still highly praised and well in demand, Sorolla understood that, without the rigour of drawing, there was no other way for constructing the base of a painting; on the other hand, the study of colour and light, required a previous one of form, without which the composition would be unstable.

The artist's impulsive speed of painting prevented him from concentrating on the patient task of capturing on the canvas every detail present in the chosen topic, with an analytic, almost scrutinizing perspective. He was never very fond of detail, of that perfect finish with which some nineteenth-century painters had triumphed in the European market, for example Mariano Fortuny (1838-1874) and the Sevillian artist José Jiménez Aranda (1837-1903).

During these months of 1888 and 1889, Jover, a Valencian art dealer living in Rome was Sorolla's main customer. In a list of works sold at that time, kept by his wife Clotilde, who carefully administrated her husband's earnings, the name of Jover appears frequently as a buyer of watercolours, something that even continued when they returned to Spain.

Otra Margarita
(Another Marguerite)
1892, oil on canvas, 130 × 200 cm
Saint Louis; Washington University Gallery of Art

Social themes, due to the influence of the writer Blasco Ibáñez, make up a number of Sorolla's works in the early 1890s, which will culminate in the canvas Trata de blancas. *The young prisoner in the custody of two policemen is also a work that can be included within the realist concept of social criticism against a society whose awareness has to be aroused.*

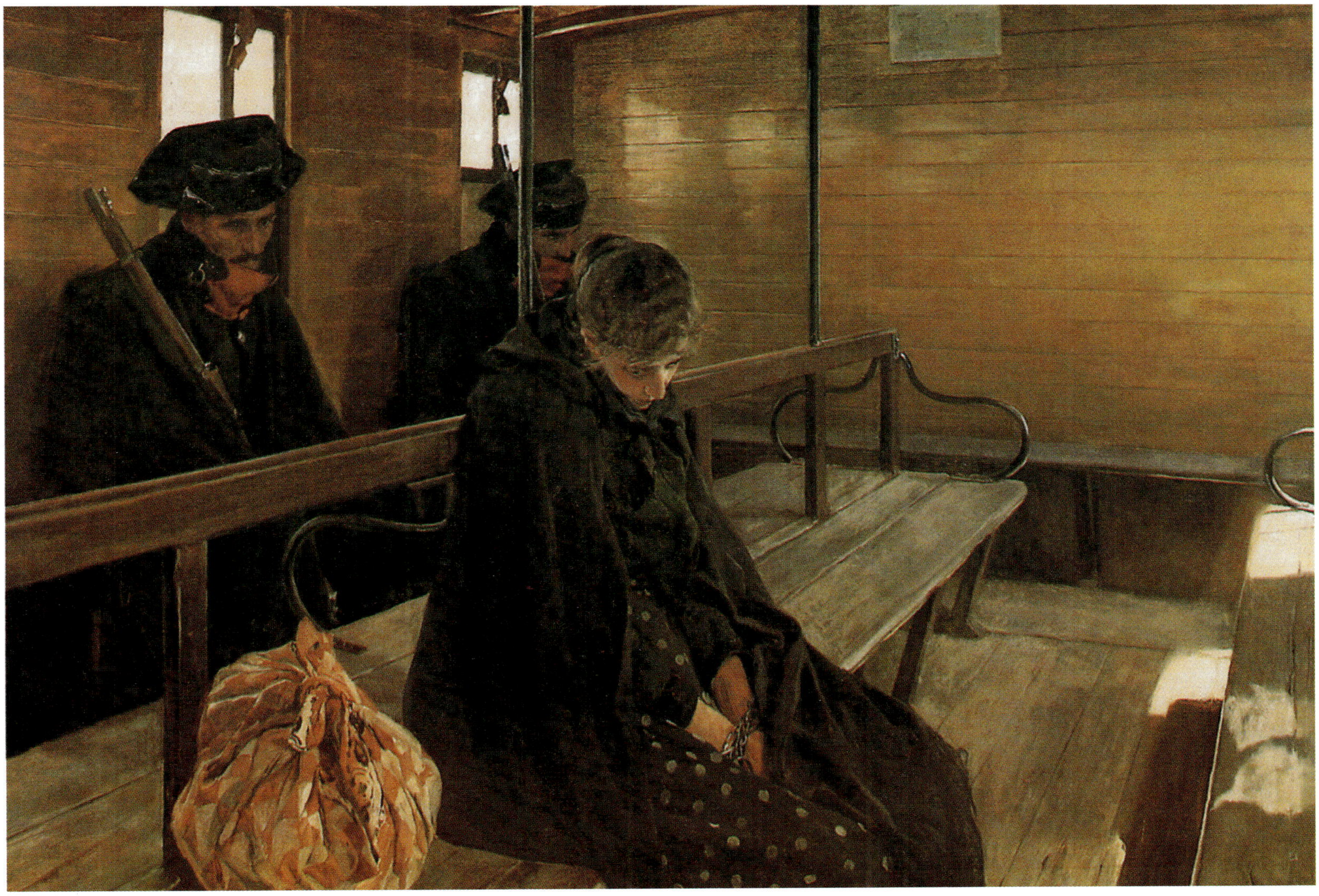

Back in Madrid

After a brief stay in Valencia, the couple decided to move to Madrid, a city with more cultural and artistic wealth, more in line with the painter's ambitions than the capital of the eastern provinces of Spain. The five years that had gone by after obtaining the scholarship had allowed him to become acquainted with everything that, until then, interested him and he needed to know in the art world, at that time feeling the urgent need and the impulse to face new challenges in his painting.

At the beginning of 1890, the move to a house and studio in Plaza del Progreso coincided with the start of an incessant and fruitful period that lasted until 1905, constantly taking part in national and international exhibitions (Exposición Nacional de Madrid, biennial exhibitions at the Círculo de Bellas Artes, Munich International Art Exhibition, Vienna International Art Exhibition, Salon de Paris, etc.) with a great many works that prove his production and his merit due to the number of medals and distinctions awarded, his work being

El beso de la reliquia
(Kissing the Relic)
1893, oil on canvas, 104 × 125 cm
Bilbao: Museo de Bellas Artes

Sorolla was not a painter very fond of religious themes, this type of work being chronologically related to those of social themes. More than works of devotion, they are portraits of a social reality in Spain at the turn of the century, still anchored in religious atavisms from days of yore.

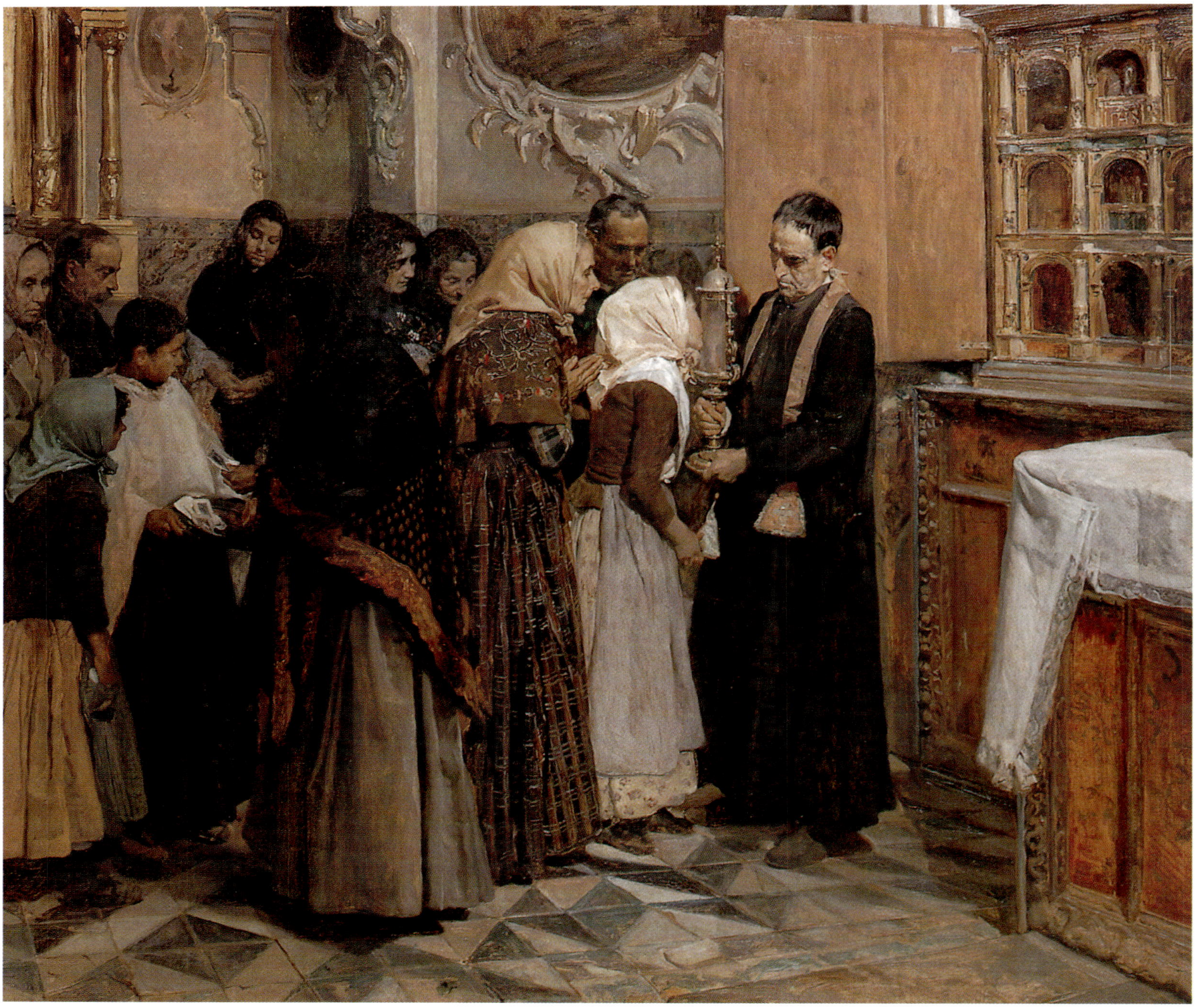

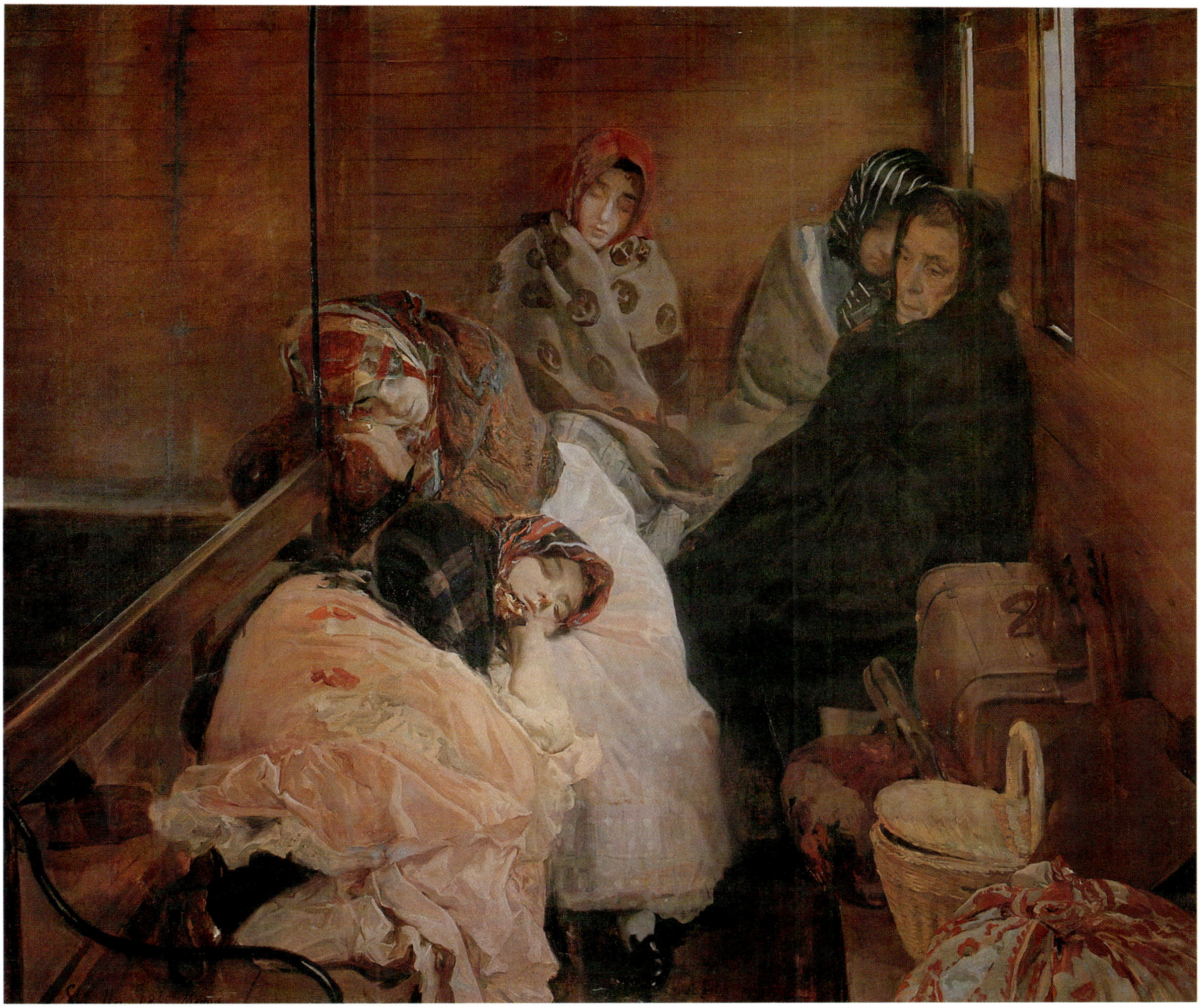

Trata de blancas
(The White Slave Trade)
1895, oil on canvas, 166.5 × 195 cm

In contrast to academic realism, Sorolla introduces a new concept of artistic form in which plastic values prevail. The skirts of the two girls in the foreground are a foretaste of what would be Sorolla's luminism.

made known as his paintings were bought by various museums. During this year he presented the following works at the Exposición Nacional: *Boulevard de París* and *Costumbres valencianas*, and five *Head Studies.* He also submitted paintings to other exhibitions in Madrid: the one of pastel drawings and watercolours held at the Círculo de Bellas Artes, specifically the watercolours *El primer hijo, La santera* and *Serenata morisca*, and the pastel drawings *El calafateo, Otoño prematuro* and *Estudio*, together with the watercolour *Fuenterrabía*; and the one held at Salón Hernández, with the paintings *Gitana, Sagunto* and *Valenciana a la reja*.

Boulevard de París is based on the sketches made five years earlier during his stay in the French capital and was finished in Madrid shortly before being taken to the Exhibition. In Beruete's opinion: "It may be an unconscious concession to the demands of the age"; but without any doubt, together with *Una desgracia* by Jiménez Aranda, it was in line with the general tendency in fashion in European art. The latter's painting was characterised by the "Grand Manner" genre and by his fine drawings which made him a worthy successor to Fortuny. Both were distinguished for their somewhat photographic approach, Sorolla's being even more

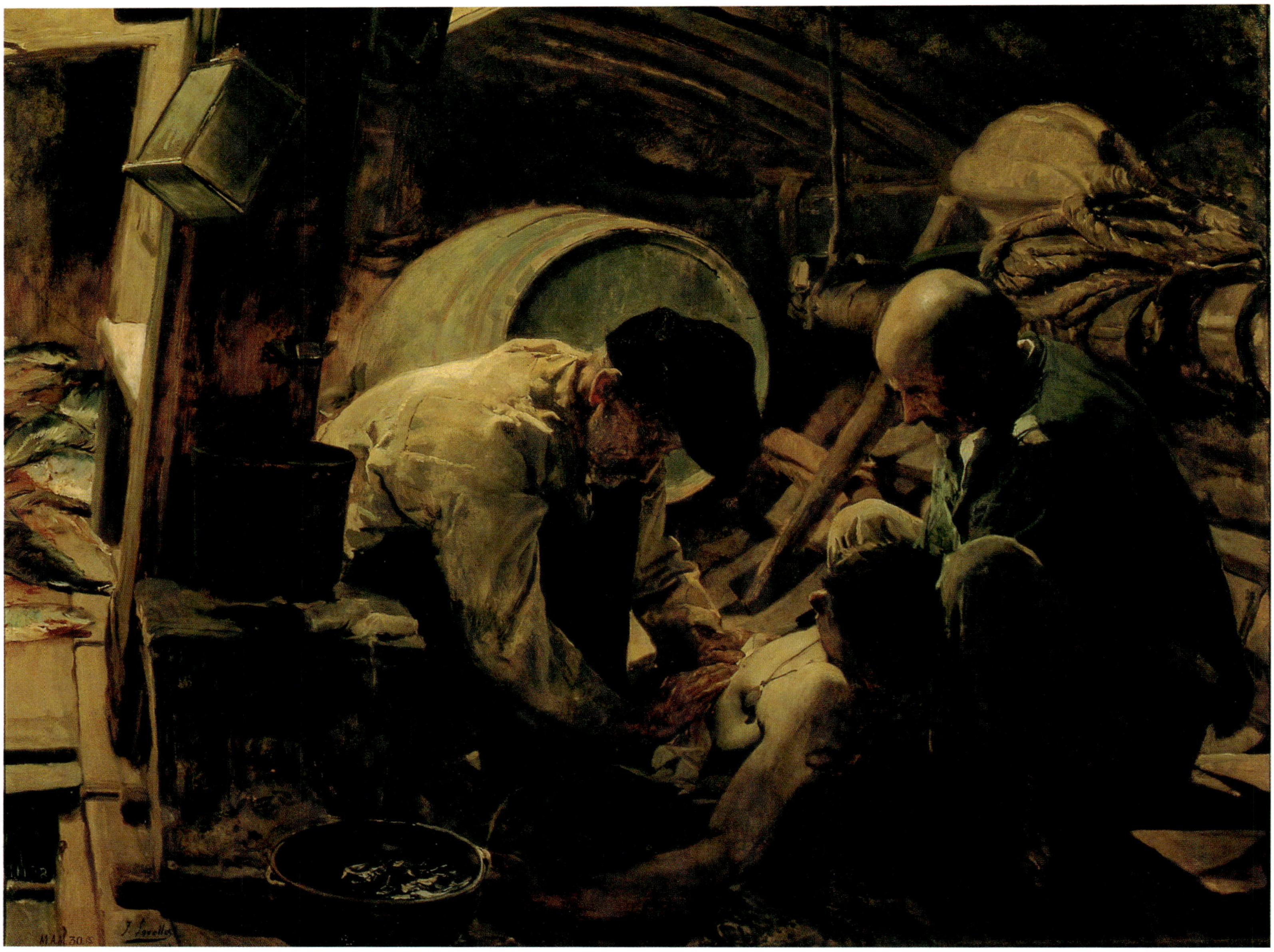

¡Aún dicen que el pescado es caro!
(And They Still Say Fish is Expensive!)
1894, oil on canvas, 153 × 204 cm
Madrid: Museo del Prado

Titles are an important part of canvases on social criticism. The dying fisherman lying in squalid surroundings being assisted by two men gives the canvas its title, emphasising its message. Bearing in mind the quality of the canvas, it isn't surprising that the works belonging to this period received so many international awards.

detailed than usual. In spite of everything, his canvas was a success and he was granted a Second Prize for its innovative nature. The critics Octavio Picón and Augusto Comas spoke very highly of *Boulevard de París* in the books they wrote on the most outstanding works of the 1890 edition of the Certamen Nacional.

On 13th April that year his first daughter, María Clotilde, was born in Madrid, which led to the exquisite watercolour, already mentioned above, *El primer hijo* ["The First Child"]. Between 1890 and 1900, Sorolla continued to take part in exhibitions all over Europe, and he also sent five paintings to the 1894 Chicago Universal Exhibition. During this period his second child, Joaquín, was born in Valencia on the 8th of November 1892, and his third child, Elena, on the 12th of June 1895, also in the same city. And so, as the family grew, Sorolla had to look after their well-being and education. He didn't give up the easy-to-sell paintings, nor did he reject commissions that were not very demanding. However, it is also true to say that he did achieve magnificent creations in both the rapidly painted works and portraits, which were so opposed to his ideal of painting.

Thanks to the success achieved at all these exhibitions, Sorolla could leave the house and studio in Plaza del Progreso and move to another larger and more comfortable one on Pasaje de La Alhambra, whose previous tenant had been his friend and adviser Jiménez Aranda. Their mutual esteem went back to that Exposición Nacional of 1890, when they became close friends, not without a certain authoritative air on the part of the Sevillian artist. In him, Sorolla found a tenacious defender of realism and drawing, which reaffirmed his painting. Having lived and worked in Paris for eight years, his work had nothing to do with the history paintings that were so highly valued at that time. He lived for less than three years in Madrid, from where he went to Seville, abandoning his production of "Grand Manner" paintings for which he was so well-known, and devoting himself to painting contemporary life scenes and characters, adapting his style of painting to the times. A meticulous study of Sorolla's canvases belonging to the period 1891-1895, for example, *El beso de la reliquia* ["Kissing the Relic"], *El resbalón del monaguillo, Fruta prohibida, Ex voto, El mamón (o Familia segoviana), La mejor cuna* and *La bendición de la barca,* reveals a clear influence of Jiménez Aranda, an influence corroborated, on the other hand, by art critics with such differences of opinion as were Beruete, Augusto Comas, Leonard Williams, Rafael Doménech, Ramón Pulido and Manuel Abril. An expressive drawing now dominates the composition, different from the academic spirit, although the chromatic palette still indicates a period of transition.

Since his return to Valencia, Sorolla had temporarily come into contact with the local republican movement headed by his friend the writer Vicente Blasco Ibáñez. For years his work was very much influenced by Blasco's ideas, who steered the painter towards a social realism very similar to that of his own novels, whilst, at the same time, he encouraged him to use his paintbrush to denounce social injustice. As a result, we have the four well-known excellent canvases: *Otra Margarita* ["Another Marguerite"] (1892), *¡Aún dicen que el pescado es caro!* ["And They Still Say Fish is Expensive!"] (1894), *Trata de blancas* ["The White Slave Trade"] (1895) and *Triste herencia* ["Sad Inheritance"] (1899).

Other canvases painted between 1892 and 1893 that must be highlighted for their portrayal of local customs and characters are *El día feliz, El resbalón del monaguillo, El beso de la reliquia* and *Una rogativa en Burgos,* the last two receiving awards at exhibitions. The great variety of themes, orientations, procedures and ways of painting seen in Sorolla's production before 1894 show us his great skill for painting, but they don't speak of a very well-defined personality. That situation of uncertainty changed when he managed to find the appropriate road to the personal and artistic demands that drove him on.

¡Aún dicen que el pescado es caro!
(And They Still Say Fish is Expensive!)
Detail

In this type of works in which a finished, but loose brushstroke is used, there is no place for what would later make Sorolla so famous: the Mediterranean light and joie de vivre.

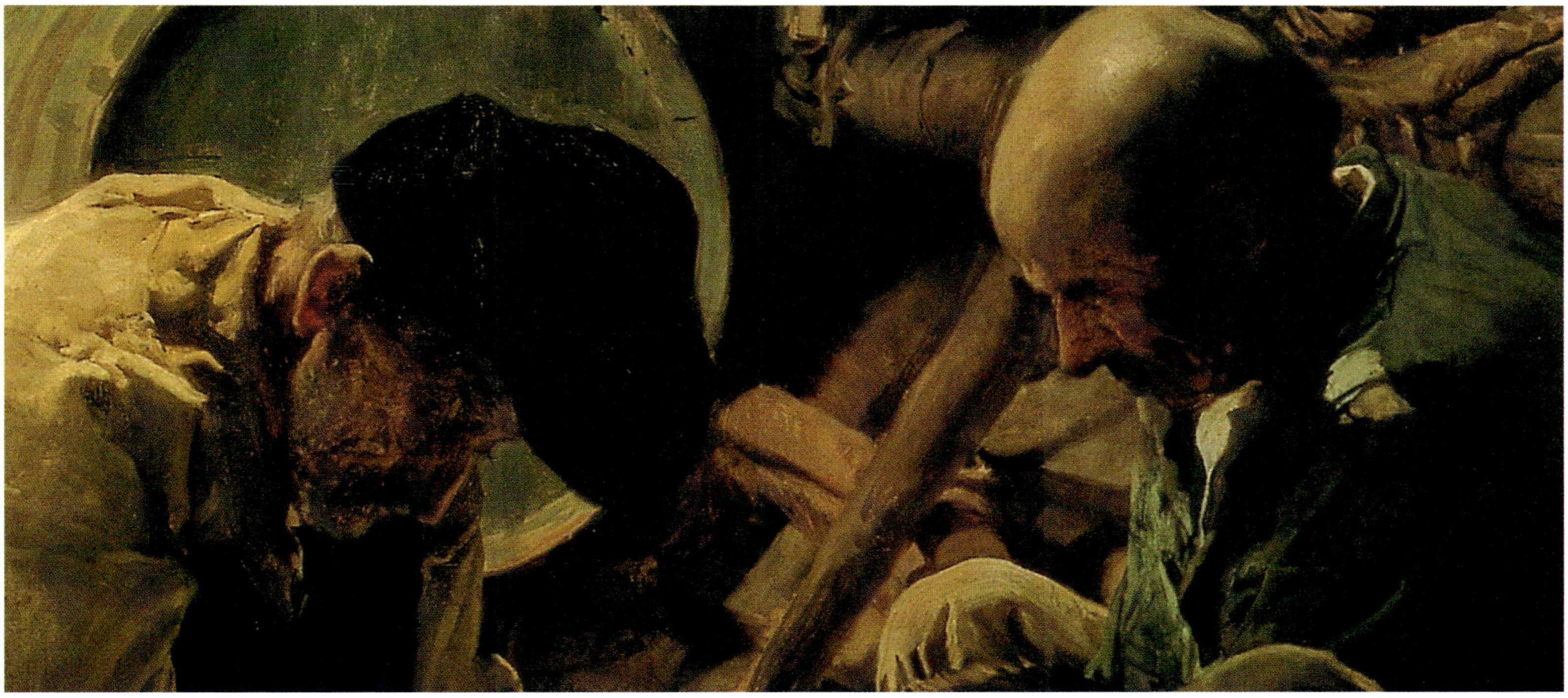

The beach, fishermen and fisherwomen: The moment of beach scenes

Living in Madrid, where he would paint portraits (*Benito Pérez Galdós*, 1894), various studies and at night watercolours for selling, he got into the habit of spending the summer in his hometown, where a large part of his family and friends still lived. By this time he was already a highly-praised artist in the capital. The gold medals received were a constant source of motivation, spurring him on to constantly excel himself. But the summers in Valencia entailed many personal incentives, many pleasant memories. And, above all, for his art, so many popular themes that attracted him for their luminosity. When Sorolla decided to paint scenes of everyday life on Valencia beach, those moments of fishing and bathing that he had observed so many times under the intense sunlight, he realised that he had found the future of his art, a theme that he would never abandon and to which he would devote himself in heart and soul the rest of his life.

In the summer of 1894, Sorolla painted three very well-known paintings on Valencia beach, not pictorially considered among the best, but for their aesthetics, and for their personal nature, being typical Sorolla paintings: the above-mentioned *¡Aún dicen que el pescado es caro!*, as well as *La vuelta de la pesca* ["Return from Fishing"] and *La bendición de la barca* ["Blessing of the Boat"], which received prizes in Paris (*Salon*), Madrid (*Exposición Nacional*) and Venice (First International), respectively. Both the first, whose title comes from the end of the novel *Flor de Mayo* (1895), by Blasco Ibáñez, and the second, show the most famous aspect of Sorolla's painting. They are not the first ones painted on Valencia beach, since he had previously painted *Las redes* ["The Nets"], *Cordeleros* ["Ropemakers"] and *El pillo de playa* ["The Beach Scamp"], but they are the first of the group making up the first stage of this modality, the two that are best known and most characteristic. Years later the artist painted better works, but the two mentioned, from an historical point of view, play an outstanding role for their characteristics.

As Sorolla himself would later admit, *La vuelta de la pesca* was also that painting with which he found himself; from then on, he said years afterwards: "With a solid base, I began to create, now fearlessly, my style of painting, good or bad, I don't know, but sincere, real, a reflection of what my eyes have seen and my heart has felt: the exact manifestation of what I have always believed art should be. Until my painting of *La vuelta de la pesca*, I hadn't exactly found what I was looking for. It was a laborious, but methodical, and reasoned gestation. It began in Assisi; it took shape in the works that I made there; it was clear in my

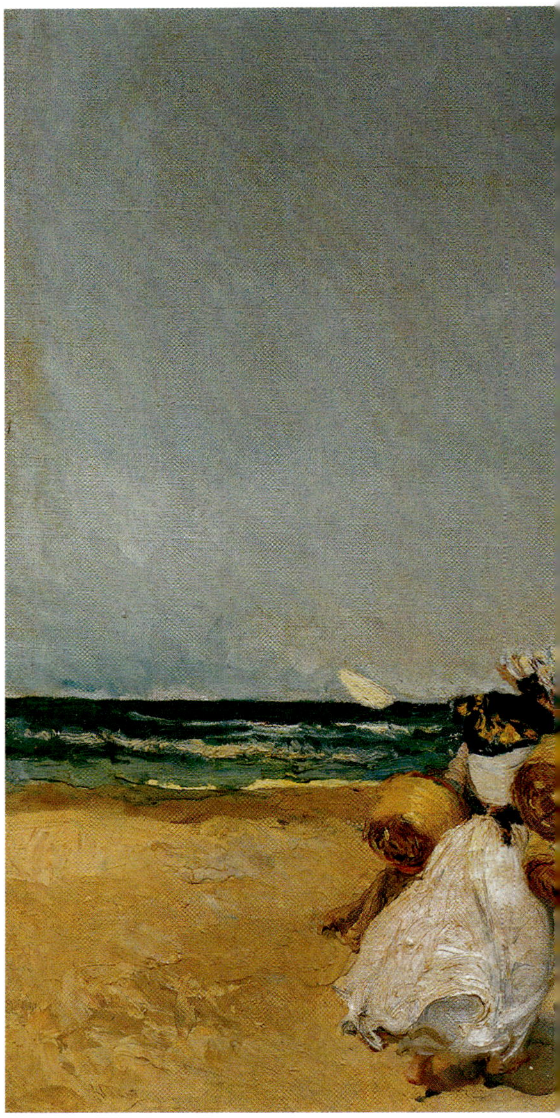

Descargando la barca
(Arrival of the Boats)
1898, oil on canvas
Private collection

This beautiful beach scene, occupying the lower third of the canvas, represents a summary of Sorolla's painting of local customs and beach scenes: the beach, the boat, the oxen towing out the fishing boat, the sailors, the fisherwomen … the whites and blues…

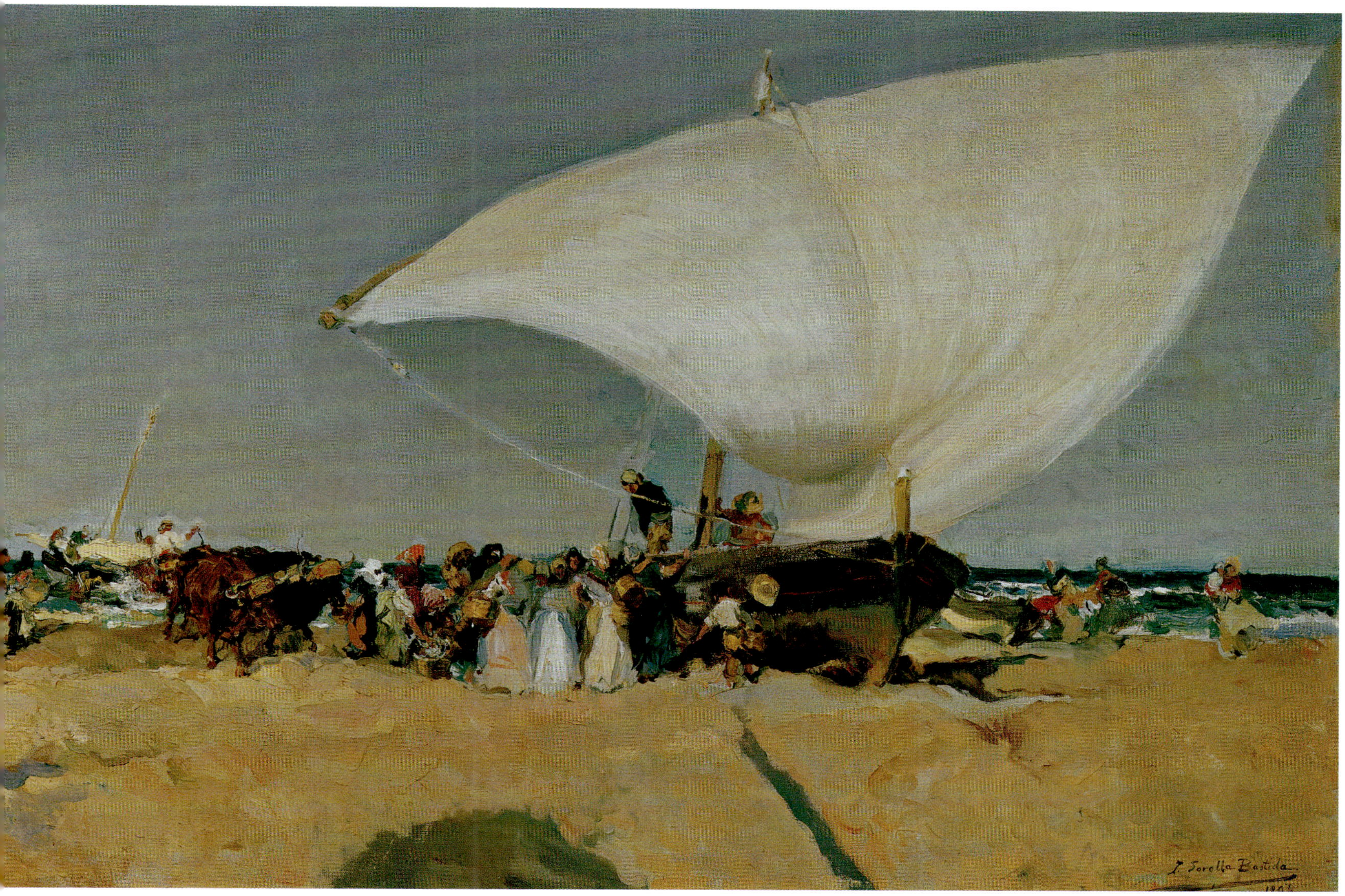

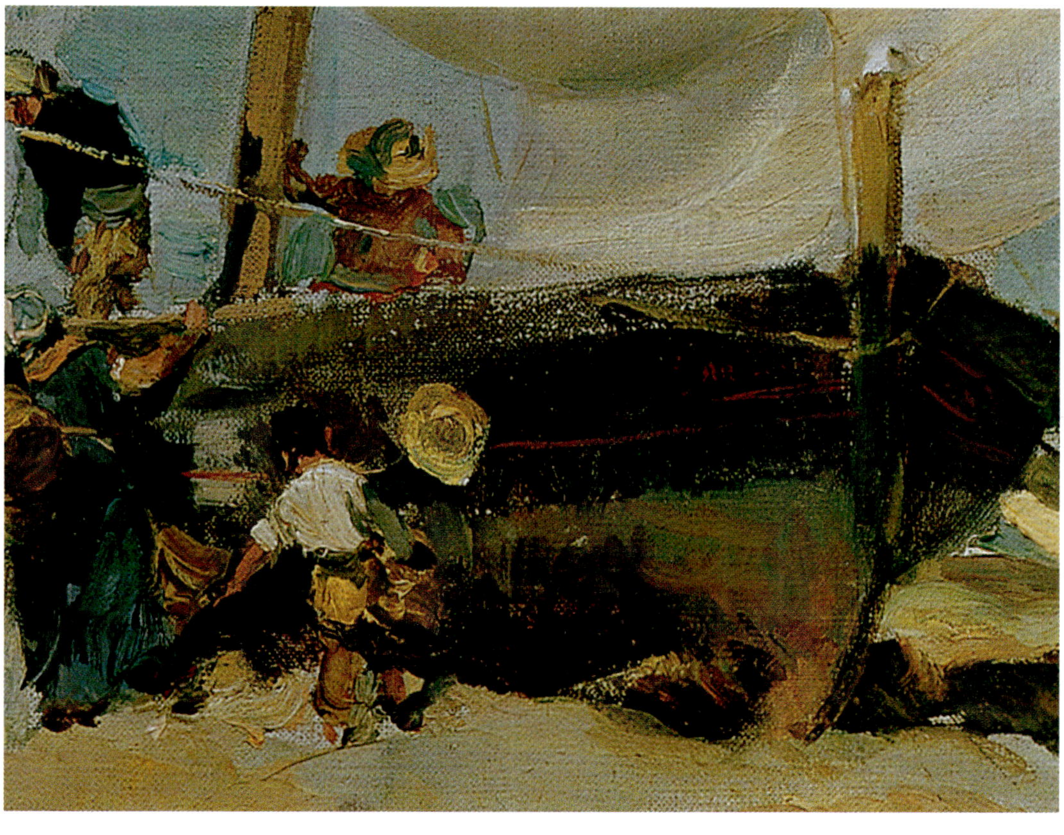

Descargando la barca
(Arrival of the Boats)
Detail

The boat, with all its connotations of the sea and work, here can be seen devoid of the strength it acquires in the representation as a whole associated with the dynamic strength of the sail.

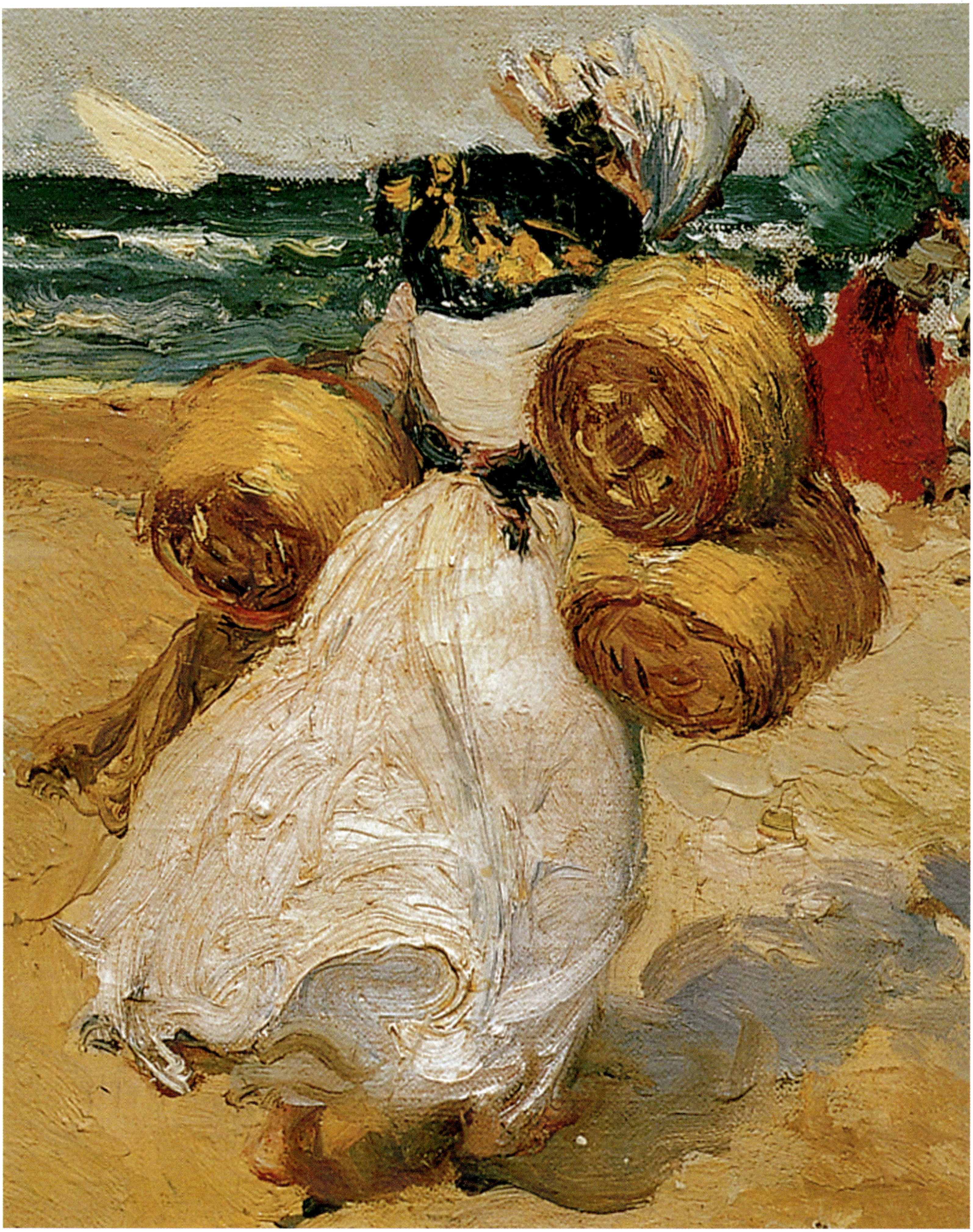

Descargando la barca
(Arrival of the Boats)
Detail

The fisherwoman, although taken out of context, is a prototype of the Mediterranean woman, proud of herself and with a very strong character. This figure is one of the axes of this great frieze which is complemented by the above-mentioned elements.

canvas *Boulevard de París*; I found it defined in *Otra Margarita*, and it presented itself as palpable, now resolved, in "the oxen pulling in the boat", in my *Sol de la tarde* ["Late Afternoon Sun"]. My only desire since I entered the *Escuela de Bellas Artes de Valencia* was to create a frank painting, a painting that interpreted Nature just as it really is, just as it should be seen... Now, in 1912, my hand obeys my retina and my feeling. Really, at the age at which one must call himself a painter: after thirty years of work!"

At that time, the artist could certainly now speak of a very personal painting.

Belonging to the same period, but to different modalities, *Una investigación* and *Madre* ["Mother"] are outstanding examples of Sorolla's work. The first one, which was awarded a Medal of Honour at the Certamen Nacional in 1897, is a beautiful interior study with artificial light painted in the laboratory of Luis Simarro, a famous name in Spanish medicine and one of the artist's best friends, who posed as a model for this work together with several of his pupils; while the second is a highly original version of the subject of motherhood, resolved by Sorolla with great tenderness in the composition.

The irresistible passion for the sea

Amongst the great beach scenes, in which Sorolla's personality and prestige were accentuated, we can highlight *Cosiendo la vela* ["Mending the Sail"] (1896), which was highly praised in Munich and Vienna, and *Comiendo en la barca* ["Lunch on the Boat"] (1898). They are two of his most important and characteristic canvases before 1899; very original compositions, splendidly depicted, full of character, light and atmosphere, apart from having been energetically drawn and painted with a long and expressive brushstroke. Both were very successful at the Exposición Nacional in 1899 and were met with warm approval.

Summer after summer, Sorolla placed his easel on the seashore and, once there, prepared his models, working untiringly long days. The canvases painted were successively put on display in Madrid and in big international centres, always attracting attention for their vibrating colouring and magnetic power of the light.

Now that opposition from some critics against the postulates of impressionism had been overcome, and a channel opened in which news artistic styles struggled to find their chance, Sorolla didn't have to support the tenacious opposition that the others suffered. His victory was resounding and quick, partly due to the fact that there were many Spanish and foreign critics who coincided in appreciating the values of his painting. Among those famous writers we have Blasco Ibáñez, with whom the artist established a reciprocal influence. At the same time as the Valencian canvases of Sorolla could be seen, the Valencian novels of Blasco Ibáñez were read. They both knew how to define and describe charismatic scenes, one basing himself on subtle wordplay and the other on the skill of his paintbrushes.

In the summer of 1899, Sorolla enriched his production with new works, highlighting among them, *El baño* ["The Bath"] and the above-mentioned *Triste herencia*, the last work of a social nature that received a Grand Prix at the Universal Exhibition in Paris in 1900. He also submitted *Cosiendo la vela* and *Comiendo en la barca* to this show, as well as *Algarrobo* and *La Caleta*. In *El baño*, like in so many other similar scenes, the sunlight and the sea breeze play an important role, in an original, daring and beautiful composition, alongside the white sheet spread out and the shivering body of the boy coming out of the water; whereas

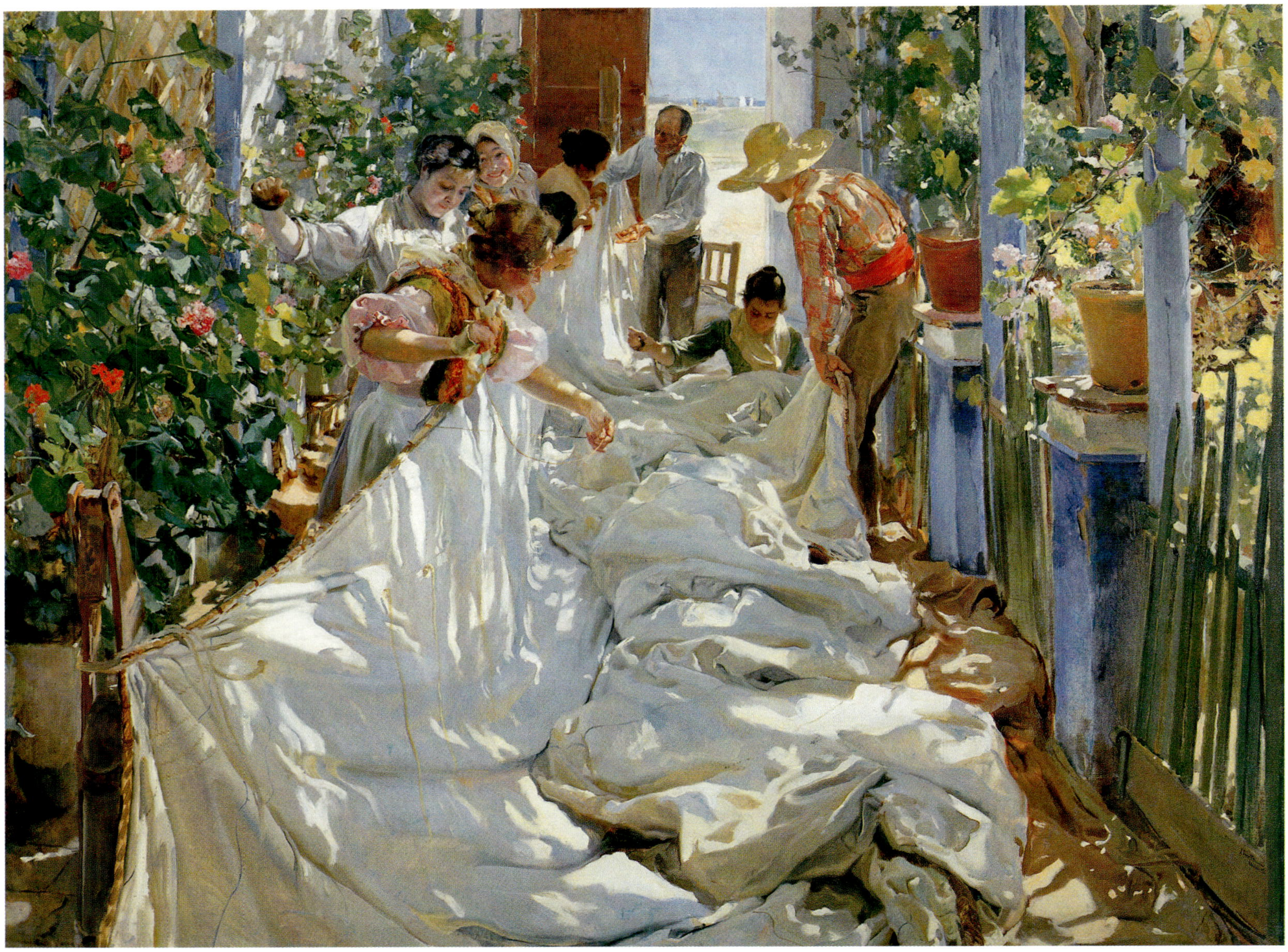

in *Triste herencia*, Sorolla put his palette at the service of the poor and sick who were taken in by the Valencian poorhouse San Juan de Dios to portray them at the time of their daily bath.

On the whole, these works are extraordinary samples of success, of original elaboration and, of course, personal artistic creation. While Sorolla was enjoying a successful career, the diffusion of his work was facilitated by the unavoidable imitators and followers of those fishing and bathing scenes, it could easily be seen how far the latter were from the master's technique and pictorial quality of composition.

Cosiendo la vela
(Mending the Sail)
1896, oil on canvas, 220 × 302 cm
Venice: Ca' Pesaro

Sorolla carries out the transition towards canvases with strong light effects at the same time as his tragic social themes. In this one, devoid of any type of dramatic element, he offers us a realistic but vibrating and luminous scene of great beauty.

Cosiendo la vela
(Mending the Sail)
Detail

Thanks to the light filtering between the flowers, the sail becomes alive, its whiteness blending with the green of nature and the soft tones of the workers' clothes.

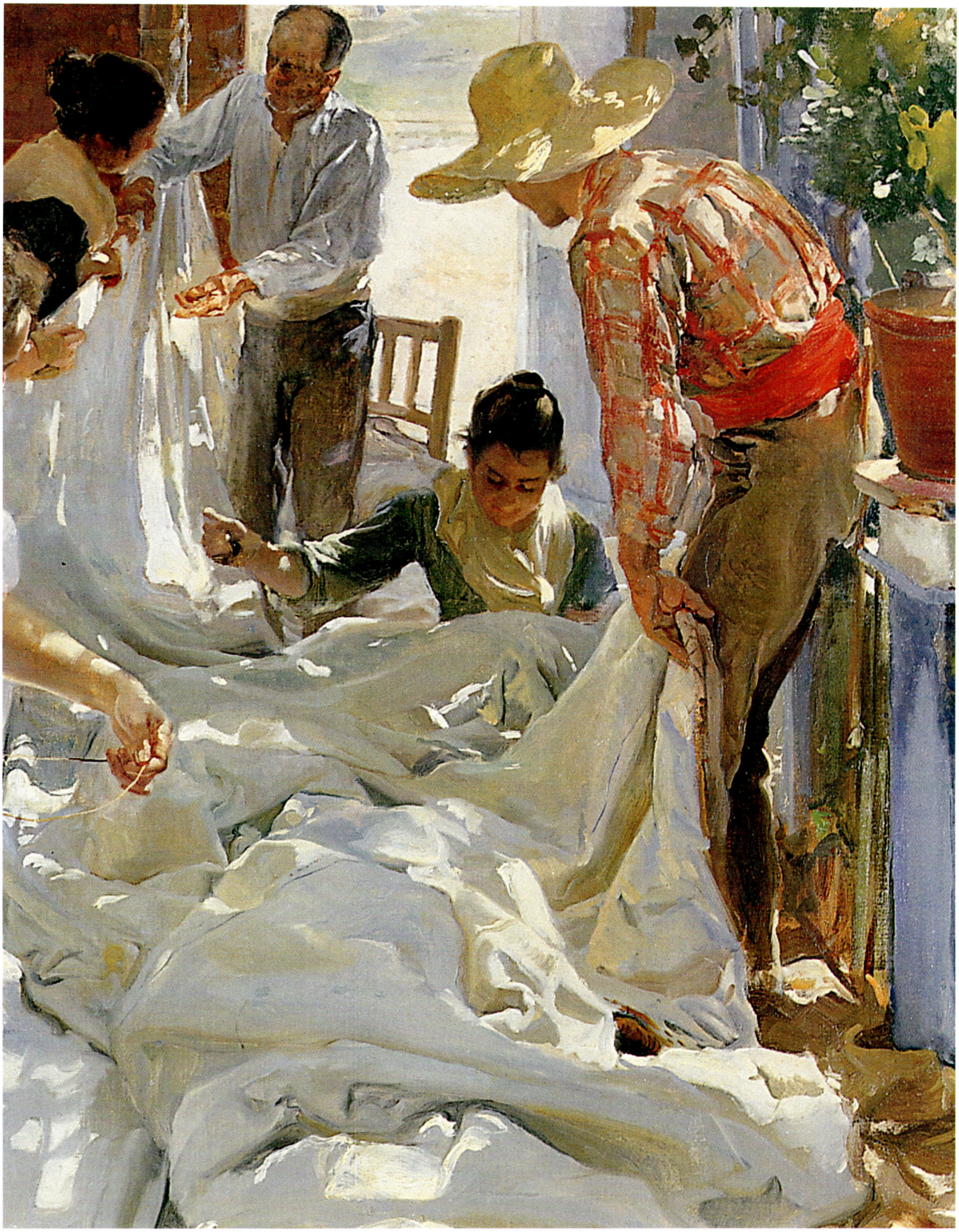

Towards an intuitively personal art

In June 1900, soon after having received the prizes, Sorolla travelled to Paris to visit that year's Universal Exhibition, together with Pedro Gil and Beruete. If years ago Bastien-Lepage and Menzel had shown him the way to realism, on this occasion it was the works of the Danish artist Peter Severin Kroyer and the Swedish painter Anders Zorn which showed him the specific way to materialize it. The similarities between the works of both painters were quite evident, with a realism based on momentariness and corporeality and with themes inspired by people and customs of their own homeland.

Zorn's works and the friendship that Sorolla struck up with him led to a significant turn in the latter's artistic career, definitively abandoning social themes in his painting and his palette becoming lighter. He devoted himself more and more to open-air scenes, with children and women on the beach, which helped him to deal with the problem of the reflection of light on water.

Once the news of Sorolla's artistic success reached Spain, his numerous admirers decided to celebrate, including Mariano Benlliure (1862-1947) in the celebrations, since he had received one of the Medals of Honour granted to sculptors at the same exhibition. The artistic atmosphere in Madrid favoured this artist who had been living there for 10 years now, having received at least 10 foreign prizes, so it was logical to expect that the 1901 Exposición Nacional would grant the Medal of Honour to a painter who unofficially certainly held a distinguished position among the artists of the period.

María o María de blanco
(Maria or Maria in White)
1900, oil on canvas, 110 × 80 cm
Private collection

This portrait of Sorolla's eldest daughter at the age of 10 shows the freedom of the artist when the model is close to him. As Edmund Peel said, "In comparison with the portraits commissioned, we can observe a greater freedom of execution as well as a more intimate knowledge of the subject. The girl's name can be seen on the left of the model and the date on the right."

The beach and children in Jávea

During the spring of 1905, year in which *Sol de la tarde* was admired at the Salon de Paris, Sorolla travelled to France and England and then decided to transfer his summer studio to Jávea, a town on the Valencian coast where five years earlier he had also spent the summer months painting various aspects of the area's local industry, i.e. raisin production. On this occasion his stay lasted two months and he painted around twenty canvases, mainly of boys bathing in a seductive chromatic play of sunlight. When drawing the scenes of raisin production, just as when later watching the bathers, the artist was mainly concerned about reflecting chromatic values and light effects, which sometimes led him to deliberately neglecting everything related with form. In the splendid beach scenes at Jávea, and particularly in the series of bathers, Sorolla, without increasing the chromatic range of his palette, which, as in all real colourists, consists of only a few colours, extended and multiplied the number of shades,

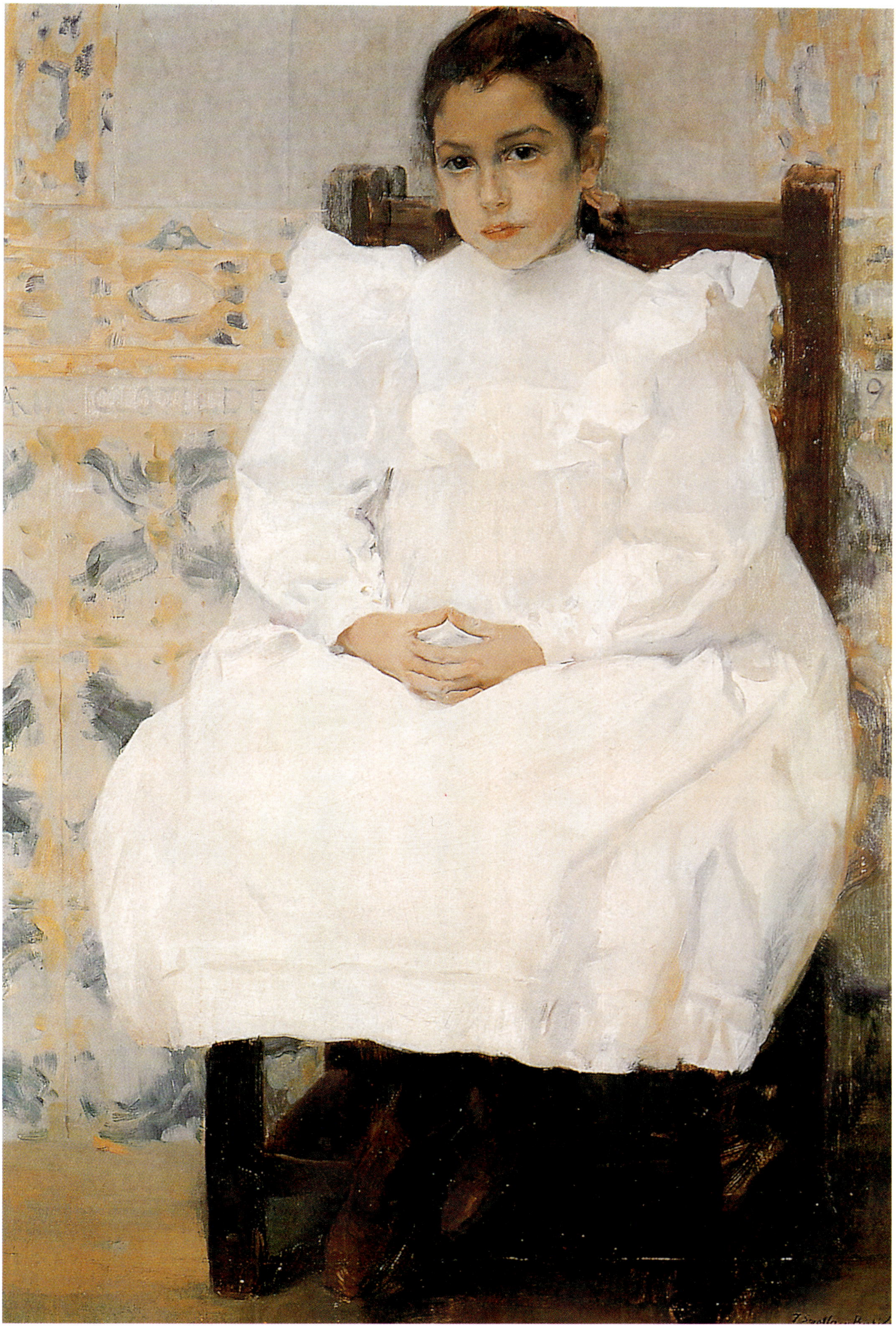

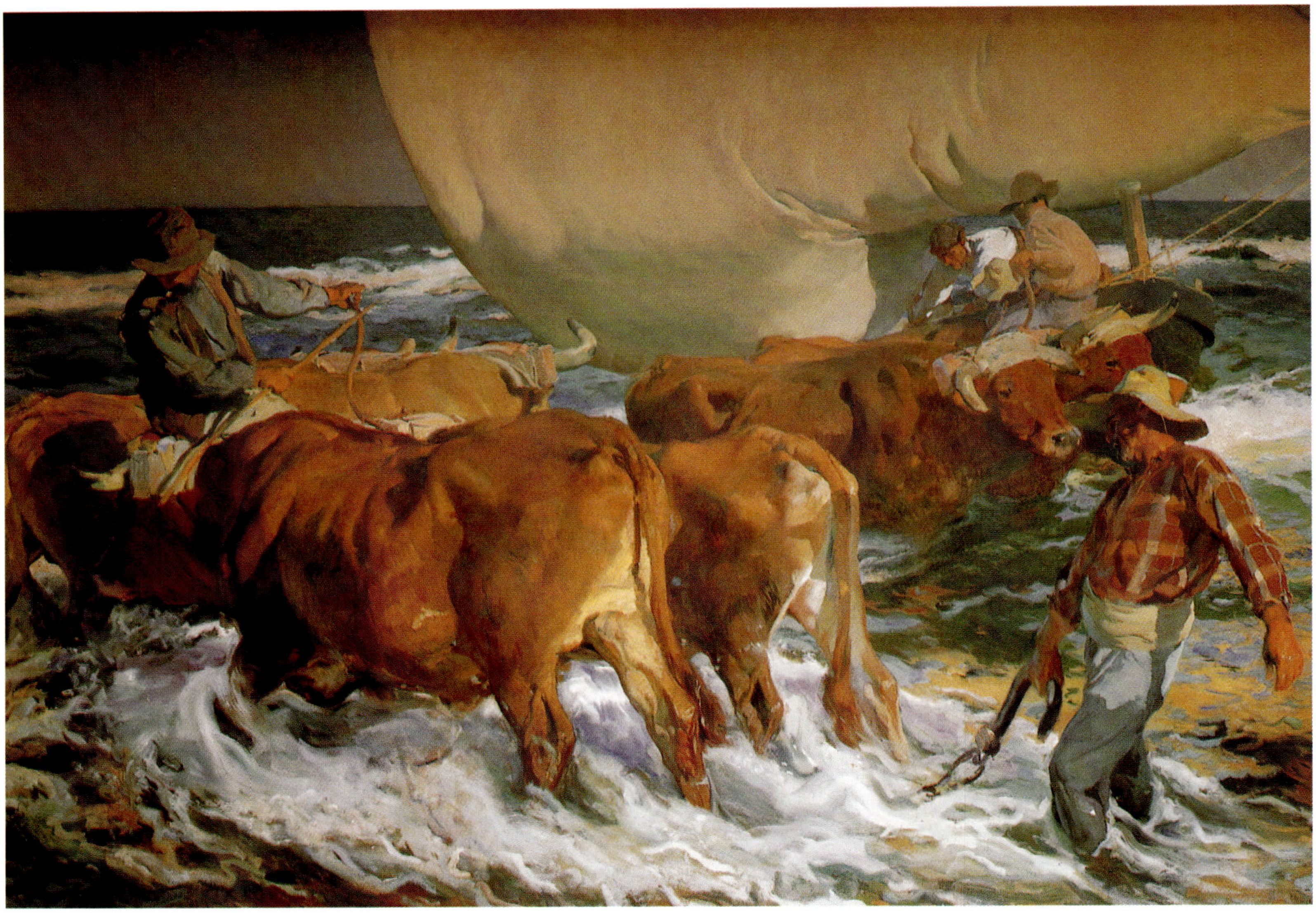

Sol de la tarde
(Late Afternoon Sun)
1903, oil on canvas, 244 × 435 cm
New York: Hispanic Society

The themes representing daily fishing scenes on the coast of Levante became Sorolla's favourite subject from the year 1900. The movement of the sails, the strength of the oxen and the fishermen would be the excuse for the artist's true passion: depicting the Mediterranean light at different times of the day. The title gives away the real theme depicted.

as well as that of bold contrasts. In this way he achieved splendid tones of blue and yellow, violet and cadmium, green and red, without forgetting the rich hues of white, a colour to which he always knew how to give a very personal touch.

However, his speed and alacrity in production brought Sorolla his share of criticism regarding the superficiality of his work. Throughout the whole of his career, there was always a certain amount of controversy surrounding his work, since many didn't accept that apparent insubstantiality and the evident optimism of his work. And so, as the nineteenth-century traditionalist conservatives, who were also opposed to the impressionists, also attacked his work for its lack of detail, various groups of intellectuals said that his natural painting was "empty of content", when the truth is that the lightness they accused him of was in fact an intentional and positive attitude.

Speaking of himself, Sorolla admitted on some occasion to the doctor, politician and writer Amalio Gimeno: "It would be impossible to paint slowly outdoors, even if I wanted to... Everything that surrounds us is mobile. The sea is constantly rippling; clouds are continually changing shape as they move along; the rope that hangs from that boat swings slowly to and fro; that boy is jumping; the branches of those saplings bend and sway … But, even if everything was petrified and motionless, the sun would still move, which it continuously does, giving everything an ever-changing aspect...one has to paint quickly, because so many fleeting details can disappear, never to be seen again!"

As a theoretical formulation, those words summed up the pure impressionist legacy. And Amalio Gimeno gave his personal view of Sorolla's speedy painting: "Our painter was characterized by an astonishing sharpness to see and capture everything he saw. His retina was like an instant plate; its corresponding cerebral centre, an automatic trigger for the comparative judgement of line, shape and colour; his will, always ready to guide the muscle, and with the muscle, the paintbrush. The fine, intricate mechanism of his neuronal threads was like the set of tense strings on a delicate instrument tuned to vibrate with the light. He was like a stenographer of colour."

In the period between 1894 and 1916, Sorolla spent more than 12 summers painting on his Valencian beach. His production during this period was immense. But contemplating the first ones, those painted five years later, the others corresponding to the next half-decade, and those of the last years of this period, and comparing them with each other, we can see that, although there is not much of a difference in the themes, there are, however, very many different versions of the same theme, revealing an artist who is a constant observer of the natural world.

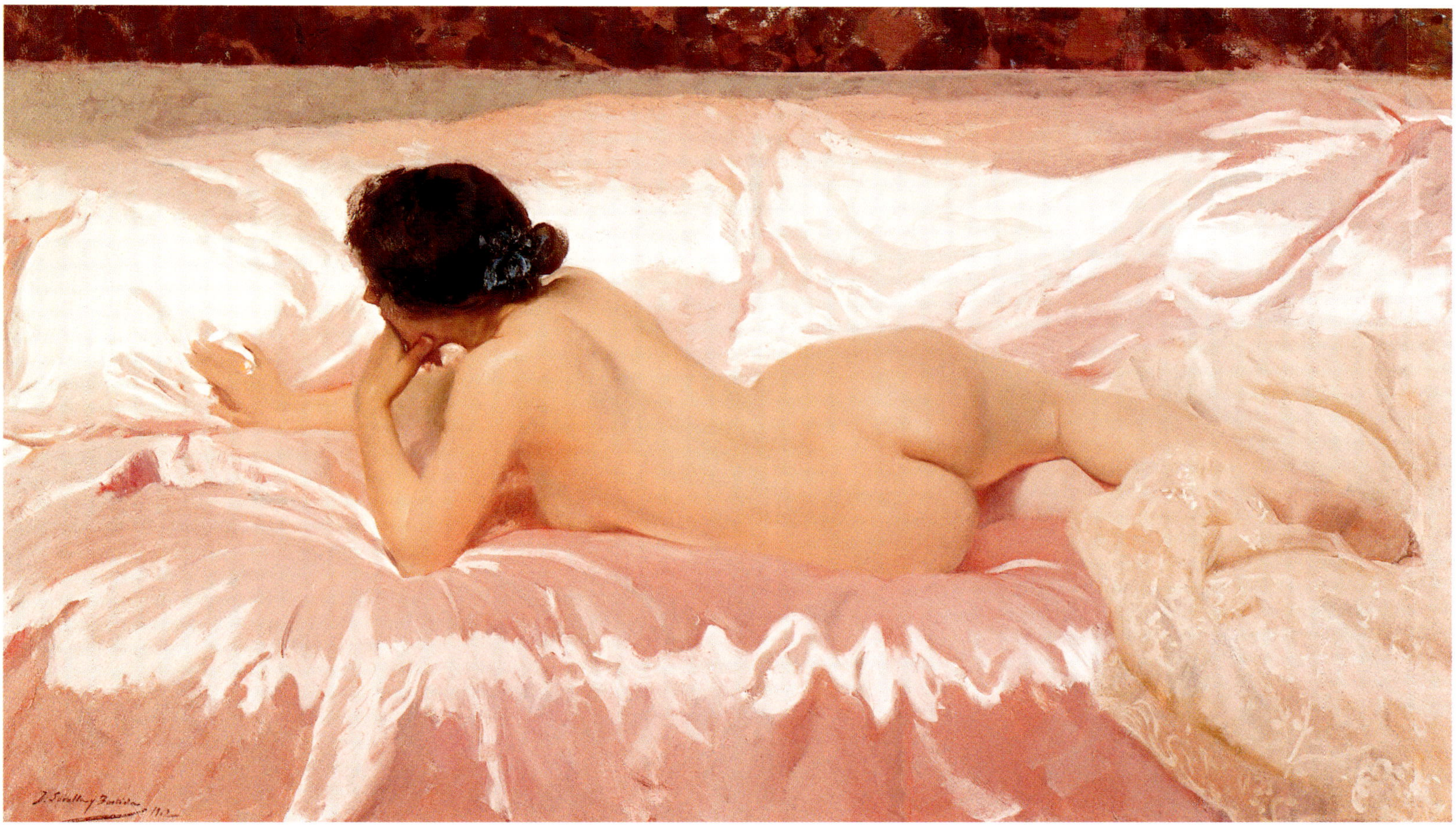

Desnudo de mujer
(Female Nude)
1902, oil on canvas, 106 × 188 cm
Madrid: Private collection

Presented at the exhibition held in Paris by the Societé Internationale in 1903, it was exhibited again in Chicago in 1922, with the title La gitana ["The Gypsy"]. *The influence of the work by Velázuez,* Venus del espejo, ["The Rokeby Venus"] *is evident. The model's dark hair tied in a bun stands out against the paleness of her body and the sheets.*

Mediodía en la playa de Valencia
(Midday on the Beach in Valencia)
1904, oil on canvas, 64 × 97 cm
Private collection

On this occasion the atmosphere has been captured with a divisive technique, using free and vibrant brushstrokes. The artist paints this composition like a huge sketch, only clearly defining part of the sunshade in the foreground.

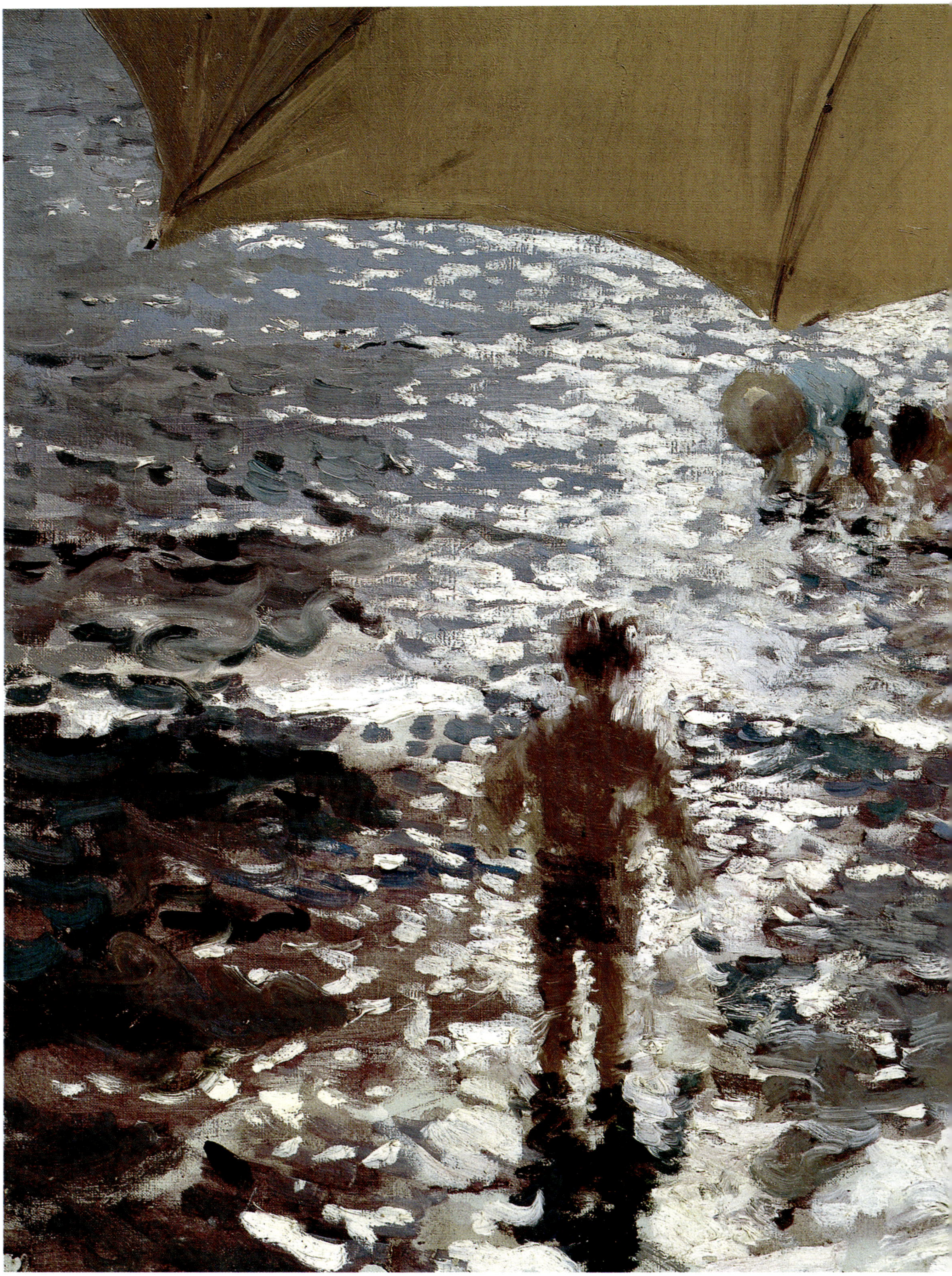

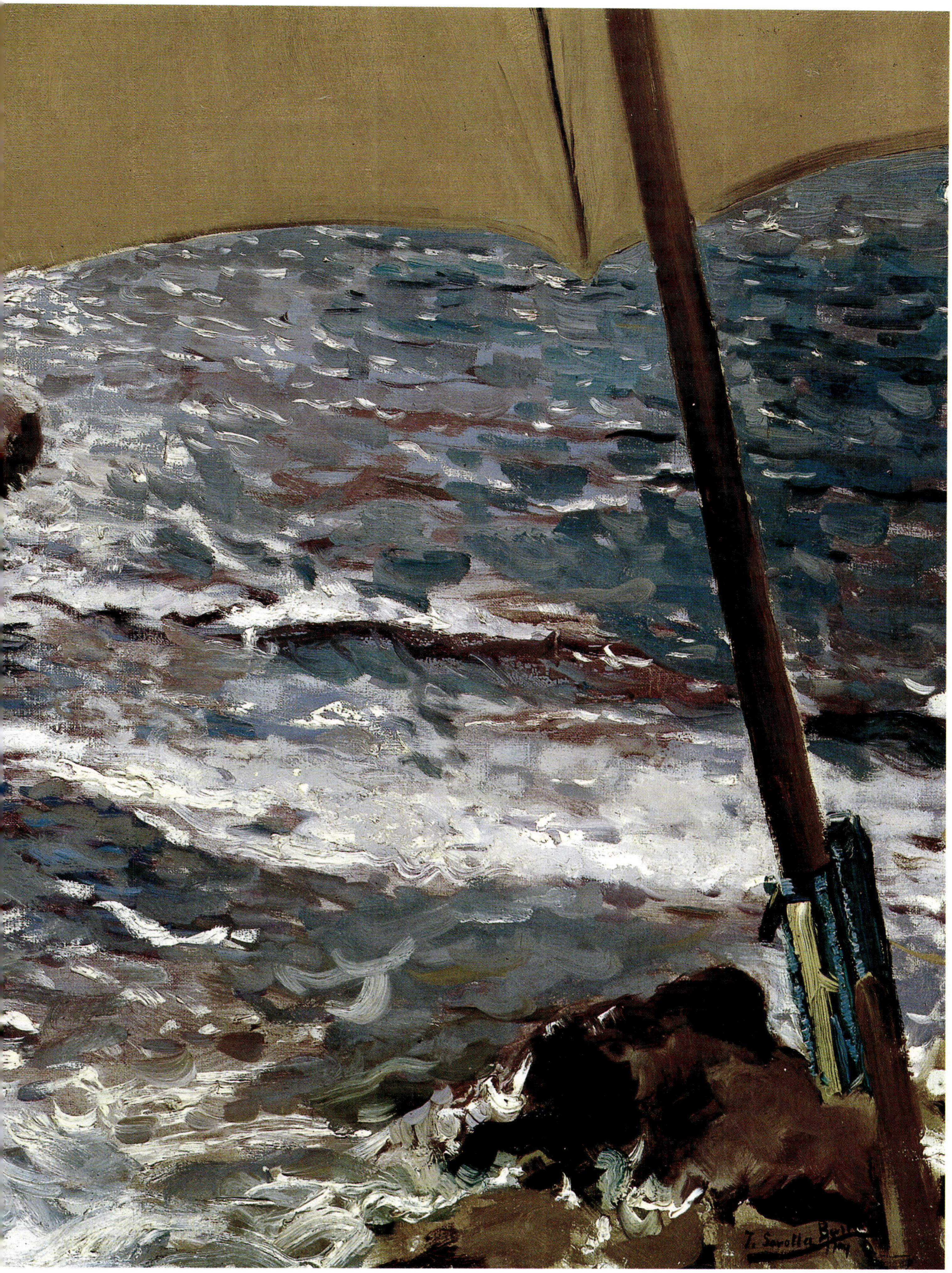

Triste herencia
(Sad Inheritance)
1899, oil on canvas, 210 × 285 cm
Caja de Ahorros de Valencia

Although this work corresponds to the artist's period of social criticism, it represents a scene halfway between his two concepts of painting. It marks the end of one period and the beginning of another, in which Sorolla will embark upon his international career encouraged by Jesús Vidal, the buyer of this work.

Paris, Berlin, London... Well-deserved international recognition

In 1906, at the age of 43 and, consequently, being in full creative flow, Joaquín Sorolla was now a renowned painter in Europe. He had already obtained a countless amount of prizes and awards, while his unquestionable artistic personality made it impossible at that time to make any possible comparison, even

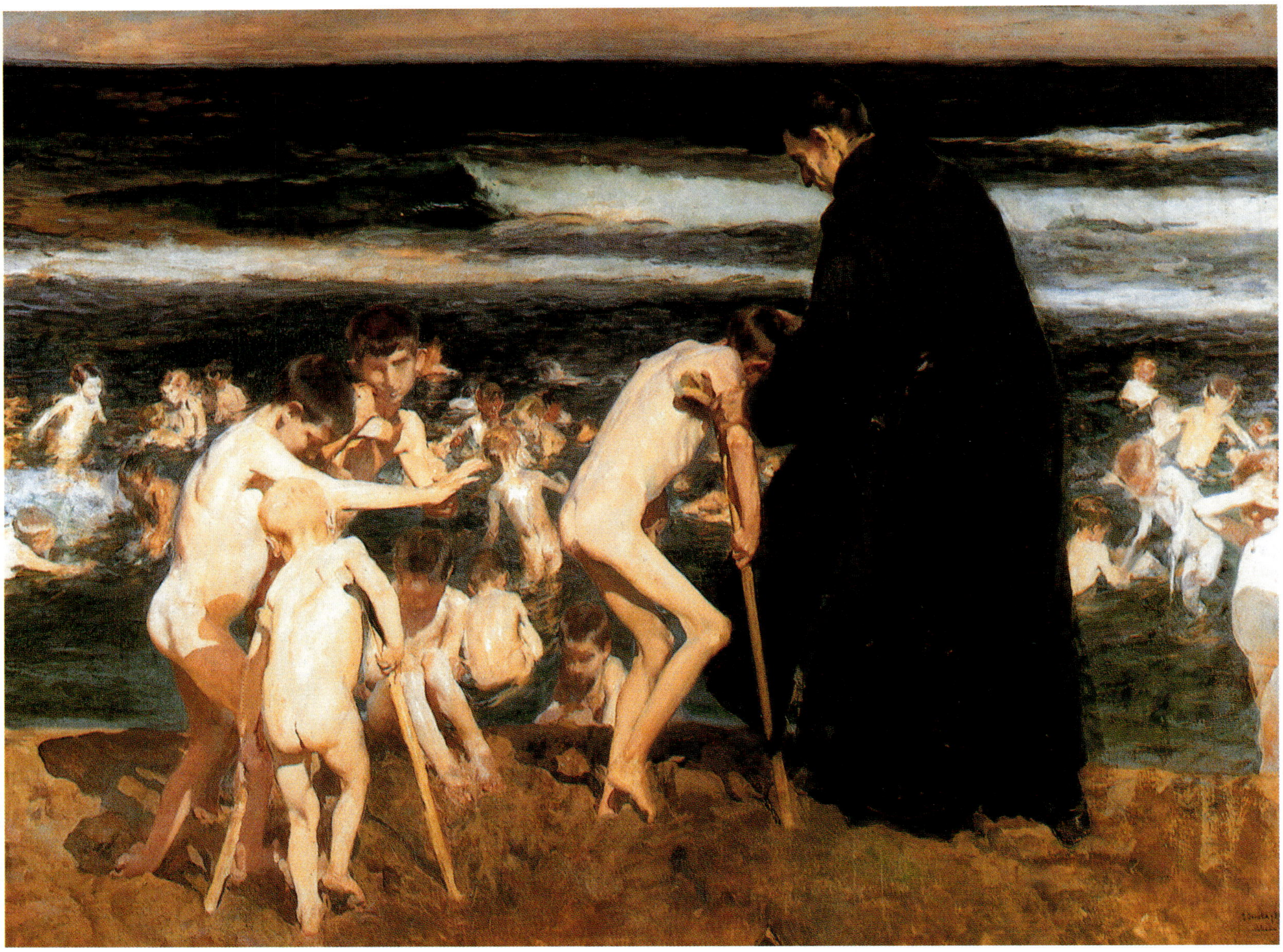

in spite of the more and more numerous amount of followers and imitators of his work who would follow him everywhere.

However, his discipline and character prevented him from being distracted by so much flattery and sincere praise; quite the opposite, the latter helped him to concentrate more and more on his work and, in a constant search for perfection and improvement, knowing that he would only achieve this goal by means of thorough dedication to painting.

Until that year, the numerous work of Sorolla had always been exhibited within the framework of collective Exhibitions, together with works of other painters. Now it was time for a solo exhibition, something not very habitual in the early twentieth century. The 1901 edition of the Exposición Nacional de Madrid had displayed as many as 16 paintings, but more than 6 had never been seen together outside Spain. Many of the painter's friends encouraged him to stage a good exhibition of his work, suggesting different cities abroad. José Artal, one of his keenest admirers, repeatedly requested him to put on a show in Buenos Aires, promising him a brilliant result and even sending him the names of people belonging to distinguished families in Buenos Aires who wanted to buy canvases or have their portraits painted for a good sum of money. On the other hand, Jesús Vidal, the lucky purchaser of *Triste herencia*, tried to persuade the artist to try his luck in the USA. Finally, between 1906 and 1911 Sorolla's works travelled to a total of 10 cities, which were, chronologi-

Pescadoras valencianas
(Valencian Fisherwomen)
1903, oil on canvas, 93 × 126 cm
Valencia: Diputación Provincial

Here the canvas is dominated by the figures in the forefront. The thickly applied brushstrokes, white not yet being the main colour used, are characteristic of the beginning of the artist's so-called period of maturity between 1901 and 1922.

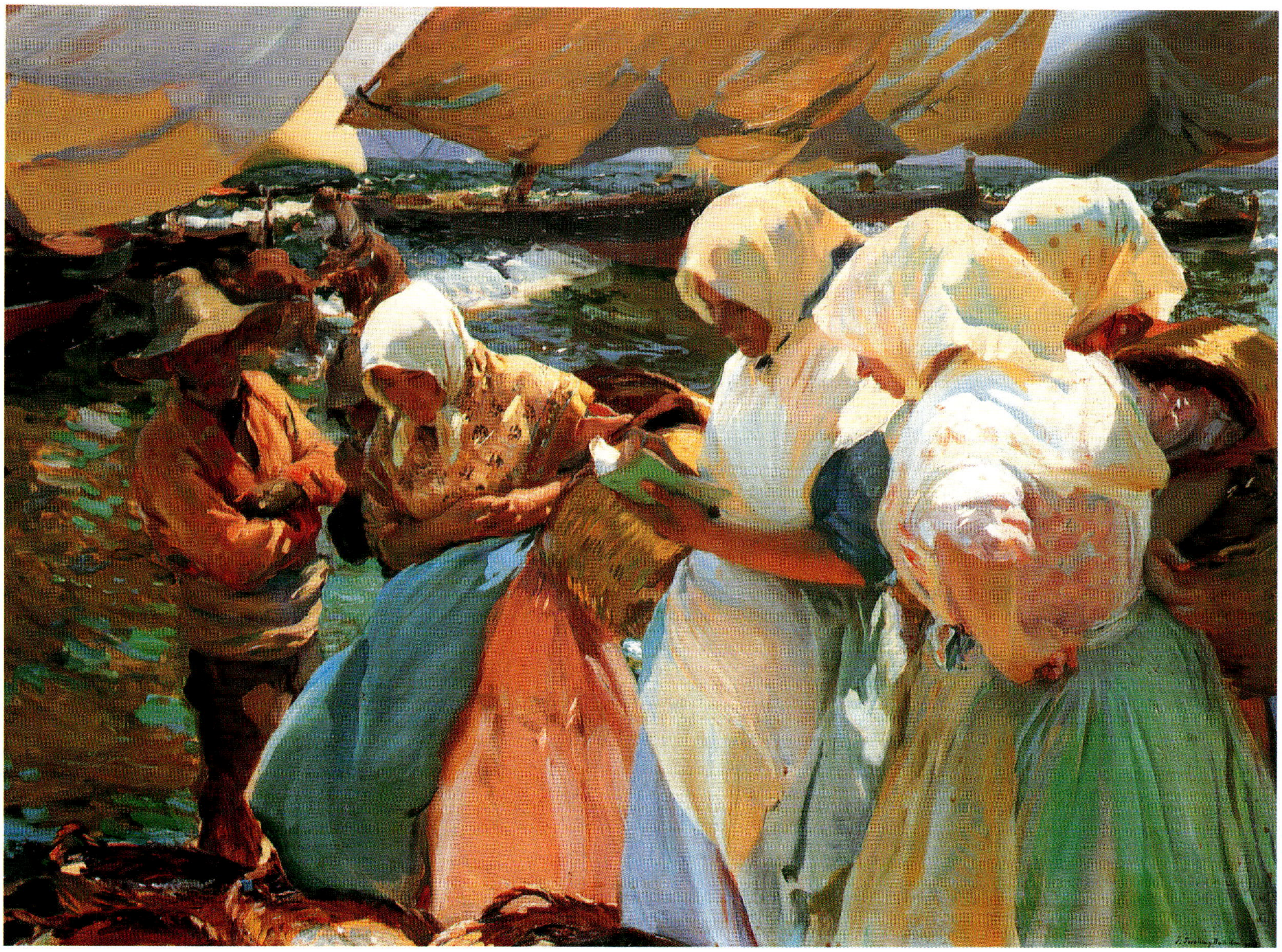

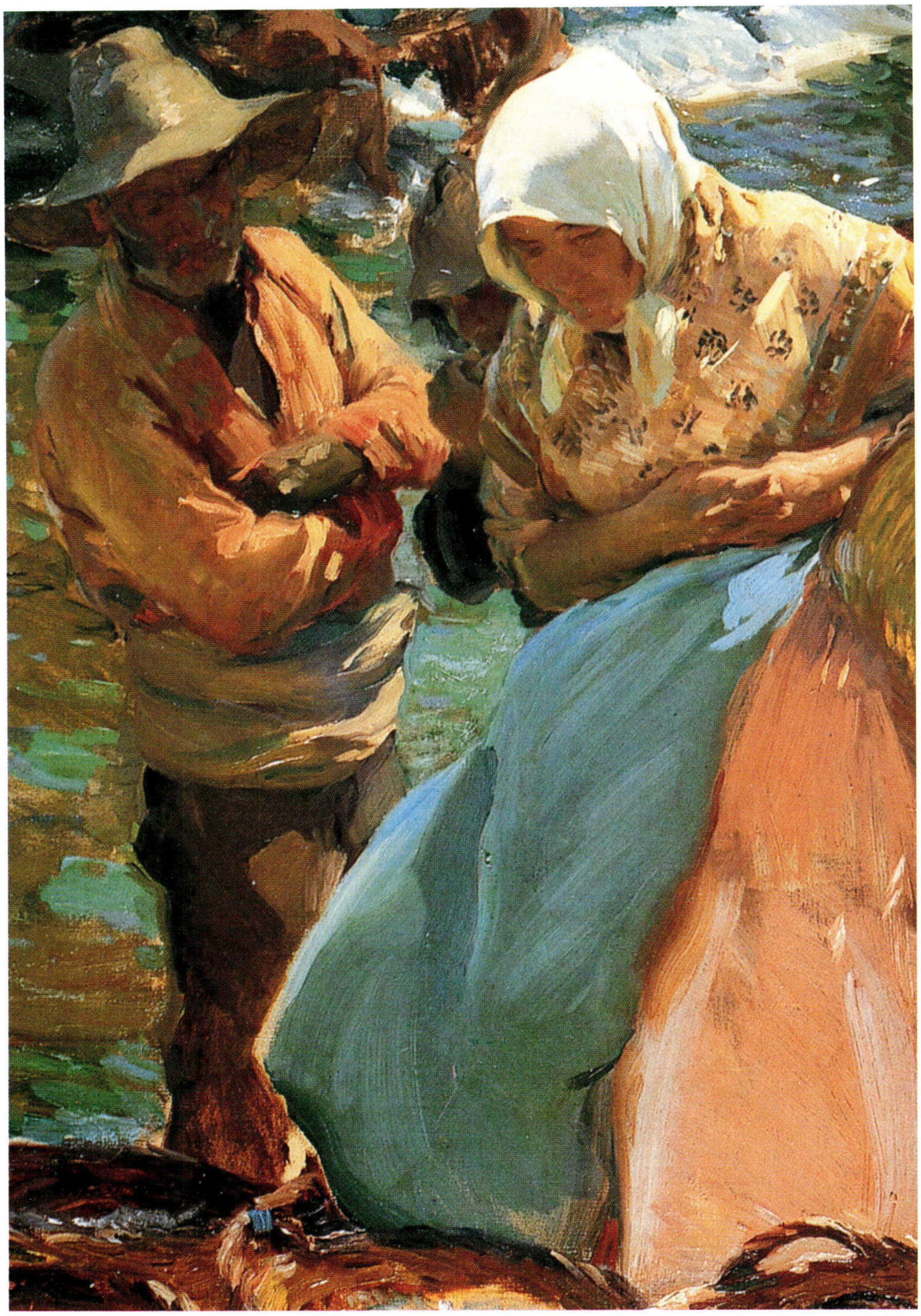

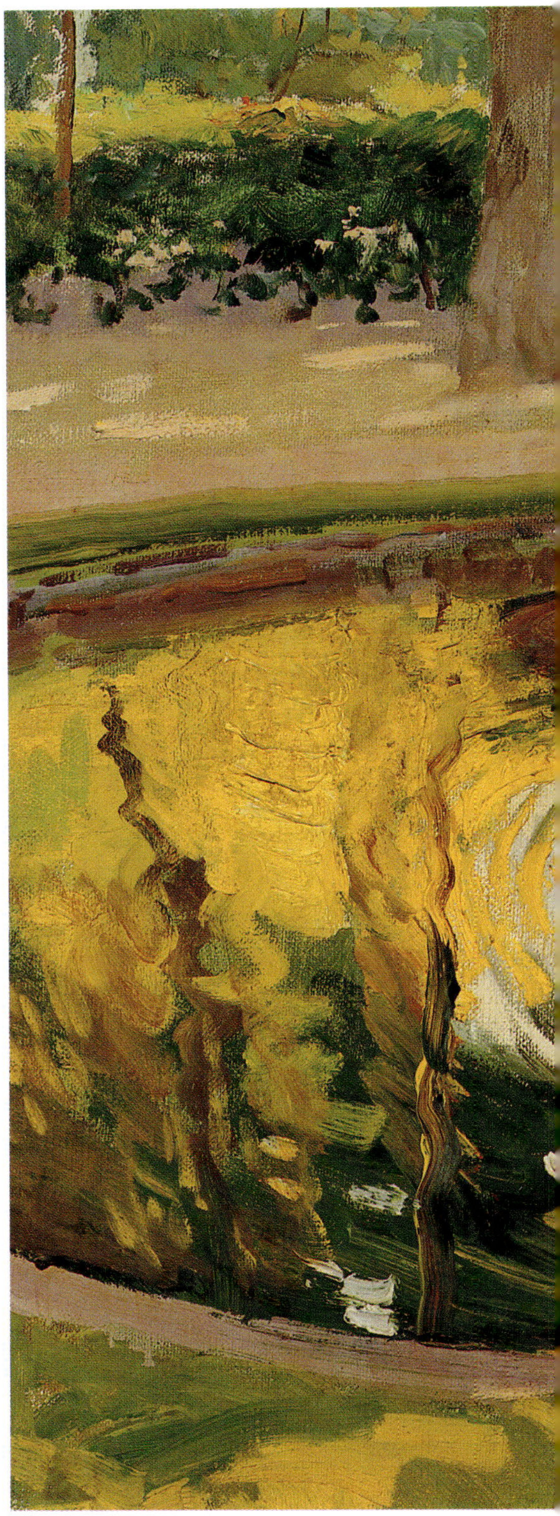

Pescadoras valencianas
(Valencian Fisherwomen)
Detail

The fisherman and woman observe the day's catch. In this detail we can see the chromatic value and the free brushstroke, characteristics that Sorolla will always use throughout his whole career.

cally, Paris, Berlin, Düsseldorf, Cologne, London, New York, Buffalo, Boston, Chicago) and St. Louis.

The exhibitions held in Düsseldorf and Cologne varied little from the immediately preceding one in Berlin. Those held in Buffalo and Boston also were the same as the one in New York, whilst the St. Louis exhibition was inspired by the one in Chicago. The exhibitions held with different paintings, although many common works were catalogued, were those of Paris, Berlin, London, New York and Chicago. The basic reason was that the painter would add new canvases painted between one exhibition and another, which explains why in 1907, in Berlin, canvases were exhibited that didn't appear in the 1906 Paris exhibition catalogue; exactly the same happened regarding the exhibition held in 1908

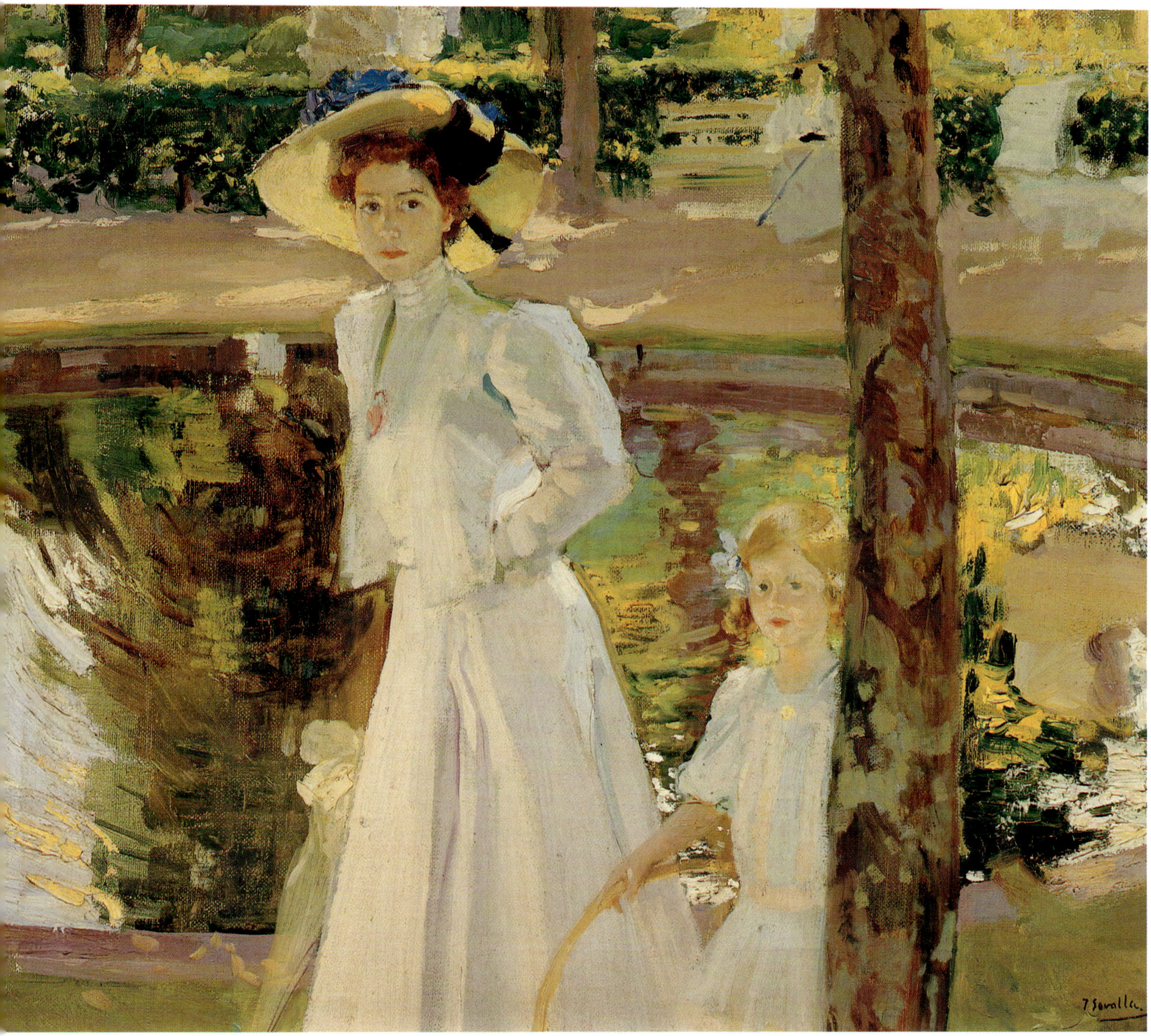

María en los jardines de La Granja
(Maria in the Garden at La Granja)
1907, oil on canvas, 56 × 89 cm
Madrid: Museo Sorolla

This scene represents Sorolla's daughter strolling with the daughter of the critic Leonard Williams, the whiteness of their dresses contrasting with the greens, blues and yellows of the background.

in London displayed canvases made the previous year, something that, on the whole, results in a very large number of works.

Therefore, Sorolla's first solo exhibition was held in Paris, at the famous Georges Petit gallery, between 11th June and 10th July. The almost 500 works exhibited, including around 300 sketches, filled the walls of the three large rooms of the gallery in a kind of anti-artistic accumulation. The attempt to make the most of the space meant that some oil paintings were literally fixed together with others. However, this didn't prevent the exhibition from arousing great interest in the city, both on the part of professional artists and public, besides being successful regarding critics and sales. The curious visitors could see how the impressionist movement was interpreted in those paintings with a certainly new

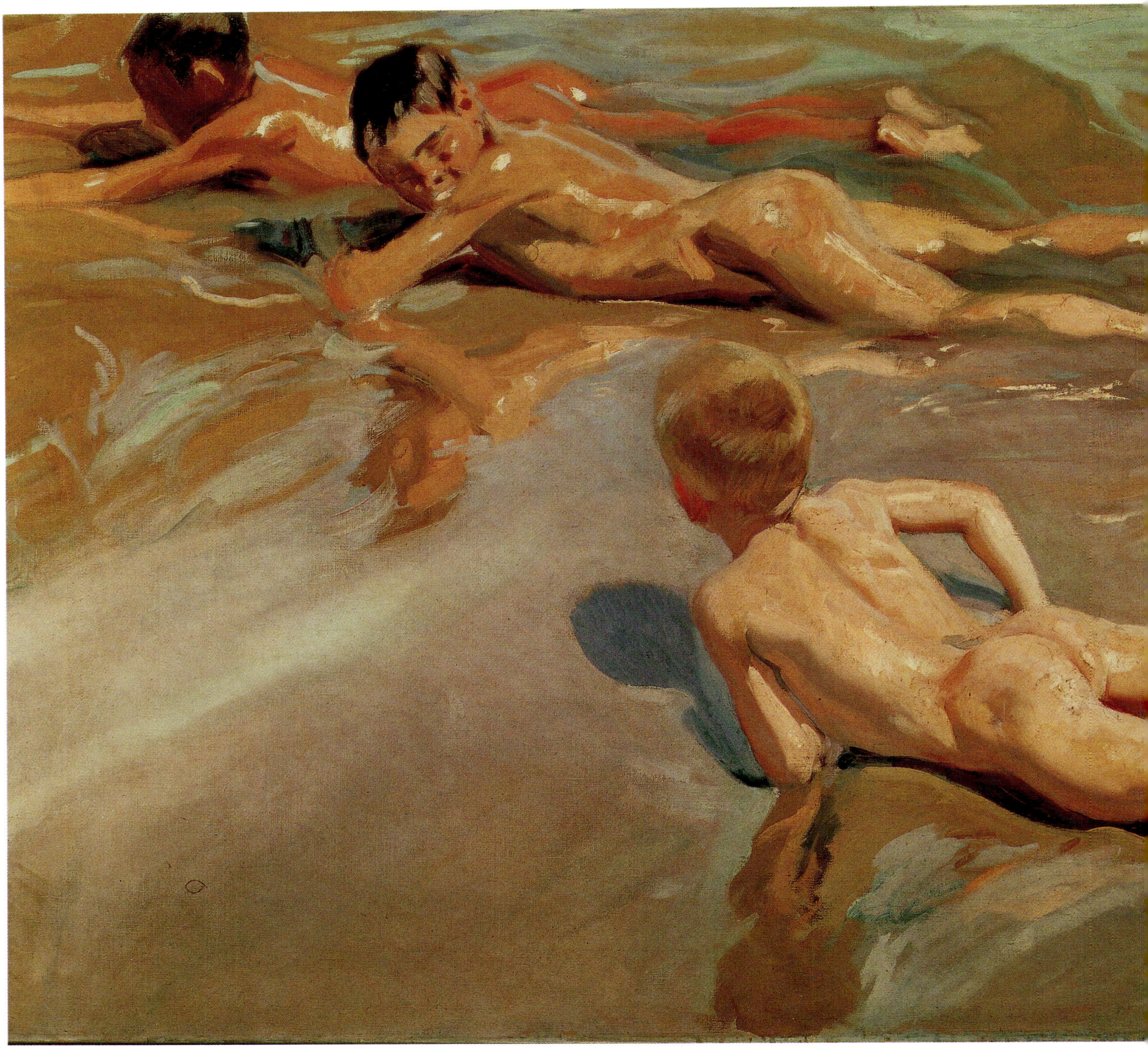

Niños en la playa
(Children on the Beach)
1910, oil on canvas, 118 × 185 cm
Madrid: Museo del Prado

With his progressive vagueness of his figures, Sorolla manages to blend the naked bodies of the three boys with the ebb and flow of the waves. The final result is close to abstraction, only broken by the anatomical references. What matters here are the rhythms, the rhythmic movement of the sea and the boys, and not the subject in itself.

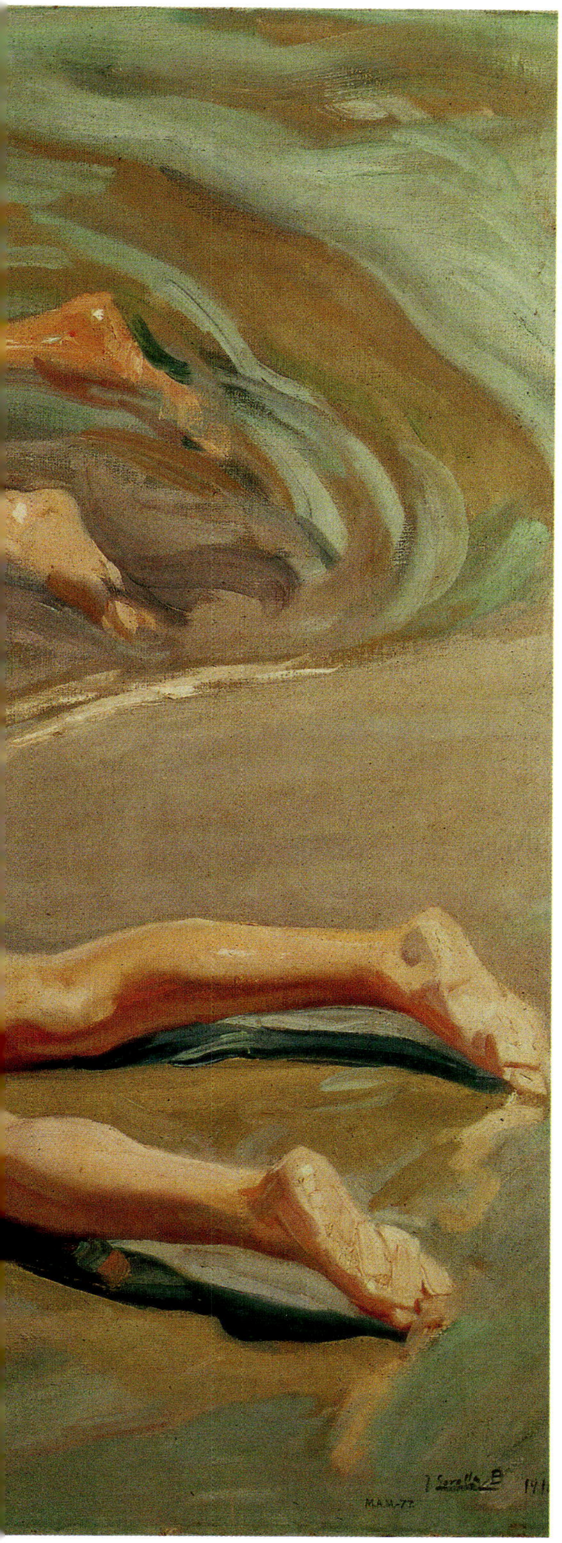

spirit and approach. Therefore, in one of the most prestigious cultural capitals of the period, a new way of approaching the treatment of light could be observed, in an original way and opening up a path to a series of expectations that would not end with those works.

And so Sorolla became the great figure of the period in the artistic movement in Paris, meaning his consecration in Europe. After that victory, he set his goals on the conquest of the demanding German market, although he wouldn't be as successful there as he had been in the French capital. The 280 works that he sent to Germany stayed in the hands of the art dealer Eduard Schulte, but Sorolla could not travel personally to the country because his daughter María was ill with tuberculosis. That's why he moved to the countryside near Madrid, La Granja de San Ildefonso, where he painted landscapes and portraits of the Spanish monarchs and aristocracy.

Success in the United States and its brilliant repercussion

At the beginning of century, the possibility arose for Sorolla to hold some exhibitions in the United States. In 1908, the painter, on the occasion of his exhibition in London, met the Hispanist Archer Milton Huntington (1870-1955), a learned American gentleman, who had been fond of painting and an expert since his early days, and who was delighted by Sorolla's works as soon as he set his eyes upon them. Although it seems likely that Huntington had previously had the chance, due to his education and travels, to know Sorolla's work before they met in London, it was his facet as a portrait painter that opened his eyes and which led him, in short, to becoming interested in another type of the artist's works.

On 18th May 1904 Huntington founded the Hispanic Society of America in New York, for a number of very specific purposes, amongst them that of disseminating Spanish arts and letters in the United States, managing to collect in a public library and museum remarkable and numerous examples of both disciplines, financing editions related with them and maintaining close and constant contact with illustrious Spaniards. Thanks to opulent economic funds, and on the contrary to other societies that failed in the attempt, he could carry out his initiatives from the very start. Two of Sorolla's canvases, specifically *Los pimientos* ["The Peppers"] and the portrait *Don Manuel Cossío*, acquired by Huntington at the exhibition in London, were the first to make up of the incipient art gallery.

It was in London, where Sorolla had been relatively successful partly due to the "very English" organization and the publicity of the exhibition as if it had been a commercial product, that the Hispanophile convinced Sorolla to take his work to his country. Huntington was convinced that his vitality, force and attractiveness, besides the cheerfulness with which he reflected the light and the colour of Spain and its people on his canvases would bring the painter resounding success. However, the artist's wariness regarding that adventure and the expenses that were going to arise from it, made Huntington reconsider the issue more calmly, an air of uncertainty now hanging over the proposal.

A few months later, in Spain, Sorolla received a letter from his friend, suggesting the possibility of exhibiting a large number of his works at the Hispanic Society. The society agreed to take care of all the transportation and insurance expenses, not to charge any fees for rent or commission for any sales made, to publish a luxurious catalogue of the exhibition and to purchase several of the best paintings for its museum. The proposal couldn't be more tempting and, from then on, all the preparations were made at full speed. This meant that, six months after the exhibition at the Grahon Galleries had ended, on 4th February 1909, that of the Hispanic Society had opened, any concern remaining in the painter's spirit and his fears regarding the American adventure finally disappearing on that day.

The great amount of works chosen by Sorolla allowed for a complete study of the artist's personality, since all types of paintings that had given him fame were sent from Europe: sunshine and open air, beach scenes, portraits, landscapes, as well as a great number of small sketches that had mostly been made on the beach in Valencia, Biarritz and San Sebastián. However, the work that most stood out was *Sol de tarde*, a canvas that had already aroused great admiration in Paris, Berlin and London, not only for its size, but for the generosity of a chromatic palette applied quickly with the paintbrush, in order to fix the effects of the rays of sun on the sky, the sea, the workers, animals and the boat which they are pulling. Alongside this painting, the Americans could see others such as *Aldeanos leoneses, Idilio en el mar, Playa de Valencia, Alegría del agua, Al baño, Pescadoras valencianas, Corriendo por la playa, Nadadores, El baño en Jávea, Después del baño*, all of them full of light and joy. As for the portraits, which were more than twenty, we can highlight those of *Blasco Ibáñez, Beruete* and *Menéndez Pelayo*, without forgetting some of those painted with the artist's wife. Landscapes and seascapes, which totalled more than 70, depicted aspects of Toledo, Seville, La Granja and Valencia, and, to a lesser extent, Segovia, El

Instantánea, Biarritz
(On the Beach, Biarritz)
1906, oil on canvas, 62 × 93.5 cm
Madrid: Museo Sorolla

In contrast with the tranquillity of the Mediterranean Sea, the waves of the Cantabrian sea at Biarritz break violently against the rocks, whilst Clotilde García del Castillo, Sorolla's wife, gets her camera ready. In spite of its size, the canvas has been painted rapidly as if it was a sketch, giving it great spontaneity.

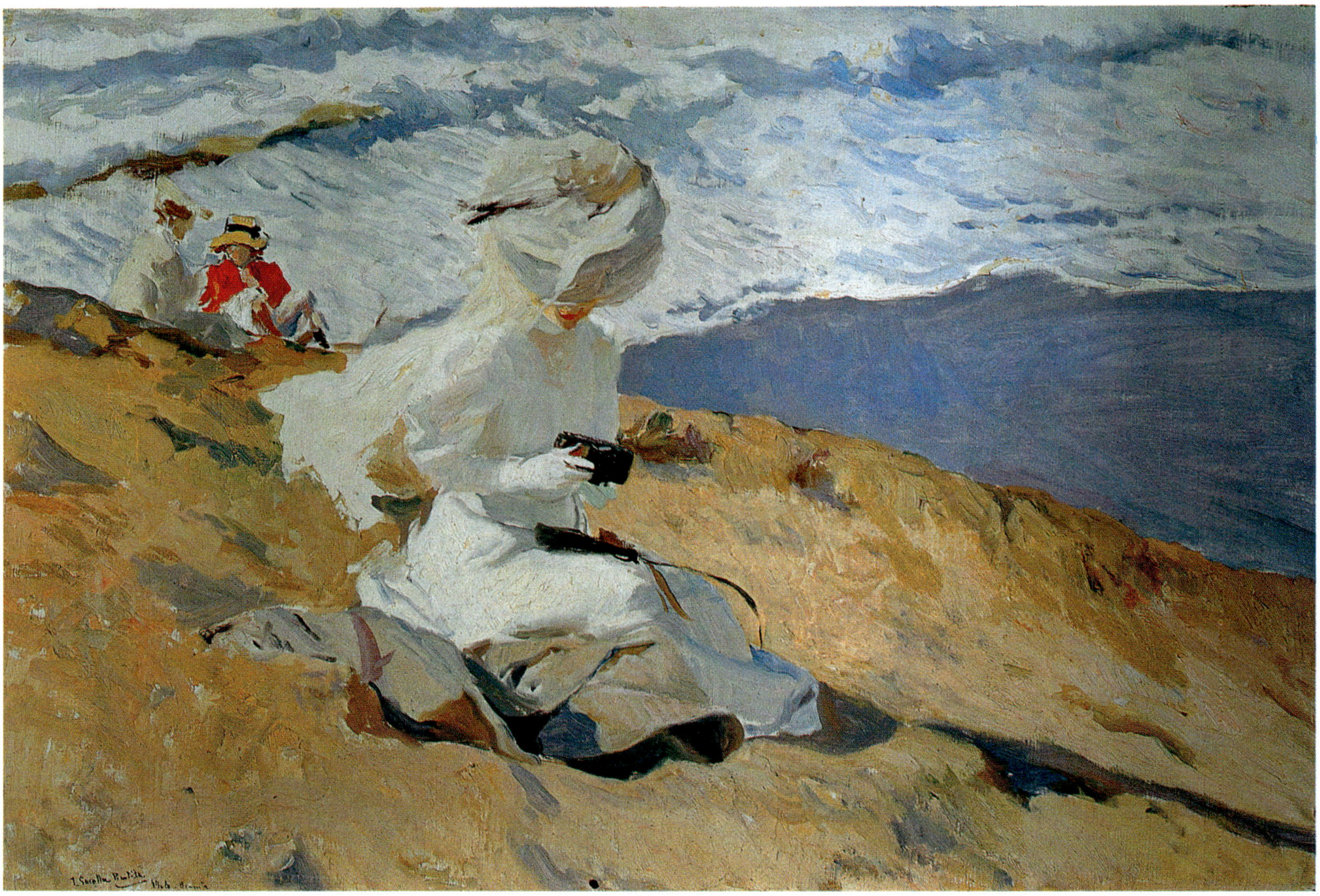

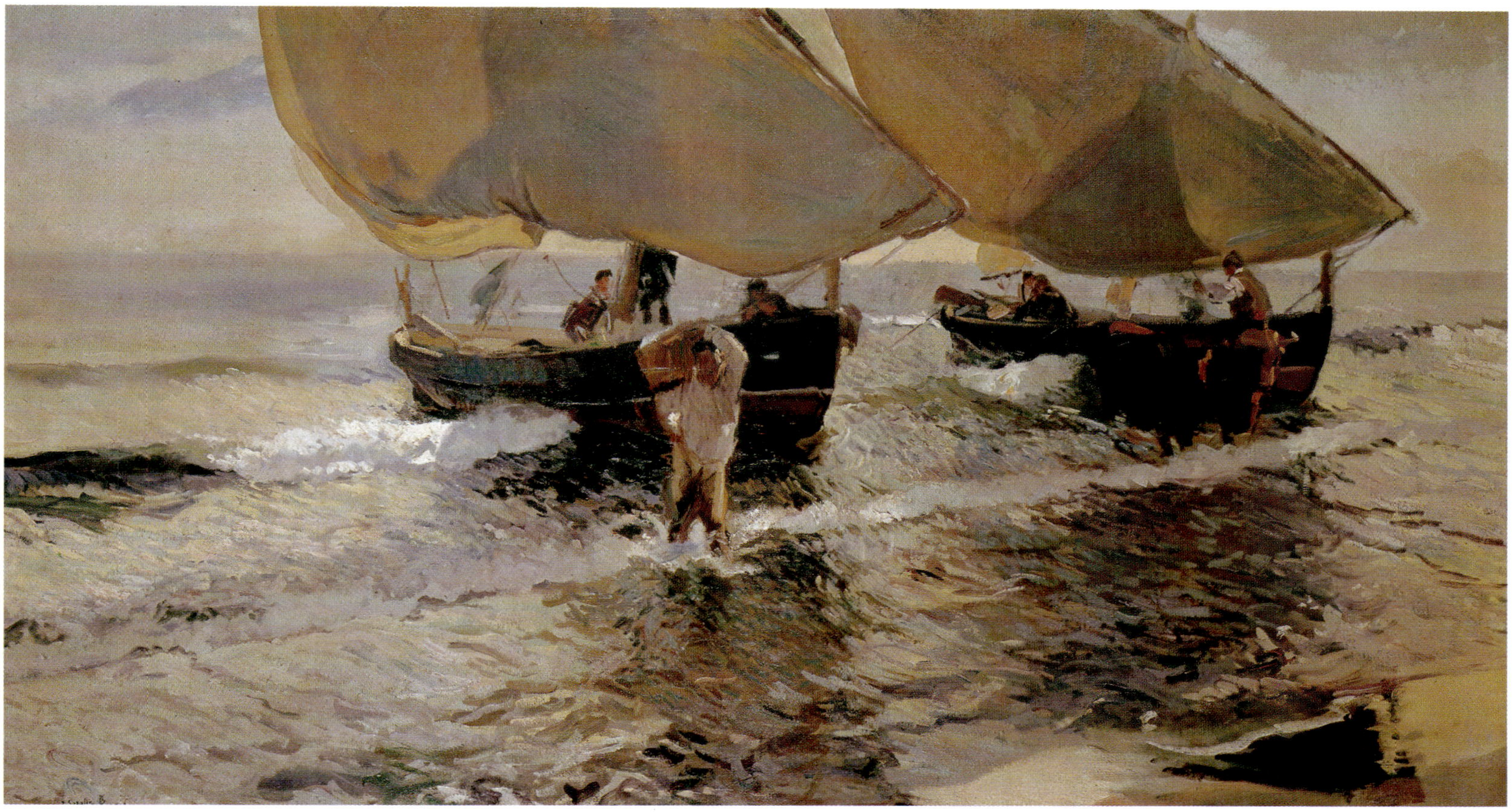

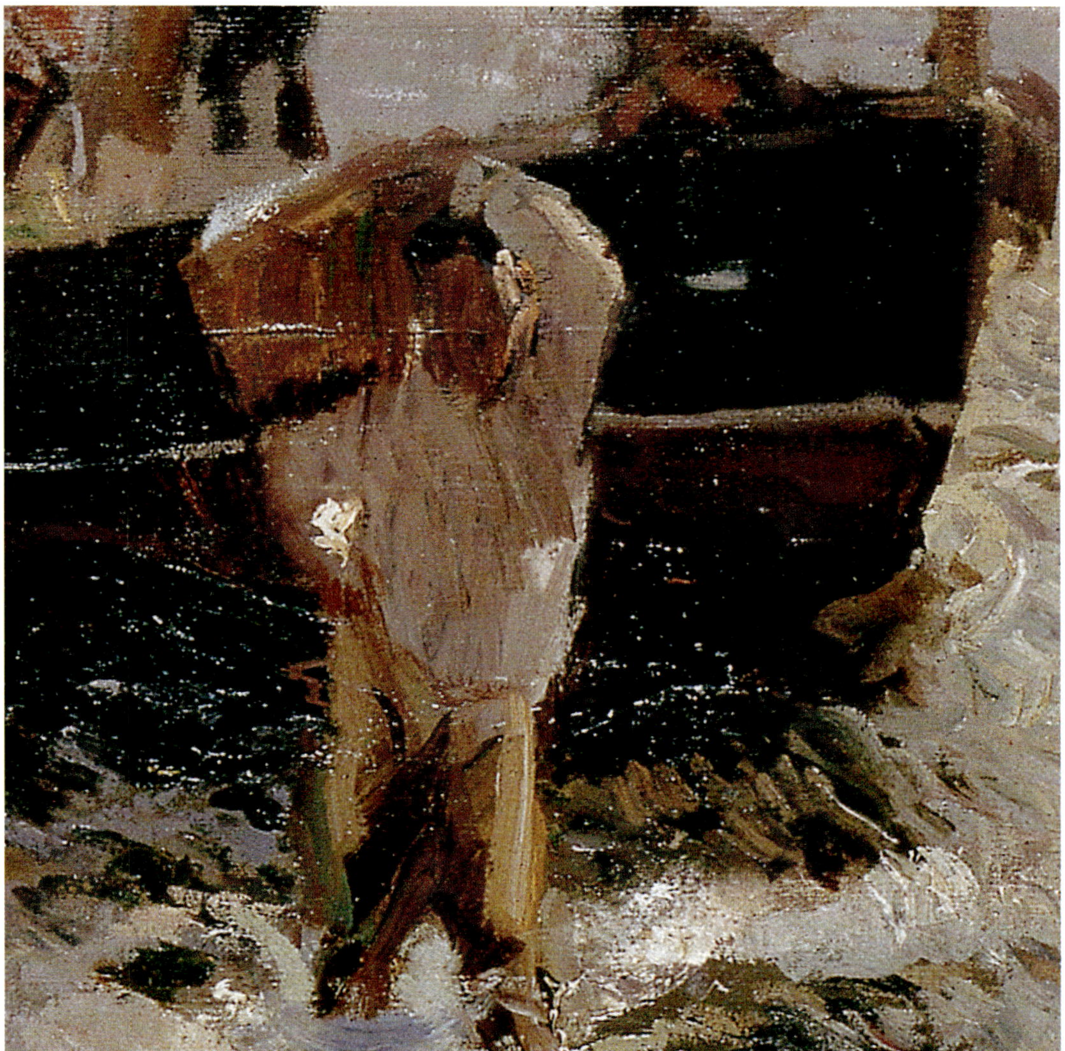

Descargando la pesca
(Unloading the Boats)
1907, oil on canvas
Madrid: Colección Botín

In this work, signed and dated in Valencia, Sorolla paints one of his favourite scenes. However, on this occasion, he is not interested in depicting the intense midday sun, but prefers a much softer light, that of the early hours of the morning.

Descargando la pesca
(Unloading the Boats)
Detail

The figure of the fisherman calmly coming ashore blends with the shape of the boat and the waves gently breaking on the sand. The shadow cast by the boat creates a chromatic symphony with the whiteness of the fisherman and the bluish-greens of the water.

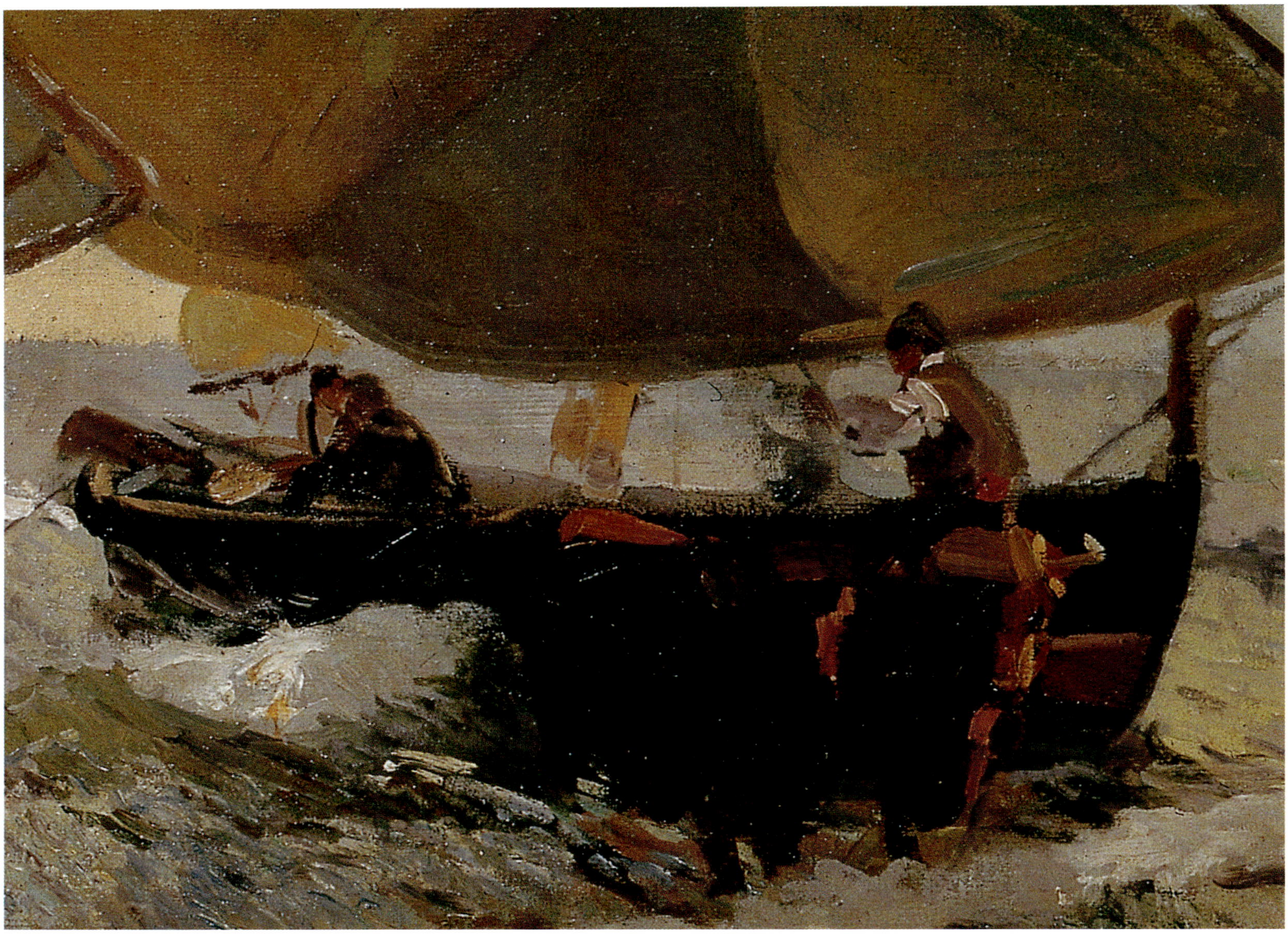

Descargando la pesca
(Unloading the Boats)
Detail

Here the oxen, protagonists in these works of Sorolla, become almost abstract elements, which blend in with the surroundings. The sail, another protagonist of the artist's seascapes, reflects the blues and ochres of the first hours of daylight.

Pardo, Jávea, Alcira and Asturias. All in all, the number of works exhibited, including sketches, was 356, appearing among them the previously mentioned *Los pimientos* and *Don Manuel Cossío*, as well as *Triste herencia*, lent by John E. Berwind, its owner at the time.

The exhibition was a resounding success in all aspects, more than Sorolla had ever experienced before and caused a great impact among the public. The huge amount of articles and opinions on the artist published during those days in the New York press (*The Evening Post, The New York World, The American Art News, The New York Times* and *The Cincinnati Times-Star*) also show its effect on the critics, which surpassed the European ones in enthusiasm and fervour. Both aspects (the public and the critics) had their logical repercussion on the sales figures, which reached more than half of the works exhibited. This success also earned him the admiration of his colleagues in the profession, from then on many American artists wanting to study with him, for example, William E. B. Starkweather, Jane Peterson, Dudley Crofts Watson and Ethel Coe. That exhibition, however, was not the first presentation of Sorolla in the United States, since before then some of his works had already been known. Examples of this were the watercolours painted in Rome at the end of the 1880s and purchased by Chilean and Argentinean collectors, as well as the canvas *Otra Margarita*, exhibited in Chicago at the 1893 Universal Exhibition, and *Triste herencia*, on show at the Church of the Ascension in New York between 1902 a 1909. Besides, the

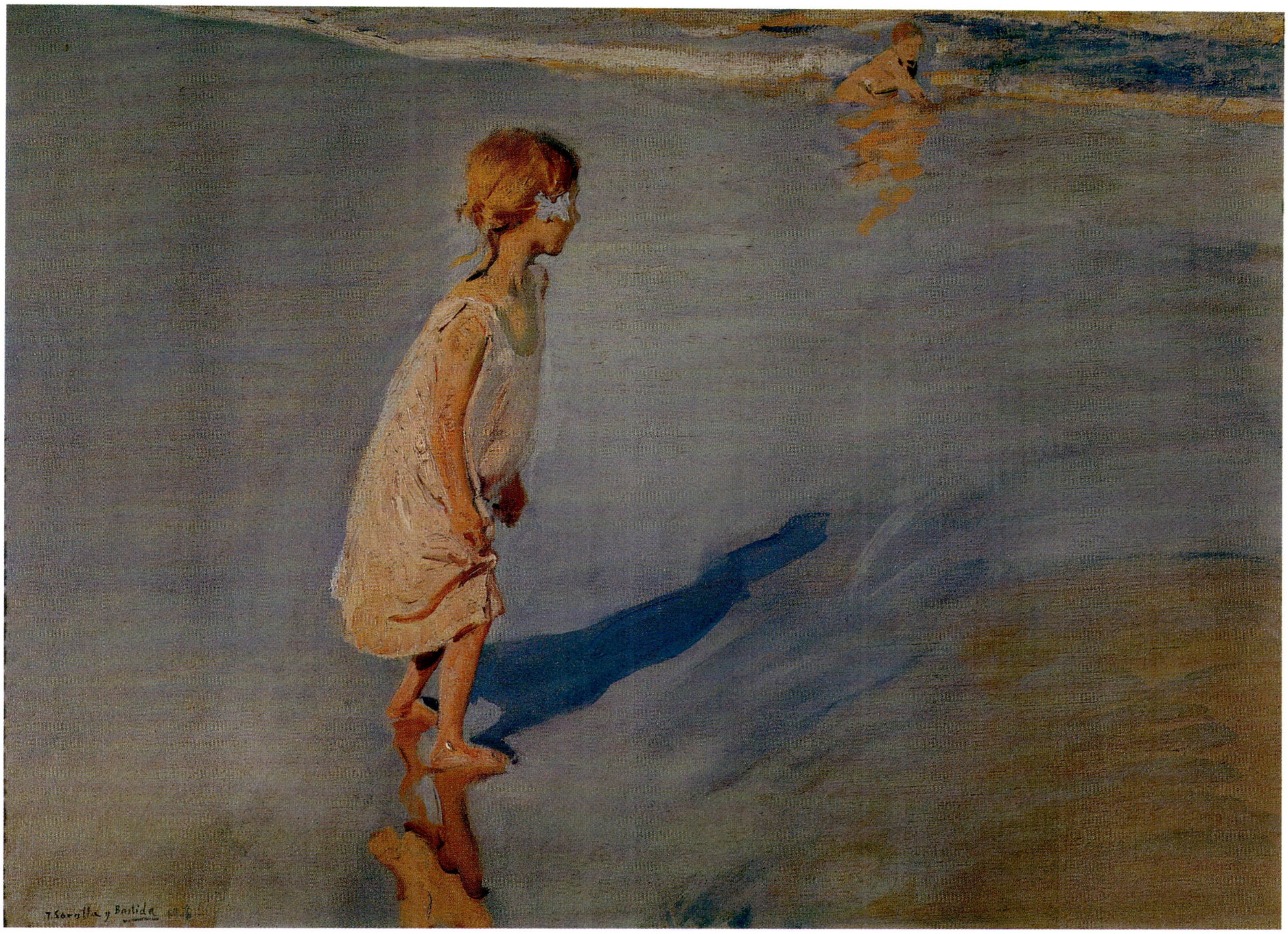

Philadelphia Museum of Art had bought *Niños a la orilla del mar* at the Salon de Paris in 1904.

Two days before the exhibition ended (the closing date was 8th March), nearly 30,000 people visited the magnificent building of the Hispanic Society.

To see so many people visiting an exhibition on only one painter, and besides a foreigner, on a single day, was not at that time, nor is it today, something very habitual. It was the most visited solo exhibition held in New York until then, well-surpassing both the Society's and the artist's expectations. The Hispanic Society itself purchased several of the portraits exhibited (*Menéndez Pelayo, Blasco Ibáñez, Beruete, Marqués de la Vega Inclán* and *Don Alejandro Pidal*) and asked the artist to continue the series, likewise incorporating others of Sorolla family members.

It also bought some small sketches and 26 oil paintings, for example *Sol de la tarde* and *Aldeanos leoneses*, *Idilio en el mar*, *Después del baño*, *Rocas del Cabo*, *Calle de naranjos* and a *Vista de la casa del Greco en Toledo*.

The Metropolitan Museum also bought a bathing scene in Jávea and a portrait of Sorolla's wife wearing a black dress.

This success led to further exhibitions, sponsored by the Hispanic Society, held at the Albright Art Gallery in Buffalo, from 19th March until 10th April, and at the Copley Society in Boston, between 20th April and 11th May, although in both cities the sales figures were notably lower. The Buffalo museum purchased

Niña con lazo azul
(Girl with Blue Ribbon)
1908, oil on canvas, 76 × 105 cm
Madrid: Colección Botín

Never has such an apparently insignificant theme (a little girl frightened by the waves and being beckoned into the sea by a boy) become a work of art. This is one of Sorolla's most beautiful and intimate works. Just the girl, the boy and the sea. So little but so much.

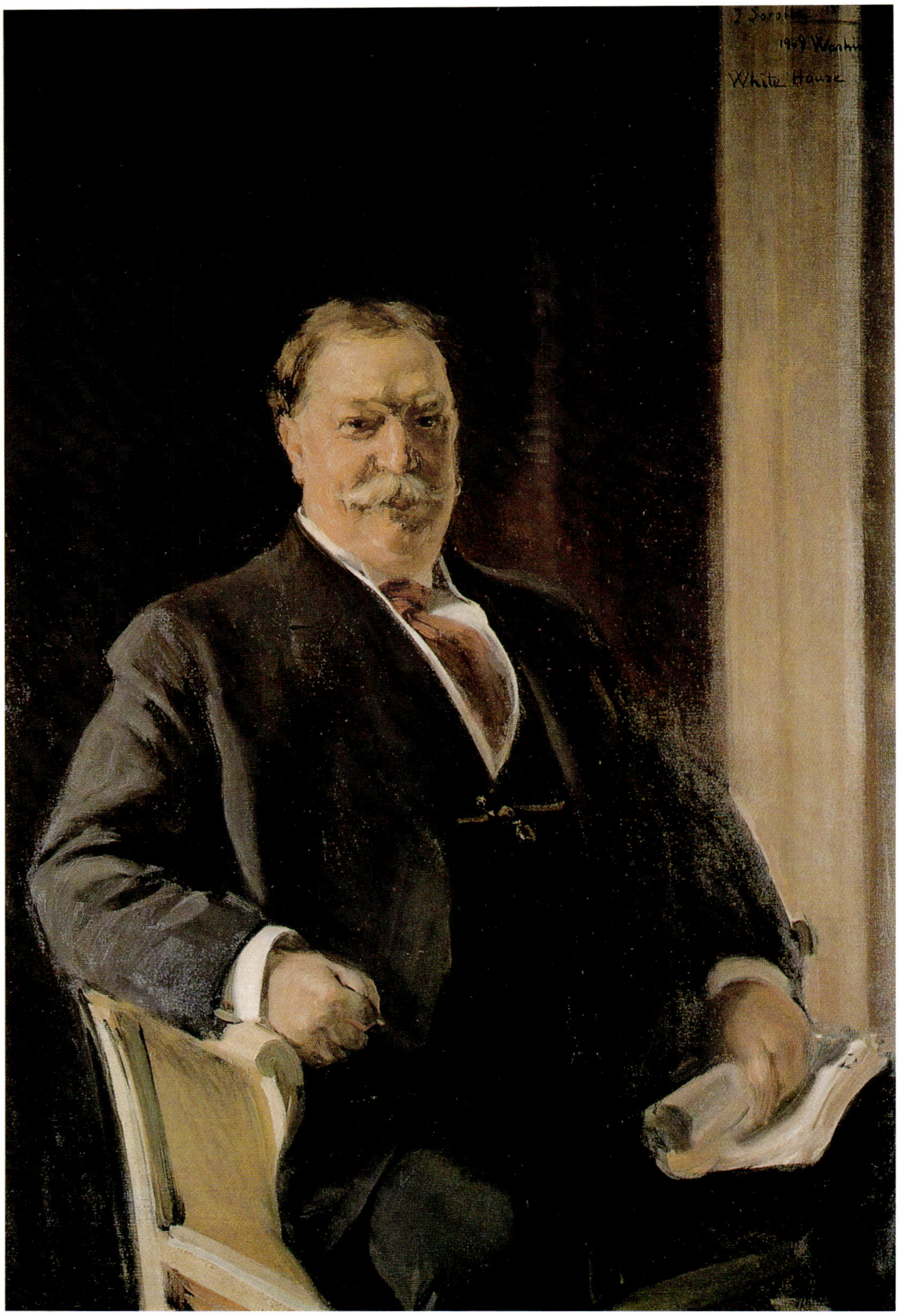

Presidente de la República, Mr. Taft
(Portrait of Mr. Taft, President of the United States)
1909, oil on canvas, 150 × 80 cm
Private collection

The exhibition held at the Hispanic Society in 1909 confirmed Sorolla's success. All the canvases had been painted in Spain; in the United States he only made small sketches and a number of portraits, of which this is one. Sorolla got on well with Mr. Taft, the president, since the latter spoke Spanish. Although this portrait is not painted as naturally and freely as those of the artist's own family, it stands out for its lack of solemnity and the skilful way in which he has reflected the jolly personality and nature of the protagonist.

Saliendo del baño
(After Bathing)
1908, oil on canvas, 176 × 111 cm
New York: Hispanic Society

An innocent sensualism reigns in this canvas, in which a smiling young woman unfastens her wet dress, while a boy looks on with a mixture of curiosity and amazement waiting to cover her with a white sheet. The reflection of youthful desires becomes the subject of this canvas, without forgetting about the portrayal of the warm atmosphere that envelops the whole scene.

one of the typical Valencian beach scenes when the boats come in, and the purchase of some of his works by the American financier and collector Thomas Fortune Ryan attracted the attention of new portrait customers. The latter also commissioned an oil painting of Christopher Columbus at the time of leaving the Port of Palos, for which Sorolla used his descendant the Duke of Veragua as a model for the admiral.

The numerous portraits painted during this period in New York, Washington and Buffalo contributed to topping up the already significant income obtained by the artist on his first American adventure. It was only to be expected that the members of that affluent society wouldn't want to miss the chance to

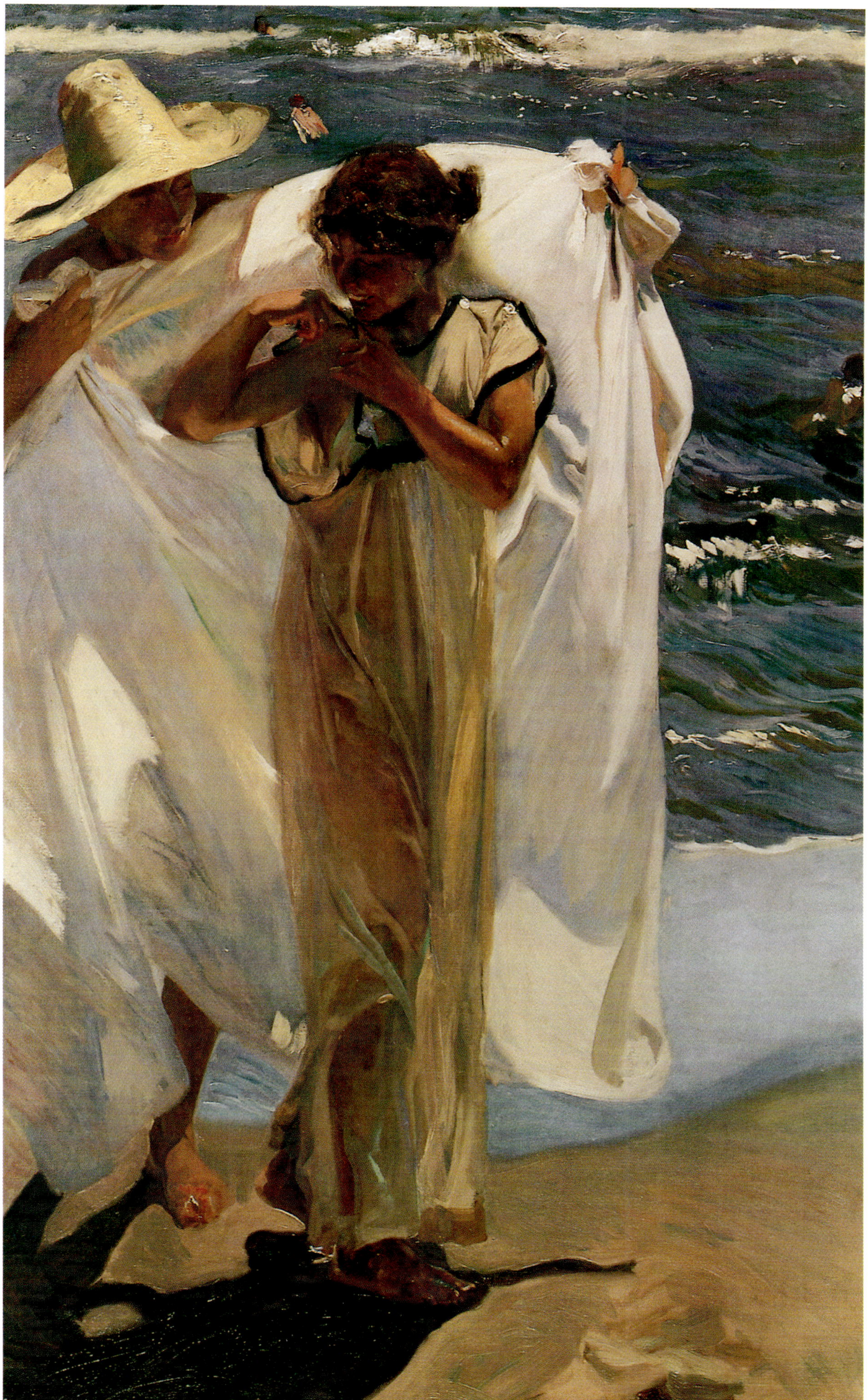

be portrayed by the artist's subtle palette. Sorolla received many commissions, more than he wished and could deal with, especially if we take into account that the summer was drawing near and that the painter only longed for planting his easel on the beaches in Valencia.

Even so, his astounding talent allowed him to paint, in the scarcely five months that he stayed in the United States, more than 20 portraits, amongst which we may highlight, those signed in New York, of *Mrs. Huntington*, *Mrs. Alexander* and *Mrs. Morgan*; *Miss Simpson*, *Miss Alexander*, *Miss Cochran*, *Miss Blodjett* and *Miss Lunjsan*, *Mr. Robbins* and *Mr. Morgan*. In Washington, the *Portrait of Mr. Taft, President of the United States*, a work that was submitted to the 1910 International Exhibition held at the Pittsburgh Carnegie Institute and which was highly praised for its success and composition, as well as that of *Señor Piña*, a minister from Spain in the capital, and, in Buffalo, that of *Mr. Kurtz*, director of the city museum; those of the Porter Nortons, and those of *Mrs. Gratwick* and *Mrs. Zanetti*.

At the end of June, Sorolla was already back in Spain, spiritually renewed. And while everybody in the artistic centres all over Spain was talking about his victory in the United States, calculations were being made on exactly how much he had earned from his sales and, in short, he had become the main after-dinner subject for one reason or another, he packed his bags and headed for that sea for which he yearned so much. And so he exchanged those hectic days spent in the United States for the peace and quiet of the Mediterranean Sea.

Some of his most beautiful and cheerful beach scenes were painted up until that summer of 1909: *El baño del caballo* ["Washing the Horse"], *La herida del pie* ["The Wounded Foot"], *Las dos hermanas* ["The Two Sisters"], *Paseo a orillas del mar* ["A Walk Upon the Beach"], *Al agua* ["In the Water"], *La hora del baño* ["Hour of the Bath"], *El balandrito* ["The Young Yachtsman"], *Niños en el mar* ["Children on the Beach"], *Antes del baño* ["Before the Bath"]... new versions, always different to the previous ones, of the themes he repeated so many times. These works would be exhibited a year and half later during a new trip that he made to the United States.

Chicago and St. Louis

During 1910, Sorolla worked non-stop. Having arranged another trip to America for the following year, he spent most of the year painting works for the two exhibitions that he had agreed to hold in Chicago and St. Louis. He also painted the canvas evoking Columbus' departure from the Port of Palos on that famous morning of 3rd August 1492, expressly moving to the Andalusian capital in order to make the best sketches for his work, apart from some portraits for the Hispanic Society's newly founded iconographic gallery, amongst them those of *King Alfonso XlII*, *Benito Pérez Galdós*, *Don José Echegaray* and *Don José Gestoso,* the latter painted in Seville.

Sorolla, since his triumph at the Salon de Paris in 1905, had not taken part very often in the Fine Arts exhibitions, and so, in 1910, he presented, *hors concours*, *María en El Pardo* at the Exposición Nacional de Madrid, a canvas that had been painted some time earlier. He also entered the Exposicíón Internacional de Santiago de Chile with his *Pescadores valencianos* and *Sol poniente*, as well as the Exposición Española de Arte e Industrias Decorativas, in Mexico, with the works *Trata de blancas, Saliendo del baño, Labradora valenciana, Remendando las redes* and *Barca valenciana*, the last two being acquired at the exhibition.

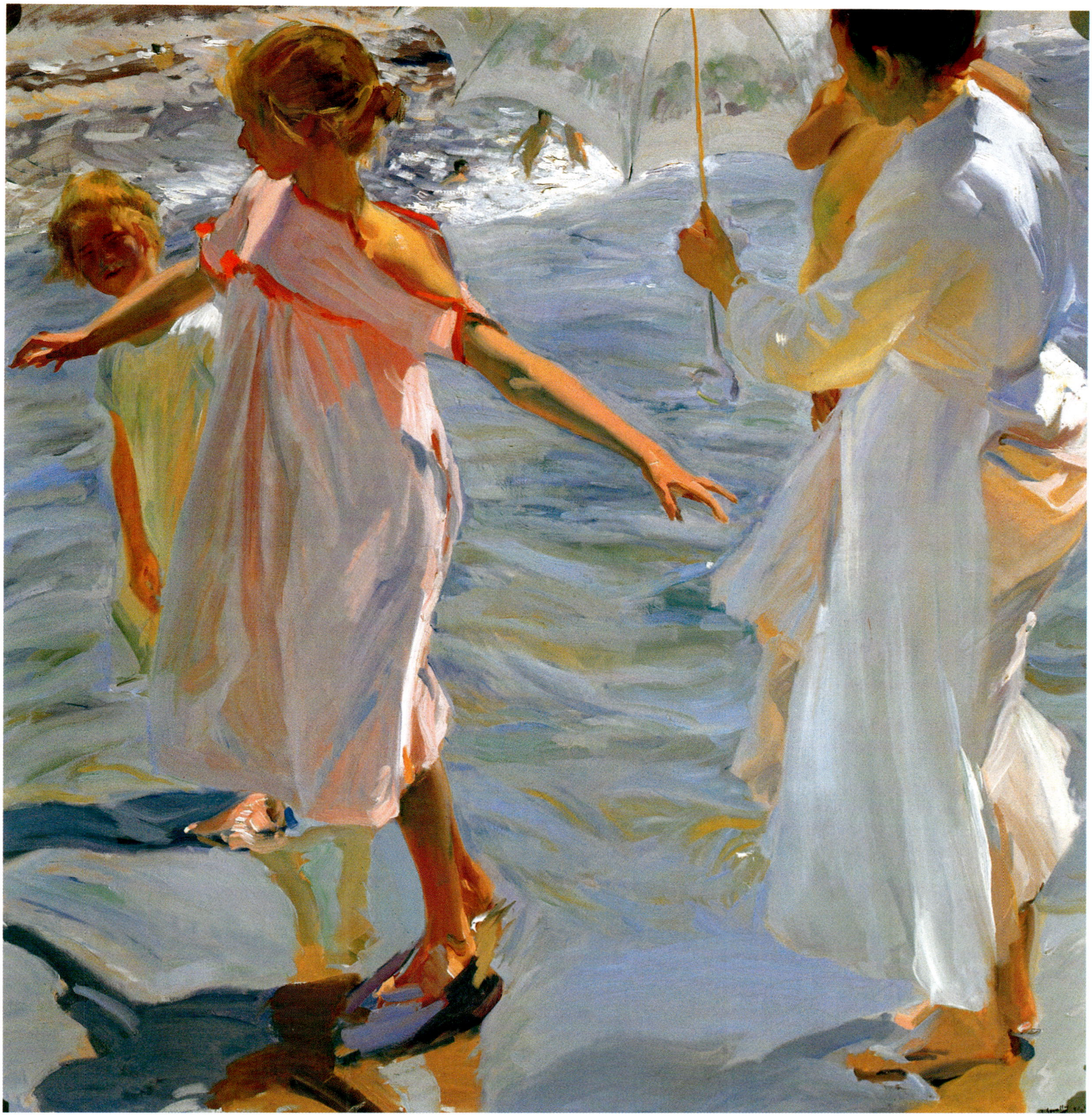

La hora del baño
(The Hour of the Bath)
1909, oil on canvas, 150 × 150.5 cm
Madrid: Fundación Museo Sorolla

The vagueness of the figures is used to emphasise the varied chromatism in which the white parasol and the pink and yellow dresses stand out. In the background, the boys' naked bodies contrast with the chaste-suggestive figures of the high society girls.

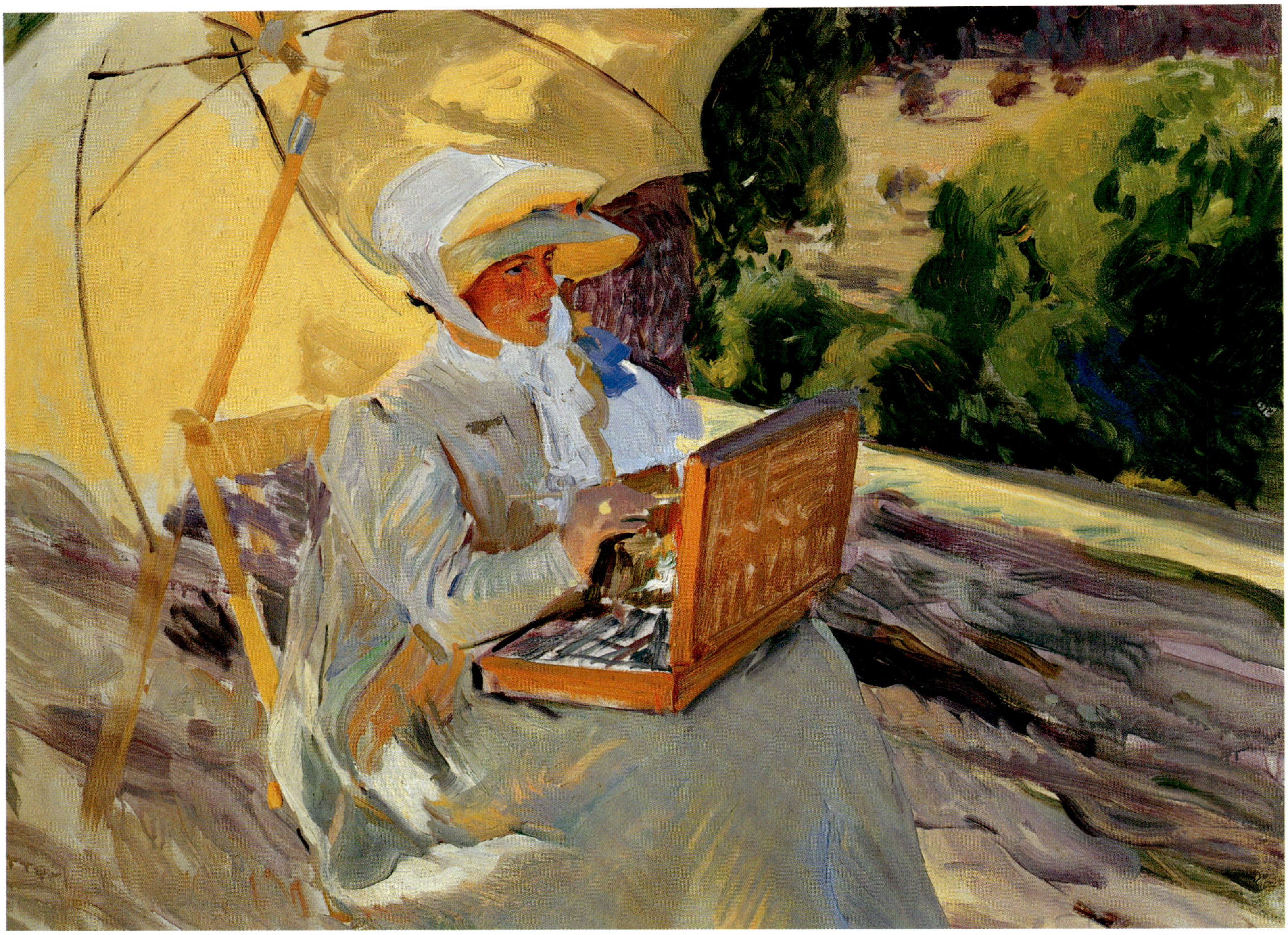

María pintando en El Pardo
(Maria Painting at El Pardo)
1907, oil on canvas, 82 × 106 cm
Private collection

The recurrent theme of the artist's eldest teenage daughter, having now recovered from her illness (Sorolla portrayed her when she was ill, wrapped up in blankets with the Guadarrama mountains in the background), sitting painting outdoors. The colours used express the painter's happiness at his daughter being well again.

Also, within his artistic career, that period also meant a significant increase in his devotion to landscape painting, a genre which he had approached alongside his interest in Seville in 1908. When he returned from the United States, and after painting in Valencia, in the autumn of 1909 Sorolla had begun a series of Granada landscapes, showing his fascination for these two beautiful Andalusian cities, especially Seville. Except for during the summer months, it was the best place for him to spend the rest of the year. And so, from 1910 onwards, the artist could be frequently seen in Seville painting people, gardens, streets and typical patios.

The landscapes of Seville and Granada, the beaches of Valencia painted in 1909 and the scenes of Zarauz, an old fishing village in Guipúzcoa, where Sorolla worked during the whole summer of 1910, made up, together with around twenty portraits, the main body of the works exhibited at the famous Art Institute of Chicago between 14th February and 12th March 1911, and then at the St. Louis City Art Museum, from 20th March till the middle of April. He achieved greater success in Chicago, where Sorolla offered, upon the repeated request of the cultural media and in way of an interesting talk more than a conference, to give a "painting lesson" to a large audience eager to receive teachings from the *maestro*.

Sorolla also painted several portraits in Chicago, highlighting the two canvases of *Mrs. Ira Nelson Morris & Her Children*, exhibited at the Chicago College Club and praised by the public and the art critics in the local newspaper

The Sunday. He sold 15 canvases at this show (the most important ones being the beach scene *Las dos hermanas*, immediately donated by its owner to the city museum, and the Sevillian landscape *Estanque de Carlos V en el Alcázar de Sevilla*), and 7 in St. Louis, *Antes del baño*, *Jardín de los Adarves en la Alhambra* and *Bajo el toldo (Zarauz)*. In addition to these sales, were two groups of paintings bought, outside both exhibitions, in New York: the four portraits already mentioned and a landscape of Burgos that was incorporated into the collection of the Hispanic Society, plus the six compositions and four Sevillian landscapes bought by the collector Mr. Ryan.

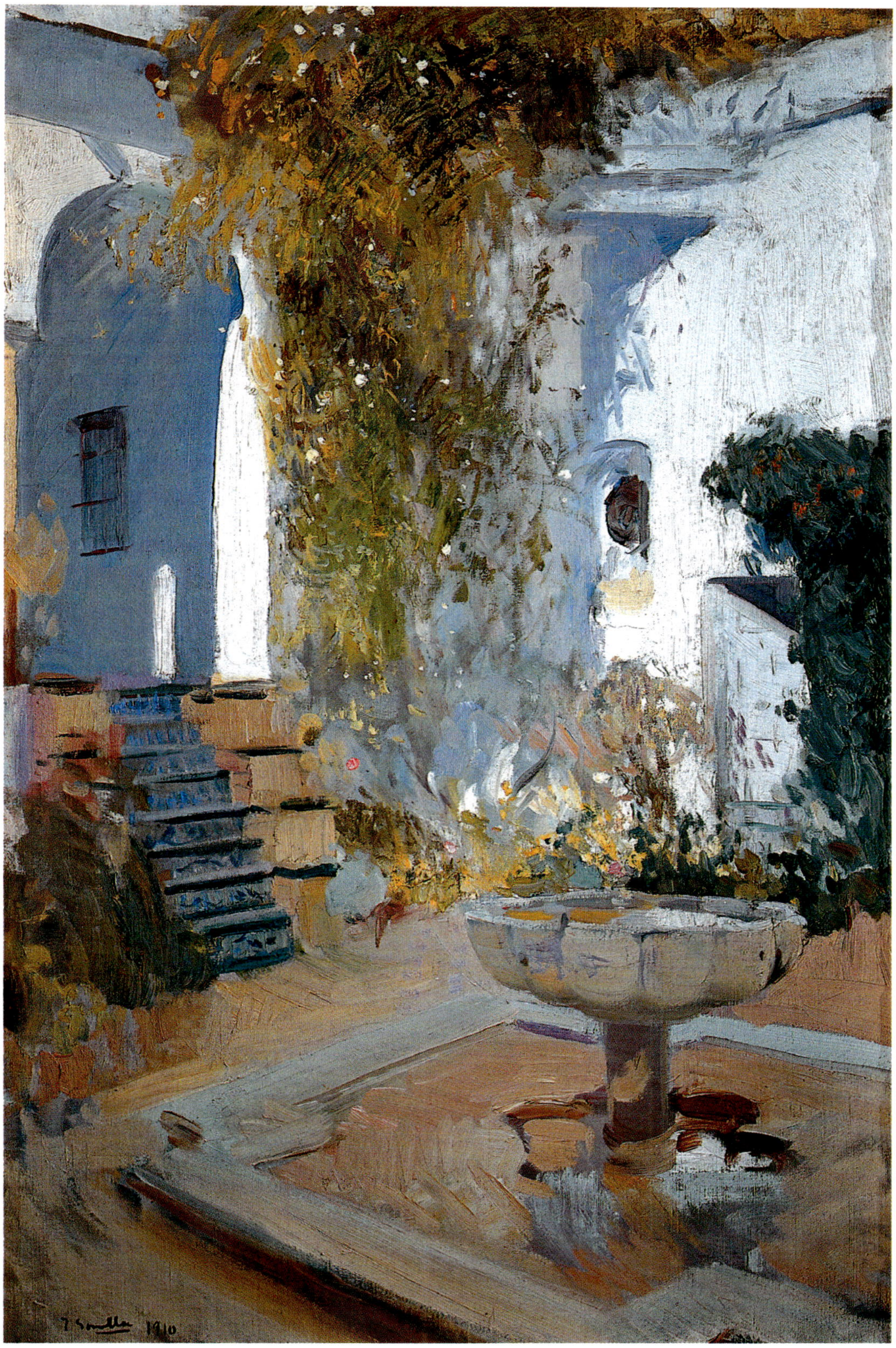

Rincón del Grutesco del Alcázar de Sevilla
(Garden Grotto, Alcazar de Seville)
1910, oil on canvas, 95 × 64 cm
Madrid: Museo Sorolla

This scene of the Alcazar de Seville reflects the light of Seville, the Andalusian patios and the coolness of the water, which all blend in with the vegetation and an intense sun. Here we can rightly apply the words spoken by Ramiro de Maeztu, "The word 'impressionism' seems to have been expressly invented to talk about Sorolla's work. The French artists to whom it is usually applied are a hundred times inferior to this Spanish painter."

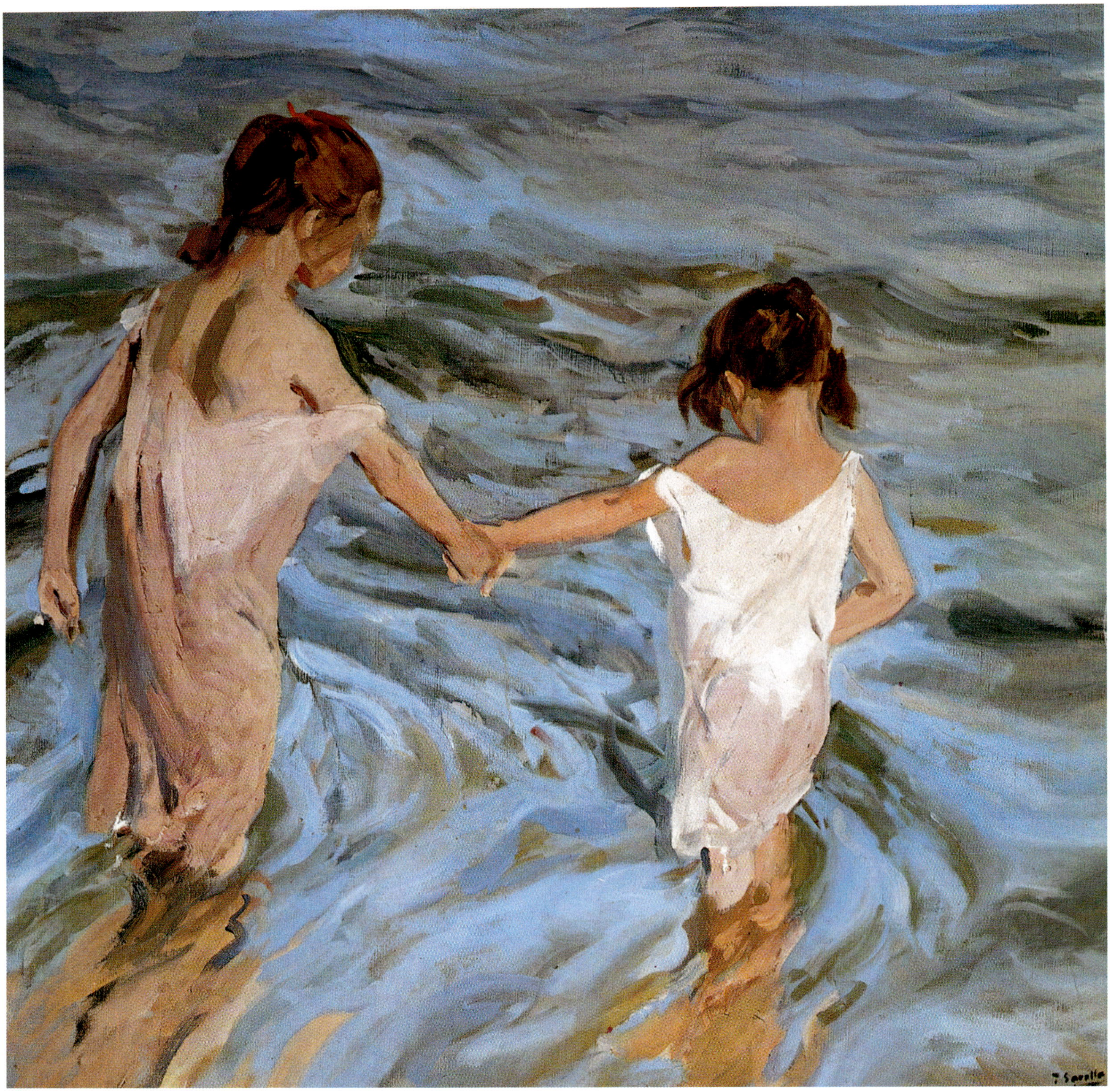

Niñas en el mar
(Children in the Sea)
1909, oil on canvas, 150 × 150 cm
Madrid, Museo Sorolla

Without any horizon or beach as points of reference, these two girls blend in with the waves of the sea in a tribute to painting in its purest form.

At the same time as the exhibitions in Chicago and St. Louis, Sorolla took part by express invitation in the Spanish pavilion of the Fine Arts International Exhibition held in Rome, also at the beginning of 1911.

He was only too pleased to accept the invitation, being able to exhibit the force and originality of his painting at one of the most avant-garde art centres. The artistic atmosphere of Rome, open to the concerns of the modern trends, was not the same one that the painter had known 25 years earlier. Sorolla sent 85 works to the exhibition, *hors concours*, which were displayed in the great hall, allowing the public to see a masterful synthesis of his brilliant creative work.

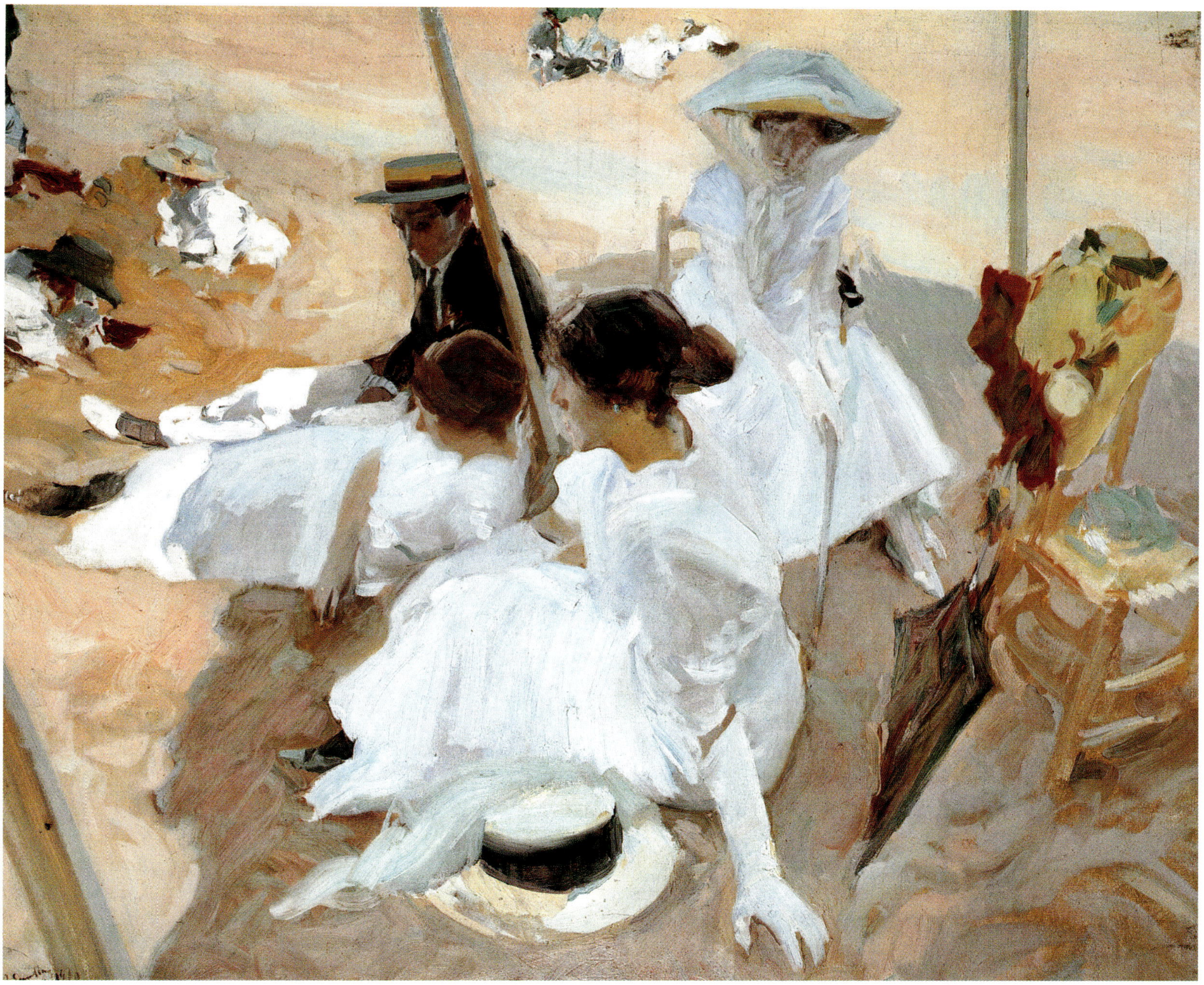

As was to be expected, the exhibition was a resounding success, and the most authoritative sector of Italian critics, with Vittorio Pica at the head, praised the Spanish *maestro*, emphasising the originality of his works, how they were perfectly in line with the pictorial movement in vogue at the time throughout Europe, his masterful skill, both in the field of colour and drawing and, in short, the outright superiority of this artist over the other exhibitors at the pavilion, amongst them being artists of the stature of Álvarez de Sotomayor, Barbasán, Benedito, Benlliure, Beruete, Bilbao, Roberto Domingo, Hermoso, Labrada, Moreno Carbonero, Rodríguez Acosta, Rusiñol, Zaragoza and the Zubiaurre brothers.

Alongside the Valencian painter, from whom the city's Museum of Modern Art bought one of the beach scenes exhibited, works presented by other painters, also *hors concours*, Ignacio Zuloaga (1870-1945) and Hermenegild Anglada i Camarasa (1871-1959), also triumphed. Sorolla who could not go from Chicago or St. Louis to Rome due to the agreement made with the institutions of those cities, and apart from his professional satisfaction and the certain chrematistic success of that new American venture, he had now received a commission for one of the works that must surely fulfil an artist's ambitions.

Bajo el toldo (Zarauz)
(Under the Awning, Zarauz)
1910, oil on canvas, 99 × 125 cm
Madrid: Museo Sorolla

Another family portrait. Sitting under the shade of an awning that we intuitively see, in the centre is Clotilde, the artist's wife, and on her right, María; Elena is reclining, and Joaquín, the only male, is sitting behind her wearing a dark jacket and a straw hat.

A tour of Spain without leaving New York: The decoration of the Hispanic Society

In the middle of March 1911, Sorolla returned to Europe and stopped off in Paris for a while, later spending the summer in San Sebastián. In the autumn, after a short trip to Majorca, he returned to the capital of France, where on 26th November he signed an agreement with Mr. Huntington, in which he would carry out a series of oil paintings for the Hispanic Society, within a certain period of time, depicting typical themes of the Spanish regions and Portugal. This decoration had to cover the walls of a large rectangular room designed as the future library, and whose approximate size was approximately 4 metres in height by 70 metres in length. As part of the assignment, Sorolla was to hand over to the Hispanic Society all the preparatory sketches and costumes used, apart from not being able to show the final decoration anywhere else first. The "contract" in question became in time one of the most important in the history of modern painting.

Before the year ended, the painter returned to his new house in Madrid, the construction of which had begun in 1909 and that, on his death, would become the current Museo Sorolla. The admiration long felt by the president of the Hispanic Society for his painting had now materialized in a challenging commission that offered him the opportunity of carrying out one of the culminating works of the century. That was his great chance, since for the first time Sorolla had received a major assignment, no other Spanish painter of the period having been commissioned anything like it before. The Society gave the work the title of *Provinces of Spain*, although not all of them appear or were painted, which is why the name given by the artist himself, *Visions of Spain* is more appropriate, since it was a panoramic view of all Spain, depicting Spanish men and women, wearing typical costumes in lively scenes, all contained in a countless number of large brushstrokes on more than 200 m^2 of canvas.

From the very beginning, Sorolla tried to portray an original view of Spain, opposed to the romantic one given abroad, basing himself on genuine locals, their customs and traditional clothes, avoiding just a simple, documented sketch of characters and landscapes.

Of the 14 final panels, some had already been decided from the beginning, while others arose as he went along. Neither had the way or order in which the regions had to appear been determined at the beginning. However, Murcia, Asturias, The Canaries and The Balearics are not represented; the two Castiles and León appear together on the same canvas; there are two canvases of the Community of Valencia; Aragón, Catalonia, Extremadura, Galicia, Guipúzcoa and

Las grupas
1916, oil on canvas, 351 × 301 cm
New York: Hispanic Society

The canvases of the series "Visions of Spain" were painted between 1919 and 1923. They arrived in New York in 1923 and have been on show there, in the same room as today, since 25th January 1926. Sorolla wished to represent the rich Spanish folklore, as well as its varied local customs and traditions. In this one, we can see a typical Valencian festivity, which is a true portrayal of the colourful and baroque regional costumes with orchards in the background.

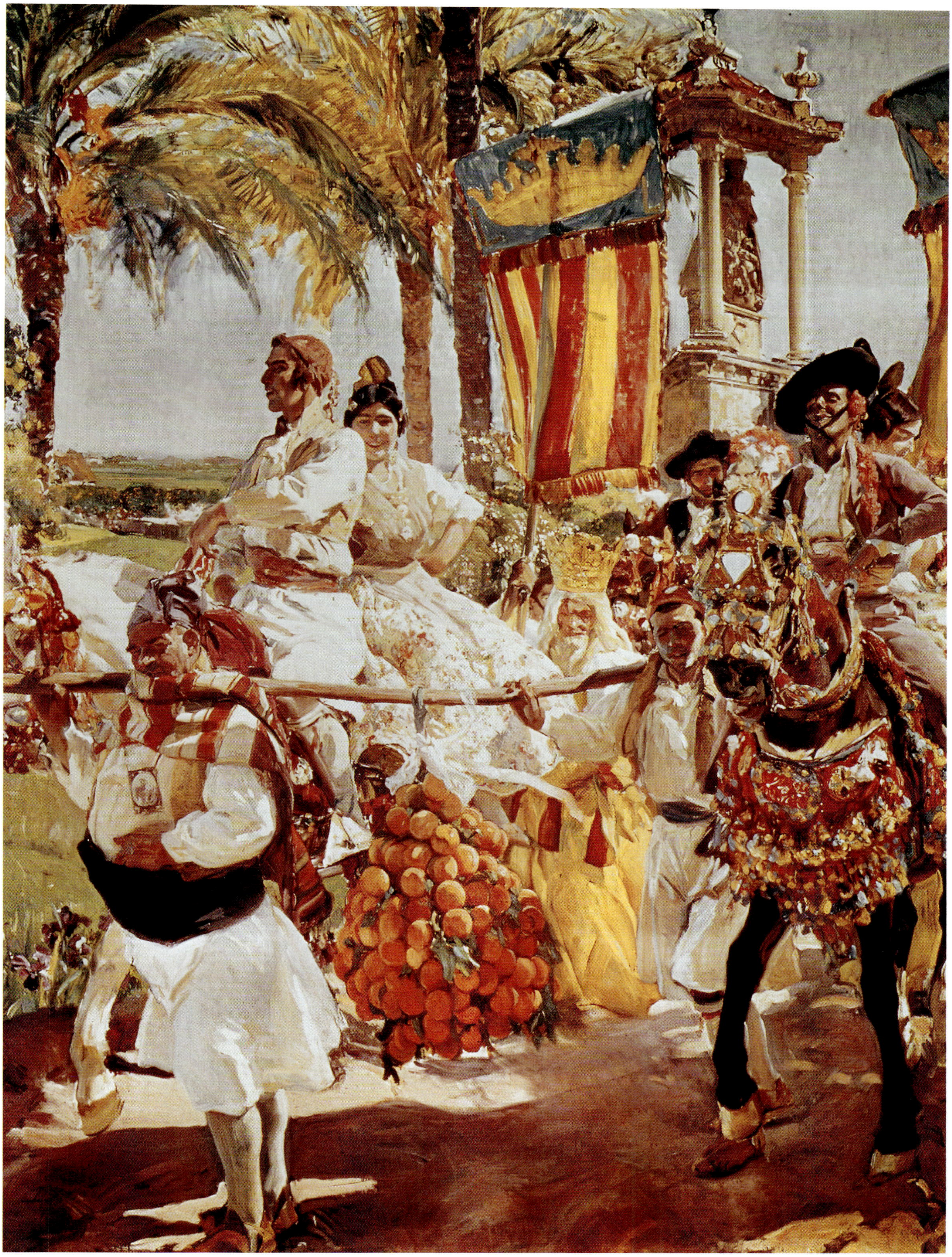

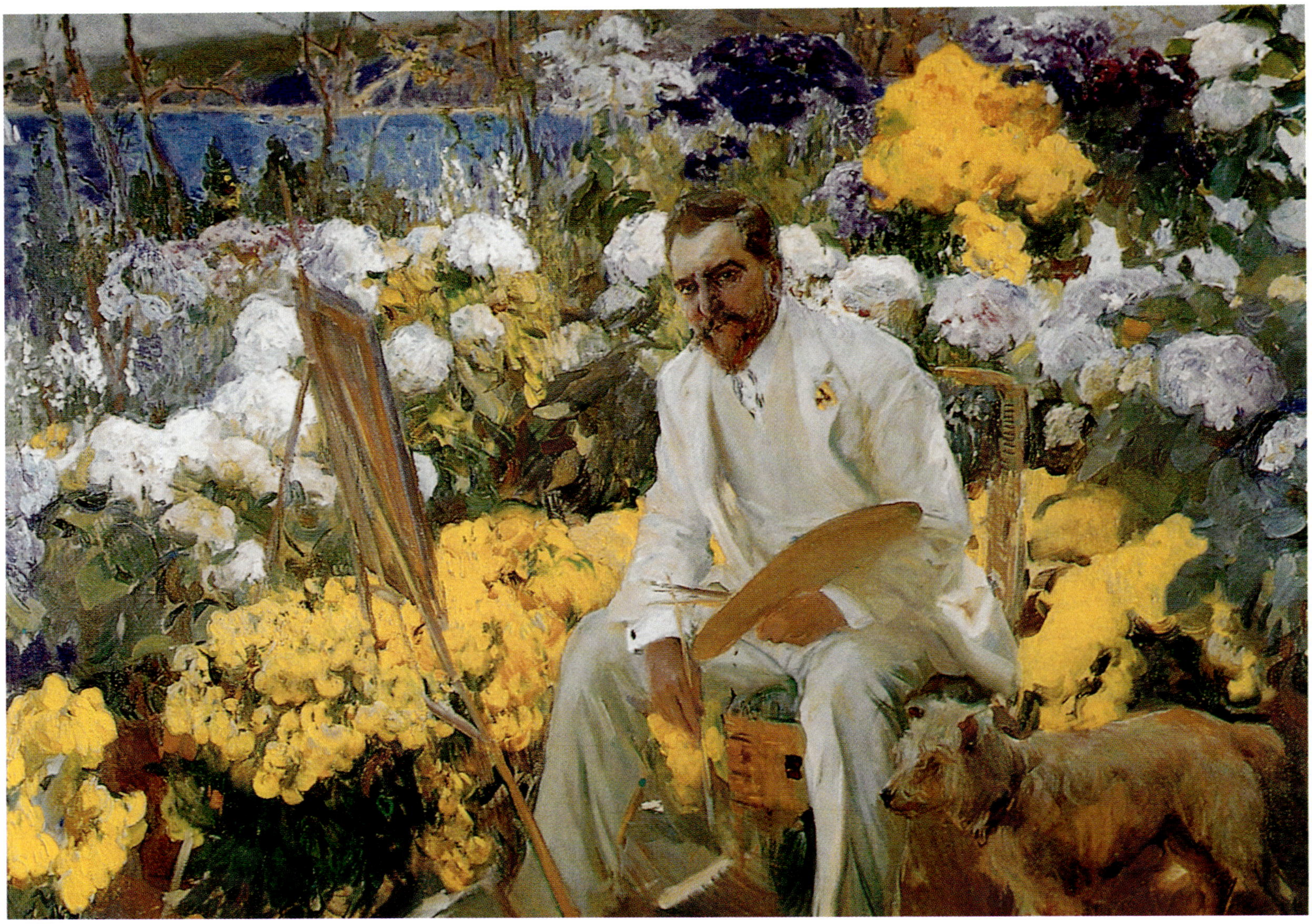

Louis Comfort Tiffany
1911, oil on canvas, 150 × 225 cm
New York: Hispanic Society

A great lover of the arts, especially painting, Mr. Tiffany is portrayed here in a luxuriant garden, sitting in front of an easel with a palette in his hand. Sorolla avoids painting the conventional static portrait and proposes what we would call a "cosmopolitan portrait", in which the painter and the protagonist portrayed show certain complicity. We wonder if it is Sorolla who is painting Tiffany or the latter trying to portray the internationally-renowned artist.

Navarre, one; and Andalusia, five, four of which were painted in Seville. Therefore, the representation of Spain appears distributed in a capricious way, responding to the artist's will in his fundamental search for picturesque motifs, those which incited his paintbrushes to work.

As for the technical point of view, at no time may we suppose that Sorolla decided to carry out any of the 14 compositions without previous analyses making sketches and partial sketches of figures. Neither would his staunch opposition to so-called studio work allow us to state that he wished to limit himself to taking regional models to his studio in Madrid to calmly paint them there, but his professional attitude must have made him realise that the Spanish scenes represented had to be captured directly in the Spanish sun. Only one mural 70 metres long was from the very first moment mistakenly set out, since it entailed making hundreds of attempts before achieving the definitive work. On the other hand, Sorolla was never a muralist; so he opted for painting large independent canvases representing the essence of the Spanish, without falsifying their natural atmosphere in his project.

In order to do so, he decided to paint each of the canvases in the region depicted and *in situ*, thus providing the effect of "speaking pages" of Spanish customs, so rich in atmosphere and character like those painted in Valencia, which gave Sorolla his fame as a sincere and truthful painter. All the panels, except one (that of the patio in Seville), are painted outdoors. The Catalan coast with its pine trees, the orange trees of Valencia, the Andalusian pas-

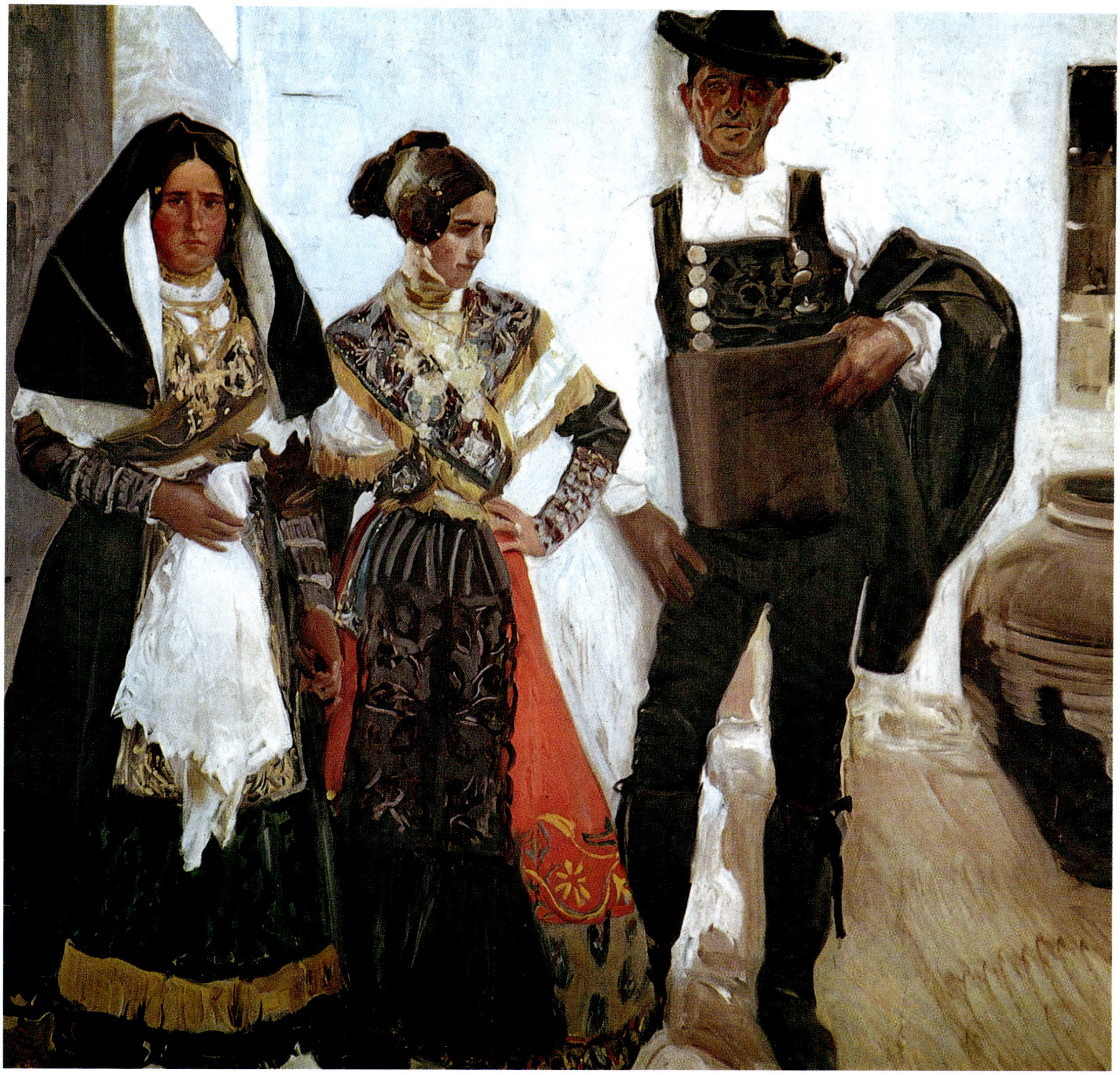

Tipos de Salamanca
(Salamancans)
1912, oil on canvas, 190 × 200 cm
Madrid: Museo Sorolla

Sorolla could not remain indifferent to the project commissioned by the Hispanic Society, starting to work on a series of studies of persons in regional costumes from different areas of the country. These people from Salamanca were painted in the village of La Alberca during the first fortnight of June 1912.

turelands with their prickly pear bushes, the Galician estuary with its chestnut trees, a village of Extremadura, the mountains of Aragón and the Basque country, the Castilian countryside, churches of Navarre, streets in Seville, the palm trees of Elche, tunny fishing in Huelva and the bullring are all part of the subject matter of the collection, which give the work on the whole its unmistakable diversity.

In search of the authentic

For carrying out this great work, Sorolla spent much of the year 1912 studying different Spanish characters. Whether he took advantage of all these studies or not, he prepared for the work commissioned, coming into direct contact with the varied and colourful typical local costumes that would give his canvases their opulent colour. He embarked on several trips all over Spain. But this was not the only thing he did, as he also gathered all sorts of information, loads of pictures, magazine and newspaper cuttings, and even wrote letters to ask where the most authentic national ethnology could be found. Between January and March he worked in Madrid, Toledo and Lagartera; in May he studied local characters in Ávila; in June he moved to Salamanca and various surrounding villages and, before returning to the capital, he painted *Vista de Madrid* ["View of Madrid"].

At the beginning of July, in Biarritz, he painted Huntington's portrait and then he went to San Sebastián, where he painted the locals there as well as those from Zarauz and Lequeitio and stayed with his family for one and a half months. Once his family were back in Madrid, in August, he went to Roncal (Alto Aragón). He spent the rest of the days in the Valle de Ansó and in Pamplona, meeting his family again at the end of the month in San Sebastián.

He returned to Lequeitio in September, where he painted two large open-air canvases of local fishermen and a preliminary study for *Pasiegas santanderinas con sus cuévanos*. It is one of a series of regional figure studies which he made at the same time as the panels. The series consists of 31 works, of different sizes, but always with full-length natural size characters. Of all these works, 22 were taken in 1926, three years following Sorolla's death, to the XV Biennale in Venice, where, in spite of the avant-garde movements prevailing at the time, most of the public and artists there admired the purity of those works. In the middle of September the family returned to Madrid, in October the painter went to Soria and to Toledo in November.

The order of painting the 4 panels is the following: in 1913 he painted the large frieze on Castile; in 1914, five panels: two on Seville and those of Guipúzcoa, Aragón and Navarre. In 1915, four: the other two on Seville, those of Galicia and Catalonia. In 1916 he only painted one, that of Valencia.

In 1917, the Extremadura one. Between December 1918 and January 1919, that of Elche, and in May and June, the Ayamonte one, the last two concluding the immense work. Looking at the dates we can see that Sorolla completed more than two-thirds of the work during the first triennium, whereas later on it took him three and a half years to paint four canvases. The explanation for this may be because exhaustion had set in due to the great effort made between 1913 and 1915.

The execution of the work allows us to establish two well differentiated periods: up until 1916, with impersonalized panels, and after that date, those of more personal elaboration. Sorolla worked arduously on the project, but the final result allows us to conclude that the preparatory studies, in which he could

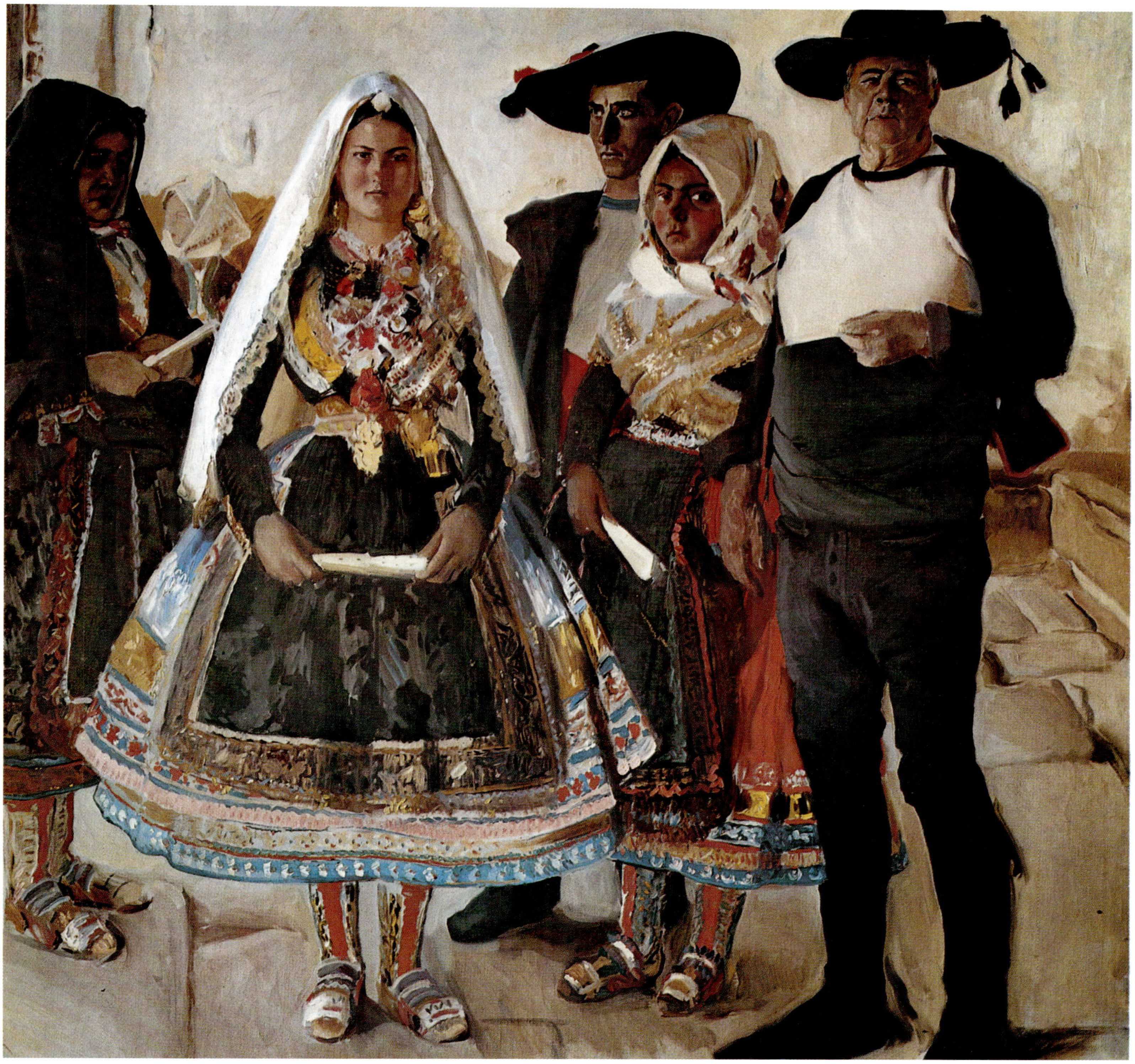

express his easiness of perception and speed of work more freely, convey more force than the definitive work. If in the first panels little spontaneity can be appreciated, the less time devoted to the last ones paradoxically permitted him to give the composition a fresher approach. The importance of the work led him to travelling all over Spain, with the corresponding discomforts entailed, such as poor lodgings, extreme weather conditions and even experiencing great difficulties for finding the most suitable places and models for his canvases. Most of the time, he would travel on his own, since he wished to spare his wife and children from these hardships.

It is also true to say that on some occasions his consolidated fame made it easier to get help from people only too willing to please him, doing all they could to make up for the countless difficulties entailed in the –at the time– hard work.

Tipos de Lagartera o Novia lagarterana
(People from Lagartera or Lagartera Bride)
1912, oil on canvas, 200 × 206 cm
Madrid: Museo Sorolla

This group of five people is a faithful, psychological, and documentary portrayal on the part of Sorolla, who, in spite of this faithful reflection, still applies his customary principles of light and colour.

In some places they offered him cosy accommodation and affectionate company, while in general he found admirers who put themselves entirely at his service and painters only too proud to be able to help out, such as Pons Arnau in Jaca, Santiago Martínez in Plasencia and Ayamonte, Andrés Parladé in Sevilla and Carlos Vázquez in Barcelona. When his wife didn't accompany him, the painter held daily correspondence with her, in order to keep her up to date with his activities and progresses. Thanks to these letters we can see how sometimes, but especially in the last days, the painter expressed concern and fears regarding his state of health, starting to suffer from fatigue, the shakes, insomnia, weakness in his legs and headaches that, in the long run, would lead to a fatal illness.

The discovery of rich Spanish folklore

Work on the Castile panel practically coincided with the Sorolla family's move to a new house in Madrid, with views to the mountains, due his daughter Maria's delicate state of health. He turned the garage at their new residence on Cuesta de las Perdices into a studio, and painted there in the sunlight. His original idea was to make one painting containing the two Castiles and León, but when he realised how difficult it was to handle a 14 metre canvas, he decided to divide it up into four pieces. The theme, in which more than one hundred inhabitants of Castile and León, women, men and children brimming with vitality, can be divided into two parts: on one side, a market, with figures at rest; on the other, a procession, with figures in motion. Apparently it represented the festivity of San Isidro, patron saint of Madrid, the profiles of the most significant monuments of that region being distinguished, such as the walls of Ávila, the cathedral and the aqueduct of Segovia, the fortress of Toledo and San Servando Castle.

The composition, if not concluded, in September 1913 only required a few finishing touches that the artist gave it at the end of the year, after a trip to Paris in the autumn with his disciple Pons Arnau, and during which he met Mr. Huntington. The president of the Hispanic Society extended the deadline for finishing the project, besides agreeing to eliminate the representation of Portugal. The next painting to follow the great panel of Castile was, at the beginning of 1914, one of those painted in Seville: *Los nazarenos*, depicting the Sevillian Easter brotherhood associations. The subject, portraying typical Spanish customs and festivities, was a must in Sorolla's decoration, and he showed his skill in representing it with great realism. Coinciding with the start of this work, Sorolla received the news that he had been unanimously elected, on 16th March 1914, member of the Real Academia de San Fernando, to take the place of the deceased painter Salvador Martínez Cubells.

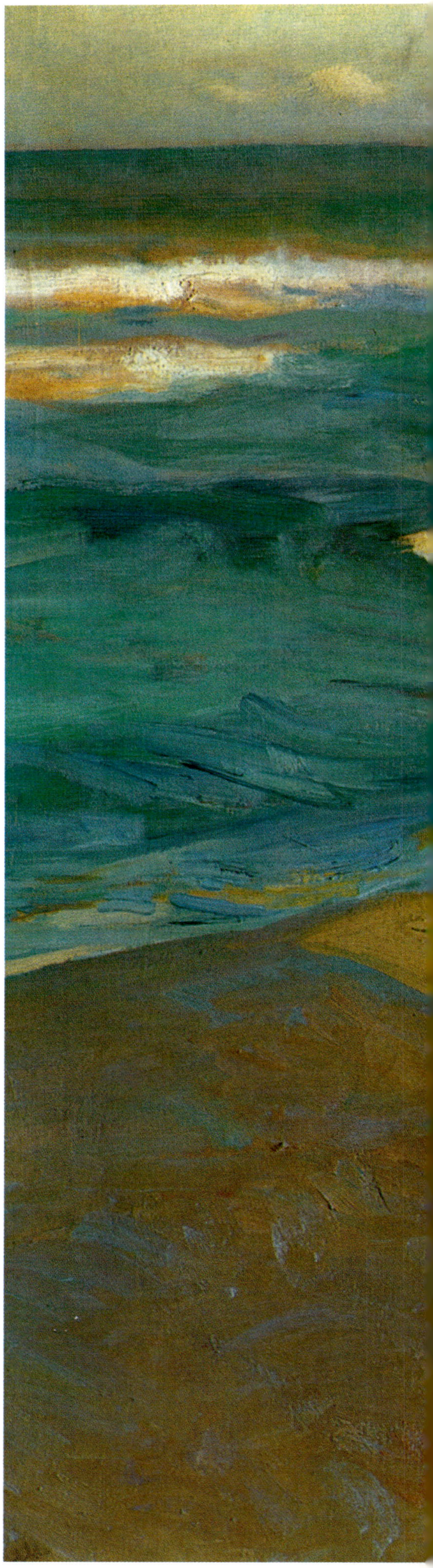

Sacando la barca
(Towing in the Boat)
1916, oil on canvas, 100 × 120 cm
Madrid: Private collection

Painted on the beach on Valencia, Sorolla does not forget his favourite themes while he carries out his works for the Hispanic Society. It is a return to his roots, a return to his native Mediterranean homeland of sandy beaches and westerly winds. Although an international painter, he would never lose his roots, always preserving his identity.

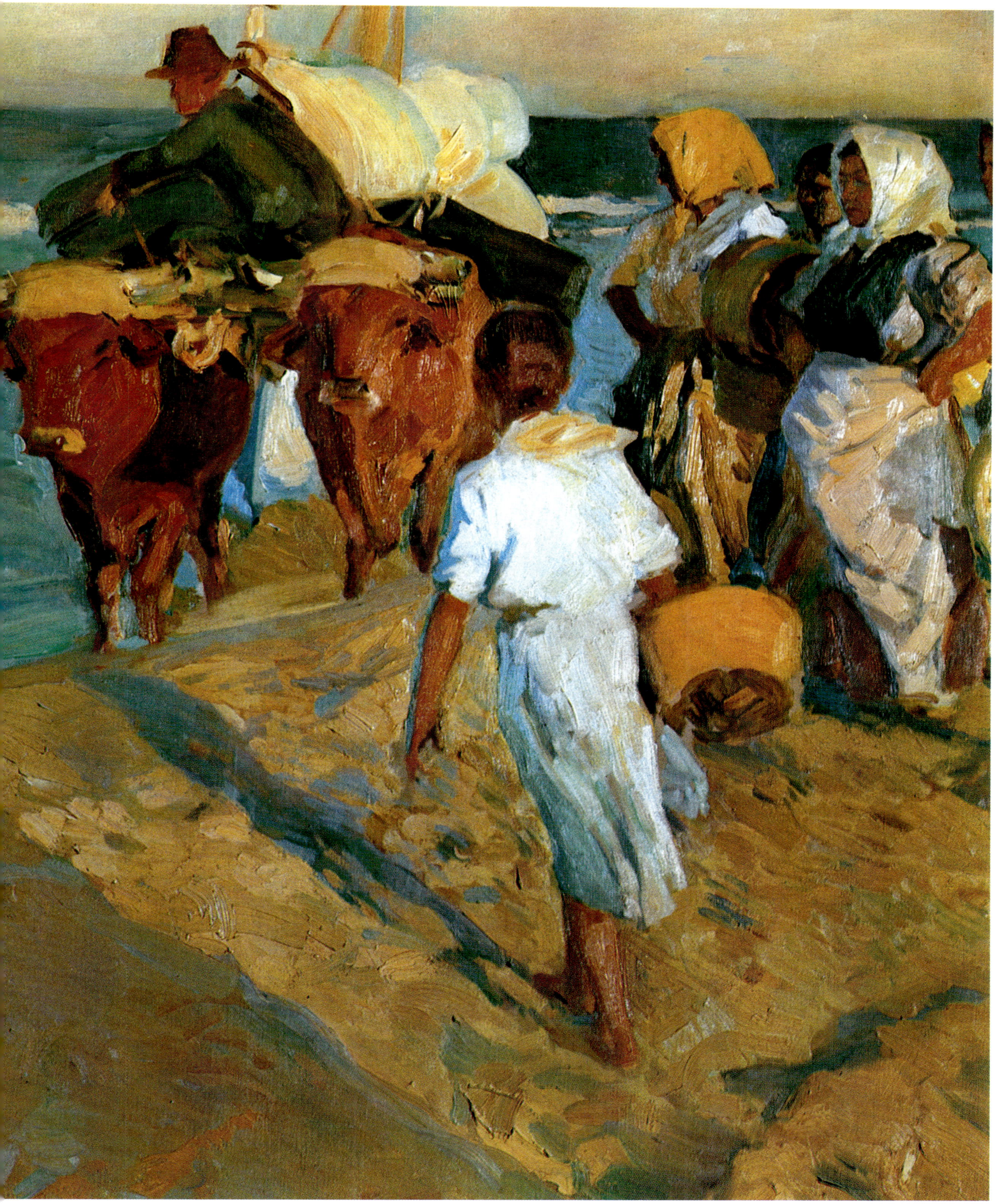

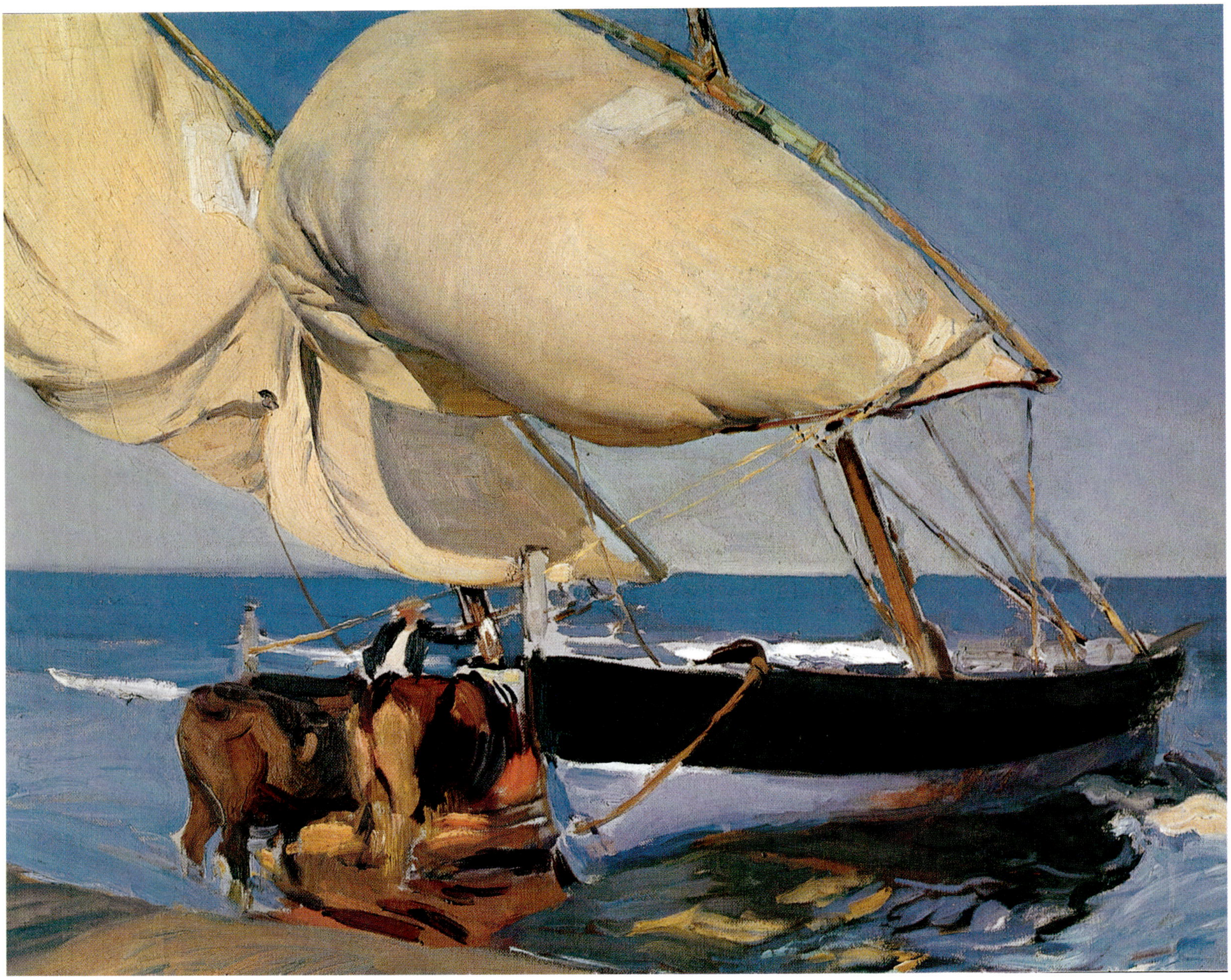

Las velas
(The Sails)
1916, oil on canvas, 75 × 90 cm
Madrid: Museo Sorolla

The recurrent theme is captured rapidly, as if it were a rough sketch. The prevalence of this type of composition led Sorolla to an almost abstract simplification on the lower part of the canvas, whereas the sails –the protagonists which give the painting its title– are much more defined.

María la Guapa
1914, oil on canvas, 125 × 100 cm
Madrid: Museo Sorolla

In 1914, the artist was commissioned to paint Baile en el Café Novedades de Sevilla *by an American millionaire. As preparatory work, he painted a series of canvases of gypsies standing in different postures, avoiding the theme of pure folklore and in line with his artistic concept of light and colour. It looks more like a portrait than a genre scene.*

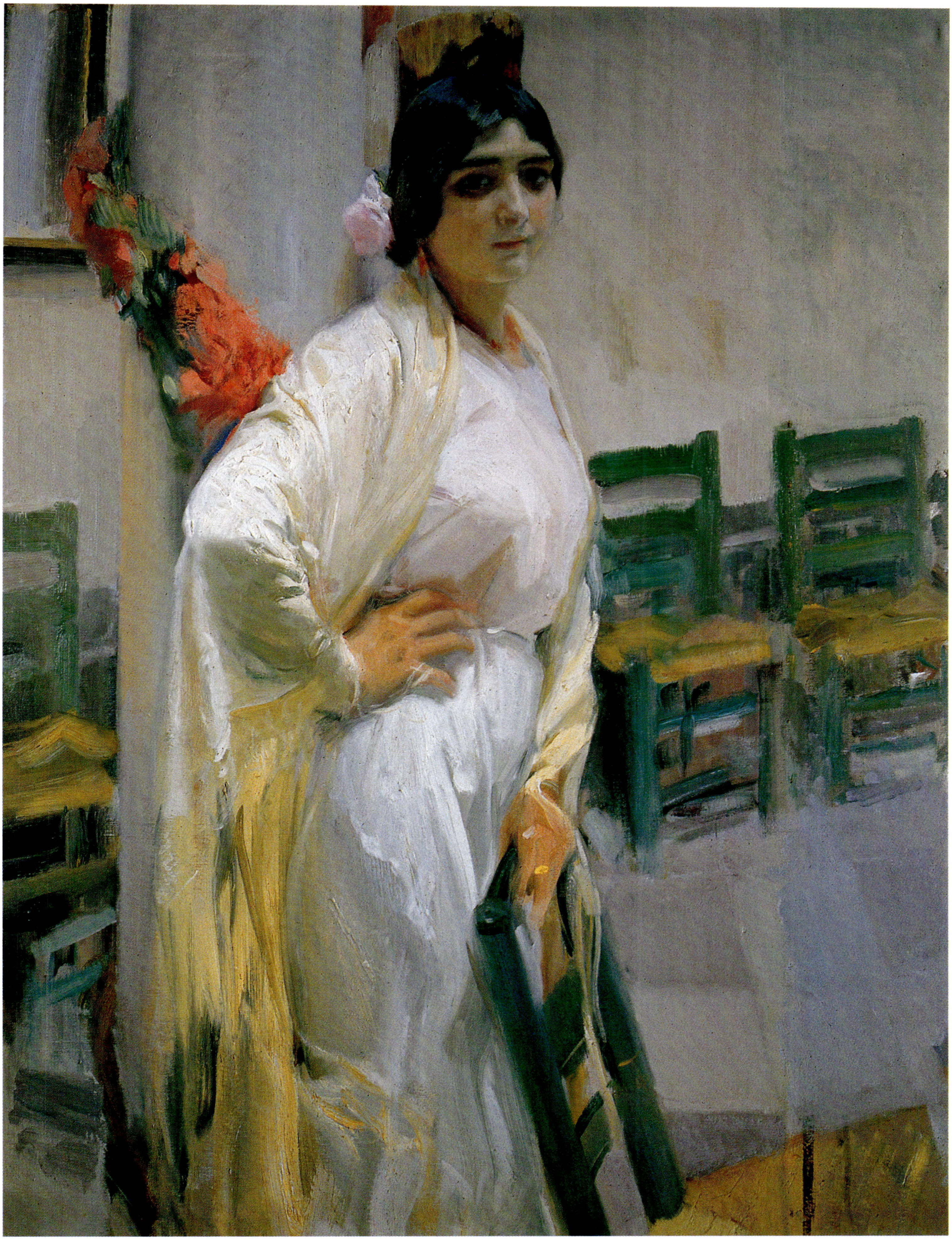

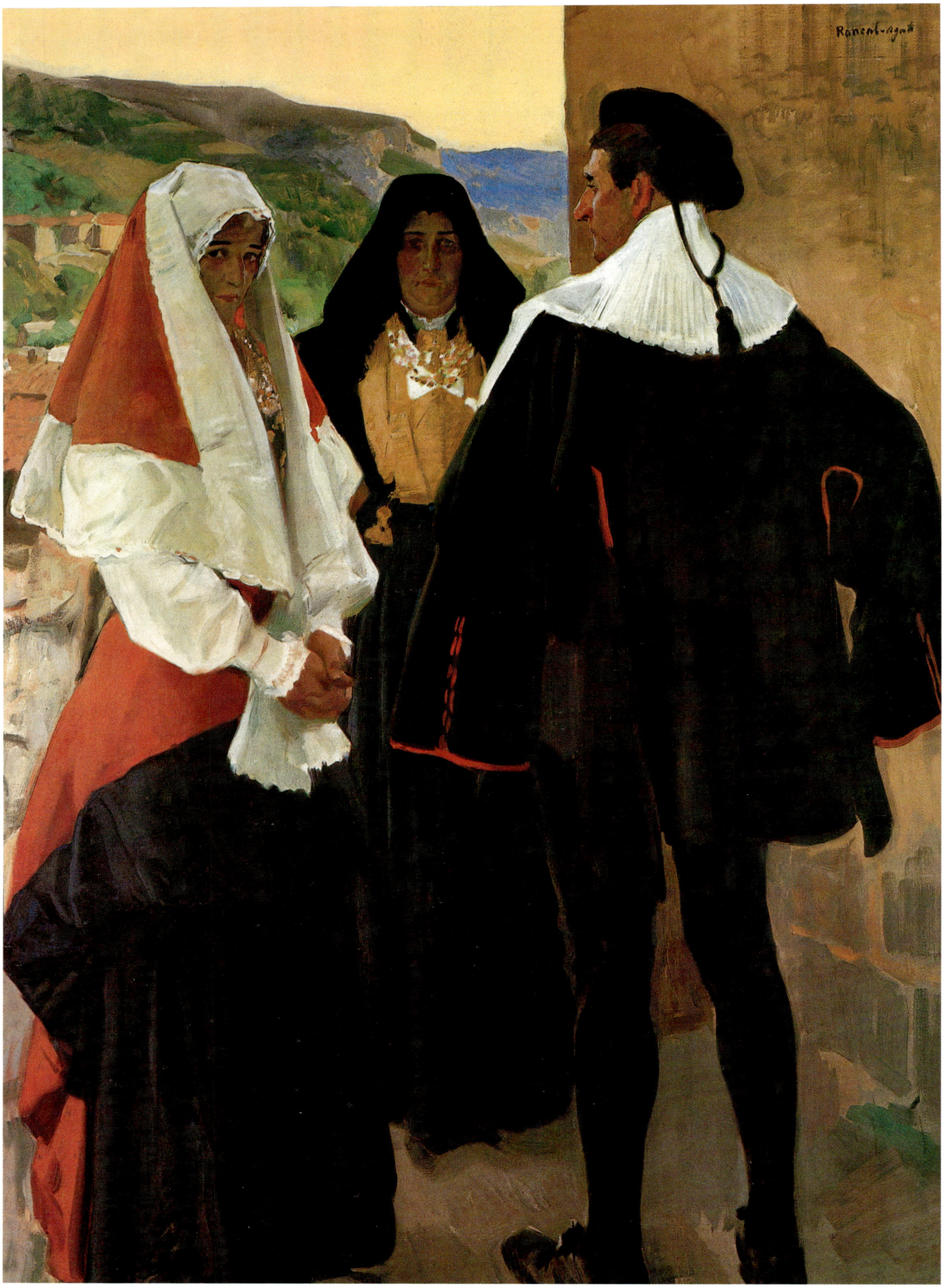
Rancel-agati

Tipos del Roncal
(People from Roncal)
1912, oil on canvas, 200 × 150 cm
Madrid: Museo Sorolla

For Sorolla each study of typical Spain would be a plastic challenge to be overcome. Therefore, as we have already seen in Tipos de Salamanca *and in* Novia lagarterana, *the characters are presented facing us, here the three protagonists form a circle, the man with his back to us, the woman facing us and the girl slightly turned toward the spectator. The background marks a counterpoint to the composition.*

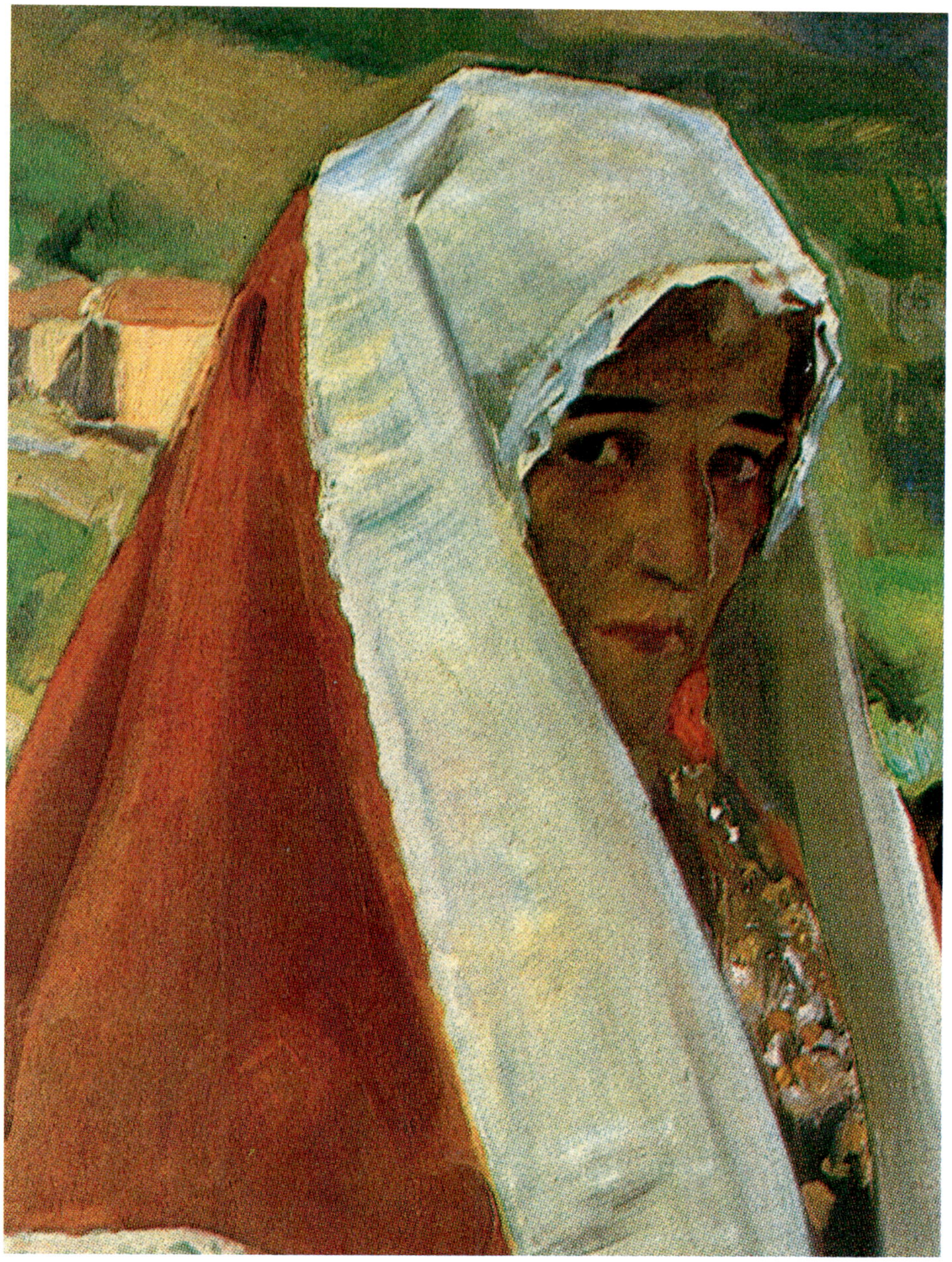

Tipos del Roncal
(People from Roncal)
Detail

In contrast to the emphasis and sobriety of the people from Navarre, the girl on the left looks at us in a half-curious, half-shy and insinuating manner. In this way, Sorolla diverges from the merely documentary aspect and introduces a human detail. His characters are not just figures; they are persons.

For the same reason, however, Sorolla never got to occupy his chair, a ceremony that was going to take place once he had finished working on the panels of the regions. Nevertheless, we know that he always had that recognition present in his heart and mind, as he started to write what would be his speech at the event, this document being one of his few autobiographical texts conserved today.

Barely six months after Sorolla's death, specifically on 2nd February 1924, Marceliano Santamaría, secretary of the painting section, gave voice to the words of the artist, who had focused his artistic reflection on the Valencia school of painting and on the tribute to six outstanding artists of the generation before his who influenced his works during his training years: Antonio Cortina (I841-1891), and the previously mentioned Francisco Domingo, Bernardo Ferrándiz, Antonio Muñoz Degrain, Ignacio Pinazo and Emilio Sala.

Sorolla always admired the artist from Alcoy, author of *Gramática del color*, who he thought was a distinguished colourist, and of whom he had written in

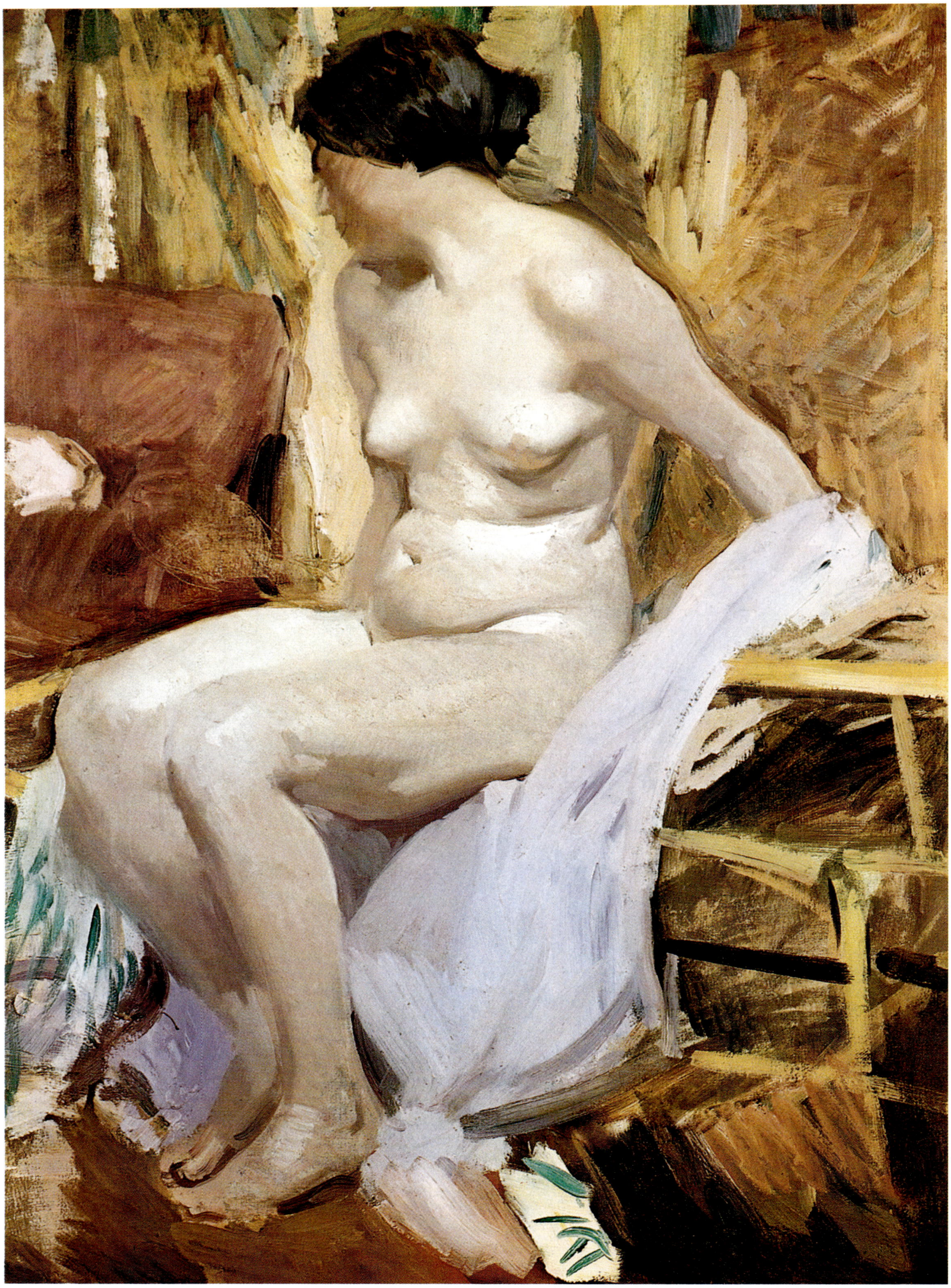

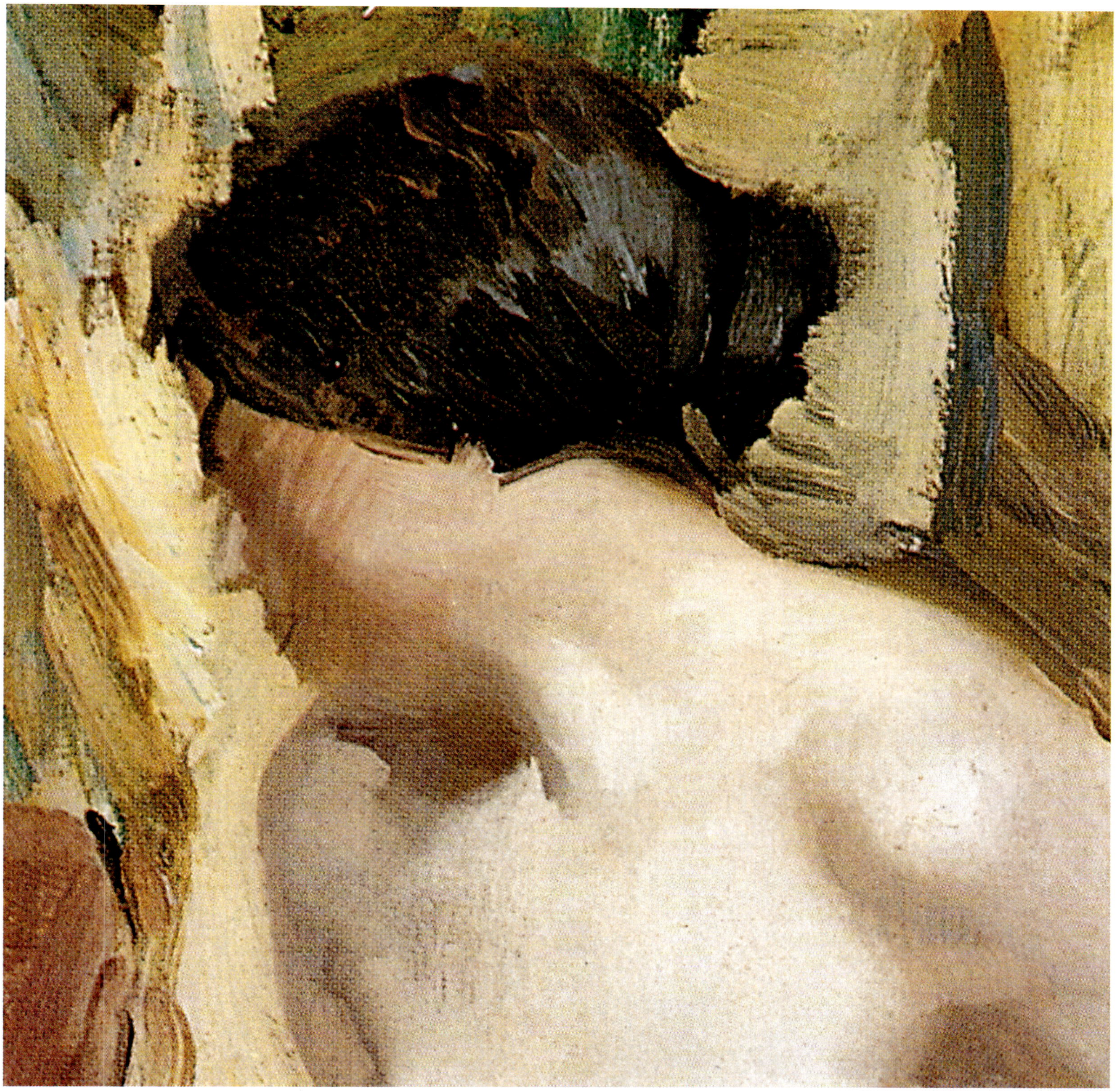

Desnudo de mujer
(Seated Nude)
C. 1914, oil on canvas, 99 × 74 cm
Madrid: Museo Sorolla

More than an academy study, this nude painted with rapid, vague brushstrokes brings Sorolla's painting closer to a certain expressionism devoid of drama. Very different to the nudes of his earlier works, he is giving us a master class in portraying a figure indoors.

Desnudo de mujer
(Seated Nude)
Detail

The only thing that matters here is the figure, and that is why the artist offers us an anonymous model who shyly turns her face away from the spectator, without losing the sensuality of her face, with her hair tied back, letting us see her neck.

the draft for his speech that he stood out "for the solid construction and complete analysis of shades ..., for his refined harmonies and taste in composition". He also had pleasant memories of the period spent at the Escuela de San Carlos, remembering Salustiano Asenjo, its director; Ricardo Franch, the engraver; Gonzalo Salvá, his landscape teacher, and Felipe Farinós, the sculptor.

When the artist had completed the panel *Los nazarenos* in late April/early May, he went back to Madrid. Soon afterwards, the family decided to spend the summer in the north, and he prepared the canvases for three more panels: Aragón, Navarre and Guipúzcoa. In July they left for Jaca, where they settled. We only have verbal references corresponding to what Sorolla painted during this period, on the part of his daughters and son-in-law, the painter Francisco Pons Arnau, (who married María Sorolla in Jaca cathedral on 7th September). Apparently, the artist used models and costumes from Roncal to paint the panels of Aragón and Navarre. In contrast to this panel of figures at rest, in which the mayor and the councilmen of the picturesque town of Roncal slowly and solemnly enter the church to ask for divine assistance before holding a council meeting according to a Navarrese custom, the one representing Aragon shows locals in motion, dancing the typical *jota*. Both canvases were completed in September. The autumn was now drawing near and Sorolla went to San Sebastián to paint the Guipúzcoa panel. On the city outskirts he painted a scene of locals playing skittles in which we can see a certain concern for placing the figures in the way of a mural painting. As soon as he finished, at the end of September, he returned to Madrid, to stay just for a few days, because he left again on 7th October, this time heading for the south, determined to paint the other Andalusian panels that he had planned without any interruptions. Invited by his friend Pedro González, he went to Jérez de la Frontera, to an estate called "El Cuco", in search of settings for the work in which he intended to depict a bullfight. However, he didn't find what he wanted, though he made the most of his time there, making some studies of vineyards with magnificent colours, and then decided to go to Seville to work on the panel *El encierro*. After an incessant search and many a talk with the Duke of Alba and the Duke of Medinaceli, he finally found the pastureland he was looking for on the outskirts of the city, on an estate called "Tabladilla".

Nearly the end of October, he now had the backgrounds prepared, with some studies of prickly pear bushes, but due to the bad weather he didn't officially start the canvas until the beginning of November, for which he had already got a good number of studies together. Whilst preparing them, he had complained of fatigue more than once, having to go up and down the ladder to reach the top parts of the enormous canvas. The problem was partly solved when they sent him his long paintbrushes from his house in Madrid. The canvas was finished by the middle of December, and is considered as being one of the most beautiful ones dedicated to Andalusia by Sorolla.

Before the end of 1914, the canvas for another of the Andalusian paintings was already on the easel, that is, the one depicting girls dancing in a decked-out patio, in front of the *Cruz de Mayo*. Two titles, *La Cruz de Mayo* and *El baile*, are usually applied indistinctly. His wife's arrival in Seville interrupted their regular exchange of letters, which reflect the everyday details and incidents of his works' progress. Therefore we don't have any comments on this panel, nor, for the same reason, on the next two: *Los toreros*, also painted in Seville between March and April 1915, and *La romería* painted in Villagarcía during the summer as the theme of the panel dedicated to Galicia. However, during this period, the sheer magnitude of the commission began to take its toll on Sorolla. His non-stop travelling all over Spain allowed him to see the rich variety of the country's customs and the impossibility of representing them all in the dedicated

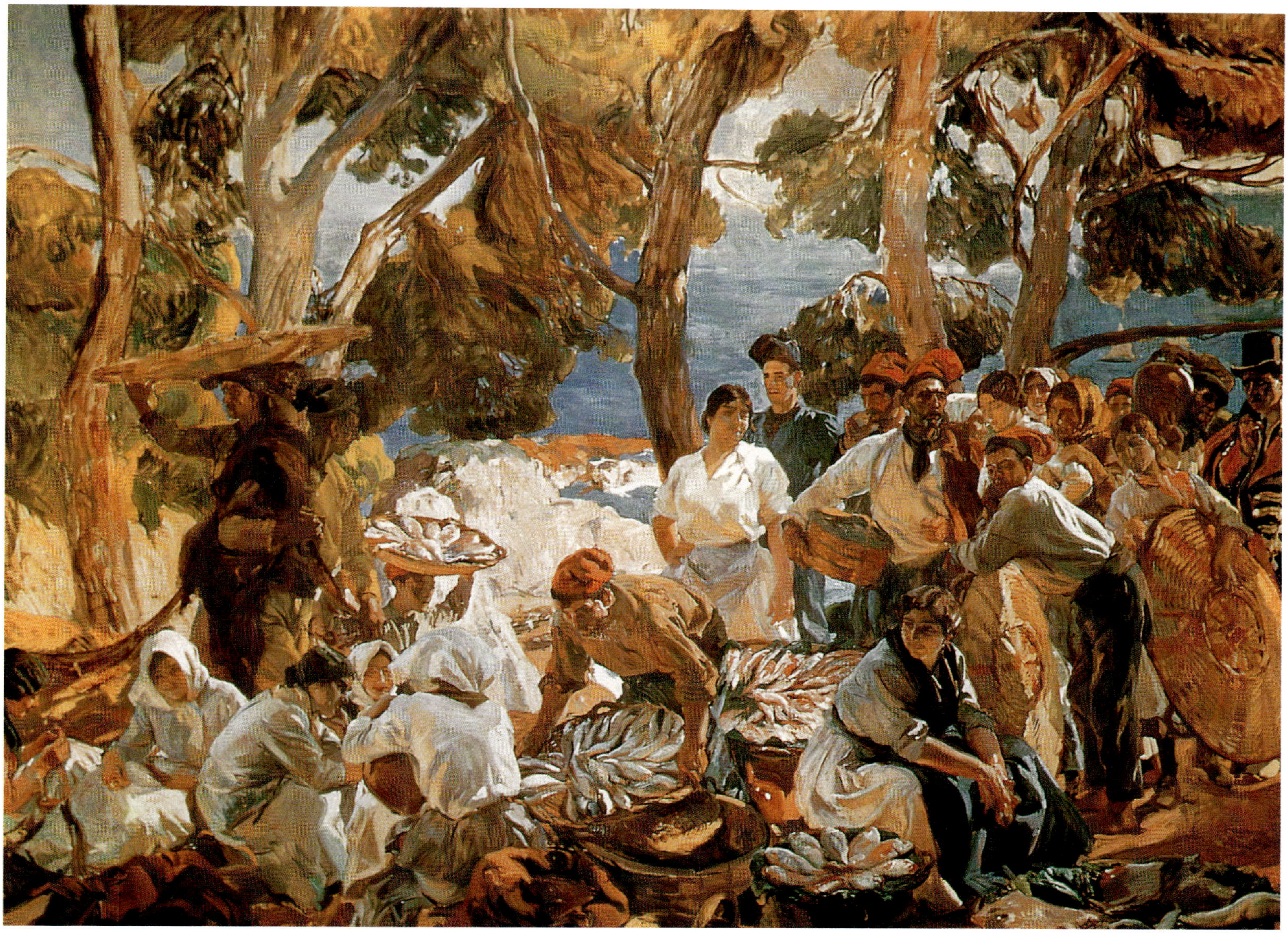

space, causing him the obvious uneasiness and anxiety that logically affected a painter of his status and professionalism.

In mid September 1915, Sorolla moved to Catalonia to paint *El pescado*, the panel corresponding to this region. He decided to paint it in Barcelona, being inspired by the old beach of Santa Cristina. After this one, he painted *Las grupas*, corresponding to Valencia, without leaving the capital, in Antonio García's orchard, after having looked for appropriate settings in Godella, Manises, Alcira and Carcagente. Begun in January 1916, it was completed in March, being a genuine song to Valencia, a canvas painted using a rich and bold palette making the result a feast of colour. Once finished, a year and a half went by without any work being done for the Hispanic Society. That summer, yearning for Valencia beach, he went there, staying and working until October, unaware of the fact that it would be the last time he would devote his soul and palette to his city. He spent the rest of the year on a pleasure trip, without painting, in Andalusia and Africa, with his wife, son and daughter, Joaquín and Elena.

El pescado
(Fish)
1915, oil on canvas, 352 × 485 cm
New York: Hispanic Society

The panel dedicated to Catalonia is, according to Bernardino de Pantorba, the most "Sorollist" as well as being, as Sorolla himself said, the one that pleased him most, because the characters portrayed are Mediterranean, like those of his hometown Valencia. The painter wrote to his wife, "I think that, in spite of its size, this one will be easier to paint than others."

The mid-point of composition

In January 1917, and with the purpose of starting work on the Extremadura panel, Sorolla moved to Mérida, Cáceres and Plasencia, but the extremely low

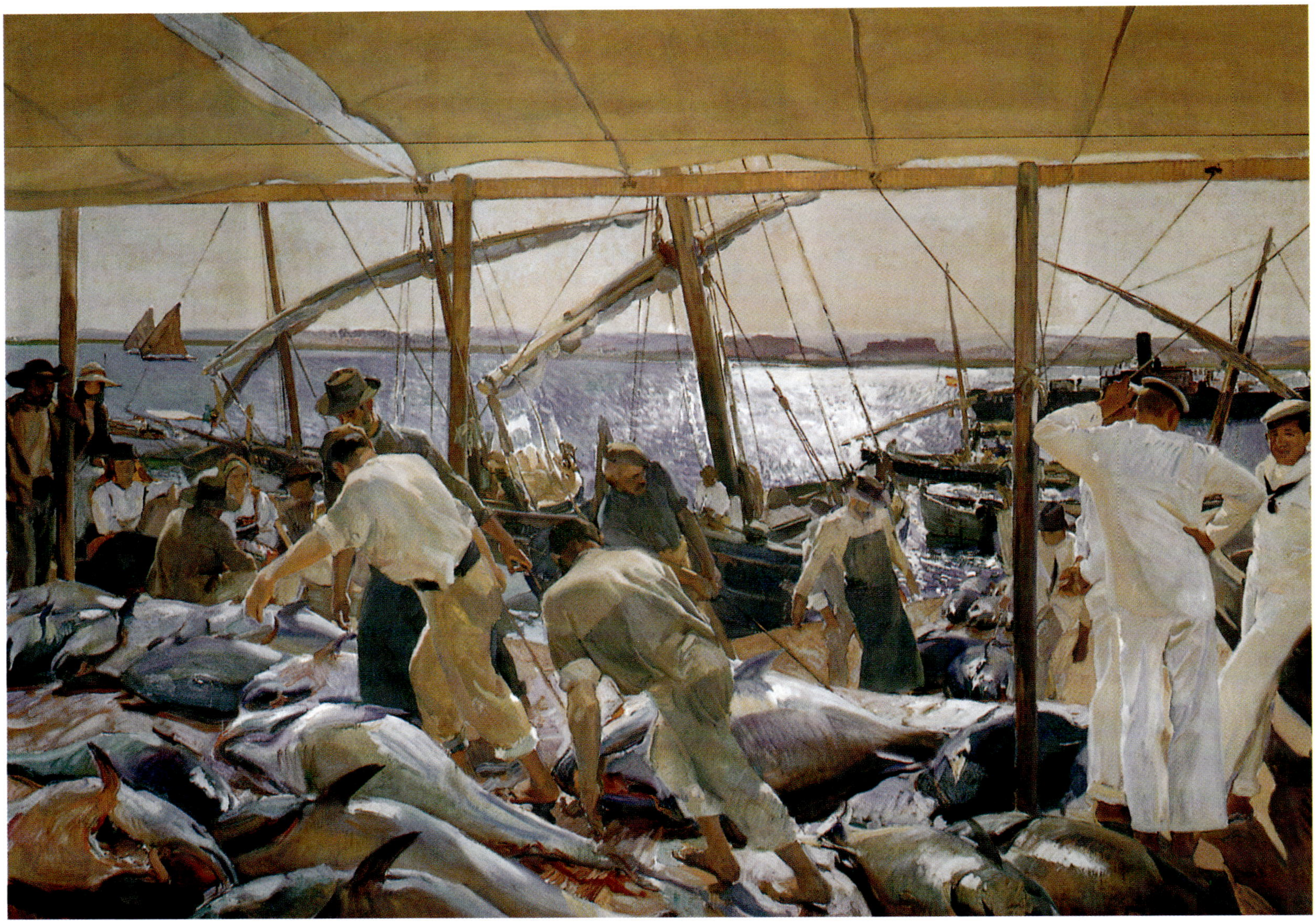

La pesca del atún
(The Tuna Catch)
1919, oil on canvas, 349 × 485 cm
New York: Hispanic Society

This was the last panel painted by Sorolla, being finished in June 1919. Exhausted after such a huge effort, he wrote to his wife, "This trip is hell. I'm exhausted [...] Ayamonte is just like Tetuan; it is the same colour [...] I don't know if what I'm going to do will be OK or not, because I don't feel enthusiastic about anything; I feel tired, old and miserable." However, as an almost posthumous work, once again we can see Sorolla's light as the protagonist.

temperatures made him postpone the work for later on. He therefore decided to return to Madrid, but during that month was invited by King Alfonso XIII to paint him at a hunt in Lachar (Granada). Neither was the weather very good there, so he decided to leave the portrait for another occasion. In mid February he returned to his house in Madrid, looking eagerly forward to the birth of his first grandson, Francisco Pons Sorolla, who was born on the 17th, and he spent that summer in San Sebastián.

Around 20th October he headed for Plasencia again, this time accompanied by his Sevillian disciple Santiago Martínez. Whilst working on the canvas, he complained about health problems and also suffered moments of depression, attributing that momentary lack of enthusiasm to the numerous months in which he had not picked up his paintbrush. At the beginning of November he finished the panel *El mercado*, and returned to Madrid with the purpose of retouching the canvas background in his studio, with which Martínez helped him, although the result was one of the less elaborately worked canvases of the series.

At the beginning of 1918, Sorolla still had two panels left to be painted, and he realised that he had to work more rapidly if he was going to meet the deadline set by the American society. For unknown causes, however, until the end of September and after having been back to Seville in March, attended his father-in-law's funeral in Valencia in July, and spent another summer in San Sebastián, he didn't go with his son Joaquín to Alicante, from where he carried

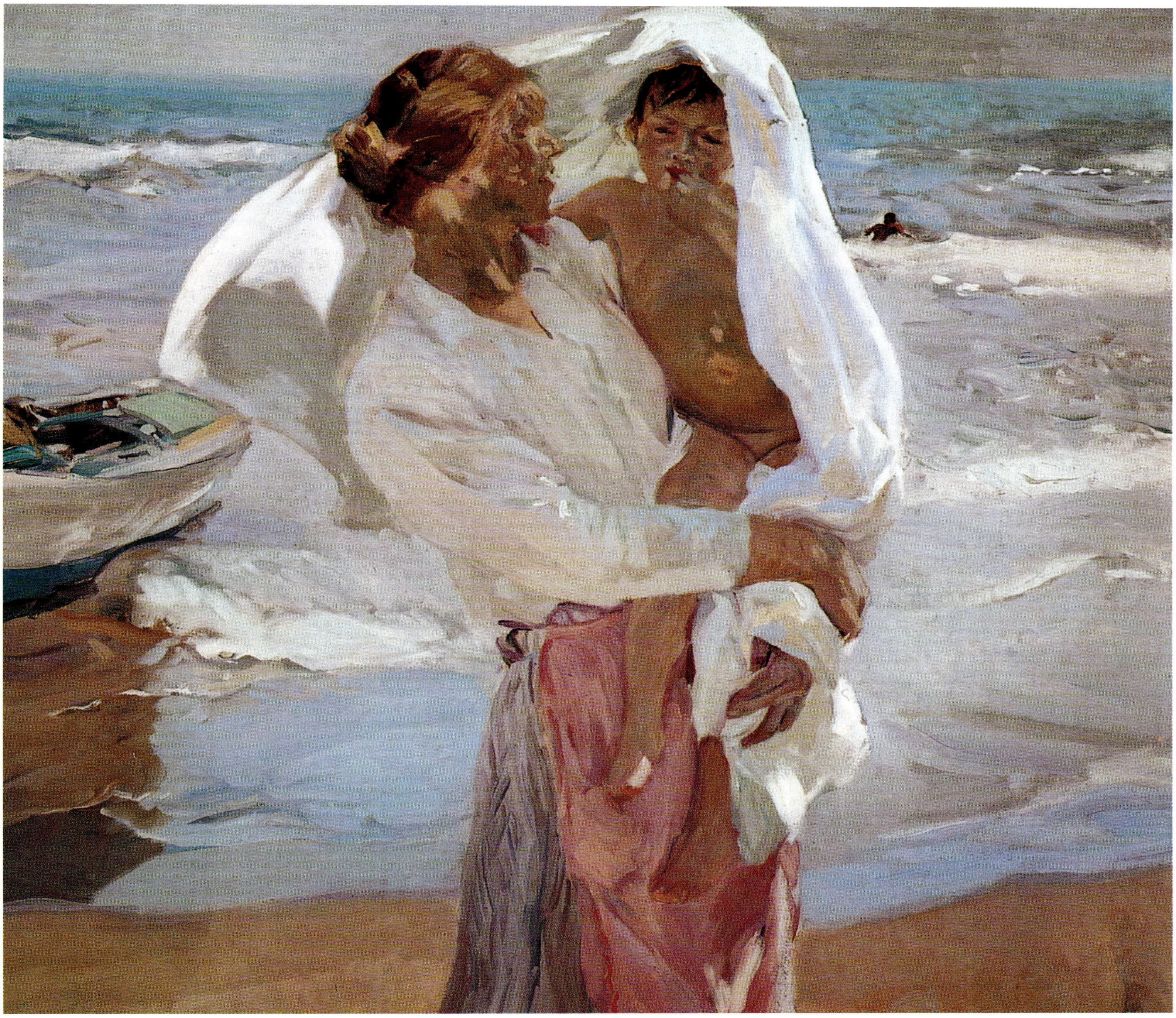

on to Elche, a town which he loved for the beauty of its centennial and famous palm trees, unique in Europe. Circumstances of a family nature obliged him to return to Madrid in the middle of the month, which meant a delay of nearly one month in his work, starting again on 25th November. At the beginning of 1919 the panel was practically finished, and he returned to Madrid at the end of January. In May he went to Seville again, where he met up with Santiago Martínez, who would accompany him while he painted the last panel of the series. In search of a suitable place, they finally chose Ayamonte where he painted *La pesca del atún* ["The Tuna Catch"], one of his most successful paintings composition-wise and in which, thanks to the geographical situation of the place, we can see a bit of Portuguese landscape in the background.

Paradoxically, and as we can gather from the letters written to his wife during this period, when days of great motivation alternated with others with moments of near despair, little did the painting of such a magnificent canvas favour the circumstances, thus putting the artist's great creative capacity to the test. He

Saliendo del baño
(After the Bath)
1915, oil on canvas, 130 × 150 cm
Madrid: Museo Sorolla

After the exhausting work of having travelled all over Spain to portray regional characters for the great project commissioned by the Hispanic Society, Sorolla goes back to his traditional themes, in which he portrays trivial everyday aspects in the Mediterranean. In this case he depicts a scene in early morning light.

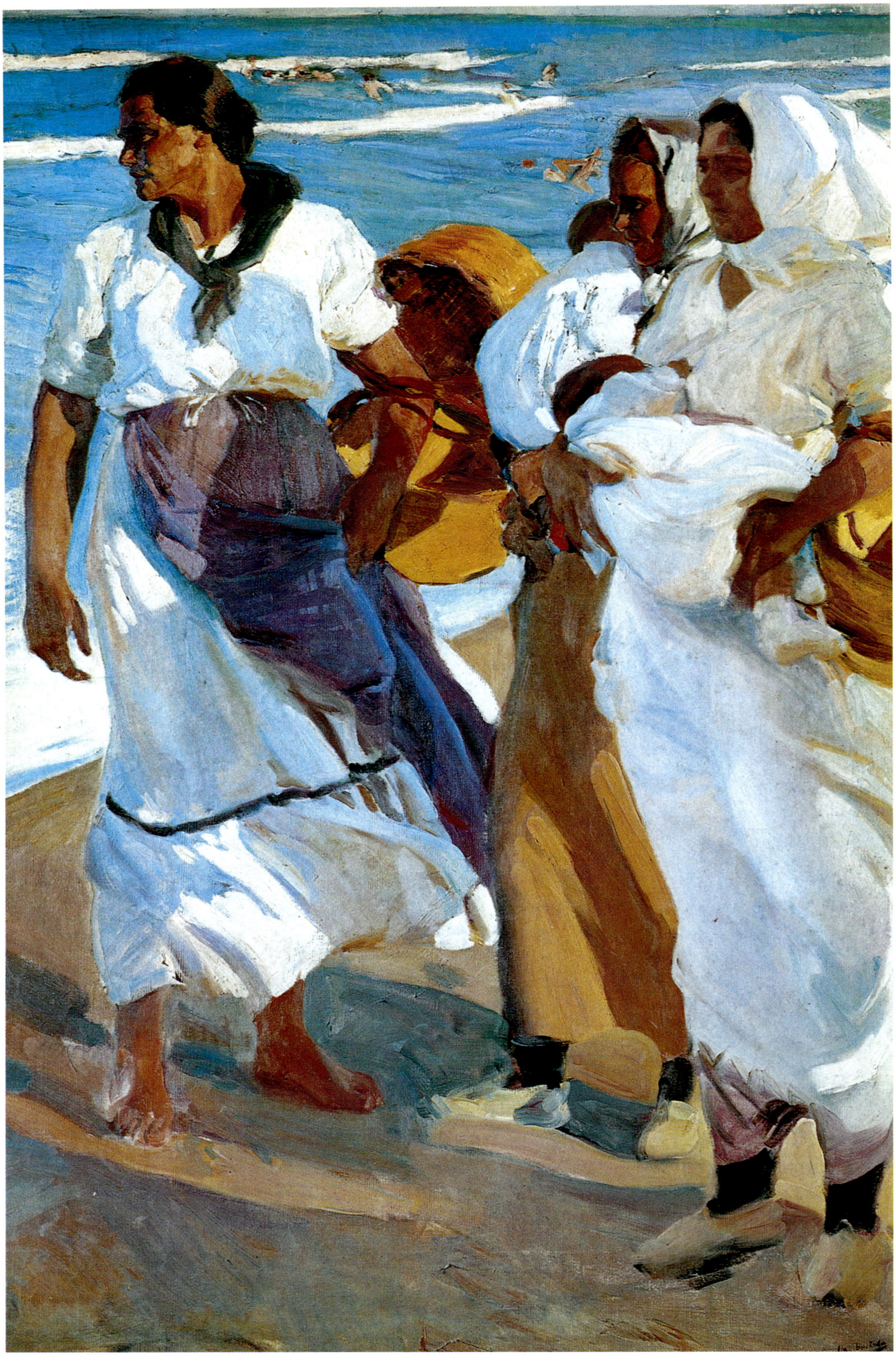

Pescadoras valencianas
(Valencian Fisherwomen)
1915, oil on canvas, 201 × 133 cm
Madrid: Museo Sorolla

The canvases mentioned on previous pages have their influence on this work in which the women, in their white clothes, stand out against the background of the sea in which children are bathing.

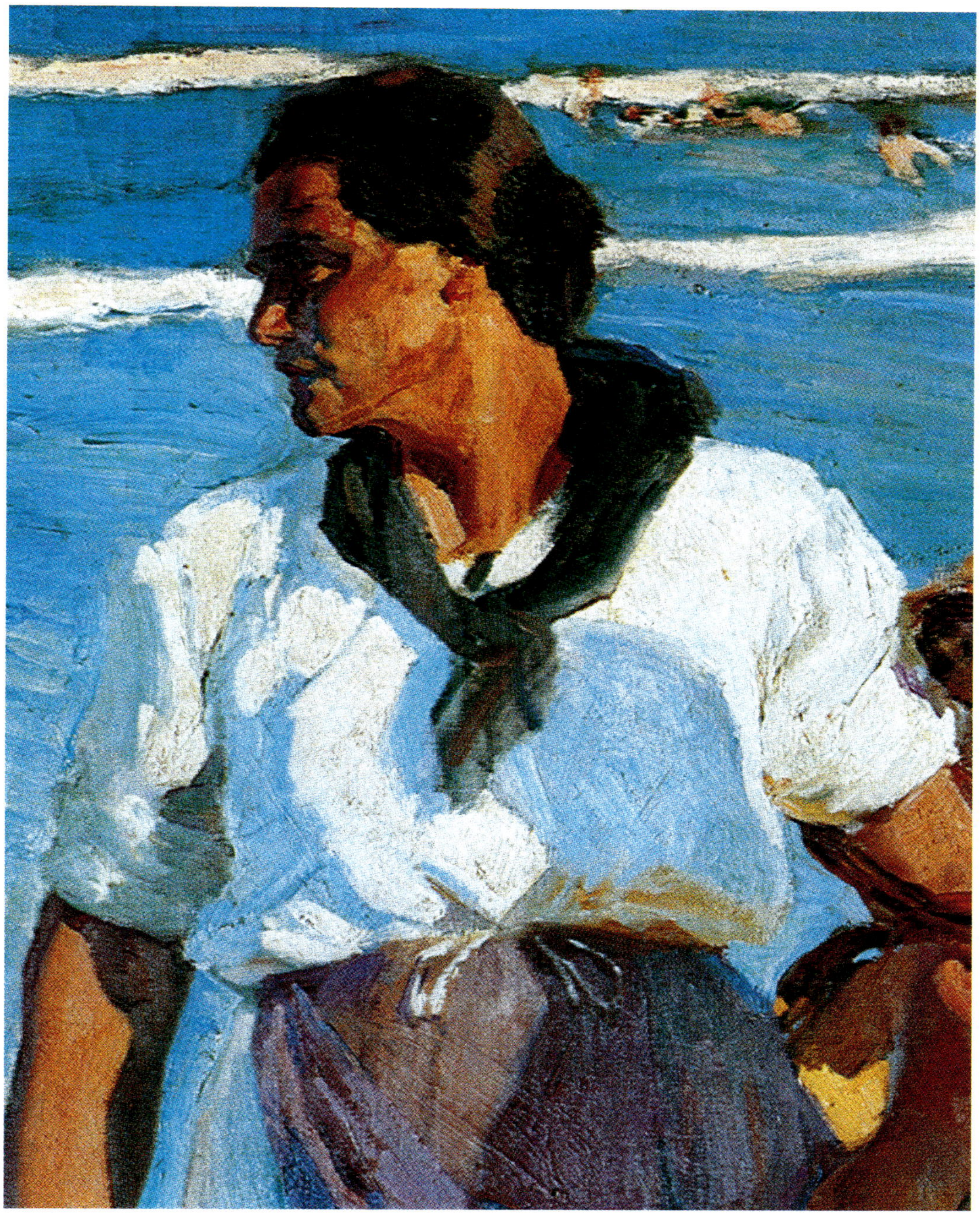

Pescadoras valencianas
(Valencian Fisherwomen)
Detail

This woman who looks as if she has been surprised by the presence of the onlooker turns her head to the right in a calm but majestic manner. Sorolla has returned to his beach scenes and he wants to pay tribute to Valencian fisherwomen, dignifying them.

often felt unwell, tired, bad-tempered and miserable; he complained about feeling dizzy, being in pain, and tiredness; he couldn't stand the heat and the mosquitoes wouldn't leave him alone, besides missing his family. His disciple Santiago Martínez described how Sorolla painted the final scene of that last panel, witnessing the effort required from the artist to paint Huntington's commission. And so, with that scene of fishermen working and of sailors dressed in white, against a setting sun that is reflected in the water, and the Portuguese coast in the background looming up out of the mist, Sorolla painted his last seascape.

At the end of June, the artist told his wife that he had given the last brushstroke to the canvas. He finished it exactly in time, because those disorders and ailments he had been complaining about since 1917 were no more than a just sign of his progressive decline in health. The words expressed by the king of Spain who sent him a telegram from San Sebastián brought him great satisfaction: "Congratulations for having finished your colossal work, which is surely to be admired by future generations as the painted photograph of 20th century Spain before our great leap forward takes place. Kind regards. Alfonso, King."

Sorolla's last years: portraits, landscapes and beach scenes

Between January 1912 and June 1919, the period comprising the great work of the Hispanic Society, Sorolla's painting activity wasn't limited to this venture alone. He painted many canvases apart from those of the project which took him almost seven long years: some belong to the same days on which the panels left their author's hands, and were painted in the same places, sometimes even using the same models. Others date from the periods in which the artist didn't work on the panels, with frequent interruptions, especially in the years 1916, 1917 and 1918. Regarding this production we may highlight, first of all, and for their quantity, the portraits. The Valencian beach scenes painted during part of the summer of 1915 and the whole of the summer of 1916, also enjoy a privileged position, not forgetting various landscapes, for example the interesting series painted in Andalusia, as well as those painted in the garden of his house.

Portraits are an important genre in Sorolla's repertoire. His activity as a portrait painter also grew at the same speed as his international prestige, and it remained until the last day of his professional life. The same as the rest of his paintings, these ones were also a point of general controversy, being praised by some and criticised by others. International criticism was never unanimous in this respect; for example, while they were not very well considered in France, in England they were even more valued than his open-air works.

Apart from the previously-mentioned portraits of *Cossío, Blasco Ibáñez, Beruete, Menéndez Pelayo*, and others of some of the most distinguished Spaniards of the period, with which the Hispanic Society began the extension of its iconographic gallery in 1909, Sorolla intensified this work since 1913. From that year, until the beginnings of 1920, he painted, in a chronological order: *Rafael Altamira, Emilia Pardo Bazán, Francisco Rodríguez Marín, Marqués de la Vega Inclán, Pío Baroja, Marqués de Jerez de los Caballeros, Juan Ramón Jiménez, José Martínez Ruiz ("Azorín"), Gumersindo de Azcárate, Maestro Bretón, Mariano Benlliure, Ricardo León, Leonardo Torres Quevedo, Ramón Menéndez Pidal, Antonio Múñoz Degrain, Jacinto Benavente, José Ortega y Gasset, José Benlliure, Antonio Machado, Miguel Blay, Manuel Benedito, Ramón Pérez de Ayala* and *Doctor Marañón, Doctor Sandoval*, as well as *Miguel de Unamuno*.

Portraits that were not painted for the Hispanic Society, but which were also made during this period are, amongst others, those of *Raquel Meller, Laura de Santelmo, Catalina Bárcena, Lucrecia Arana, Esperanza Iris, Francisco Giner de los Ríos, Amalio Gimeno* and the painters *Federico Ferrándiz* and *Fernando Viscaí*. In short, with his portrait gallery, Sorolla managed to offer a modern, intellectual and dynamic image of Spain, represented by illustrious personalities from

Rosas blancas del jardín de la casa
(White Roses from the Garden)
1919, oil on canvas, 96 × 64 cm
Private collection

In contrast to the great themes recently finished for the Hispanic Society, Sorolla approaches one that is new to his artistic production. Bearing in mind the approaching illness that would mean the end of his painting days, these flowers painted with thick brushstrokes and vibrating colour are a fine example of his painting skill, which makes an apparently trivial theme a work of art. For Sorolla the theme is only secondary; what matters is painting for painting's sake: colour, light and strokes within space.

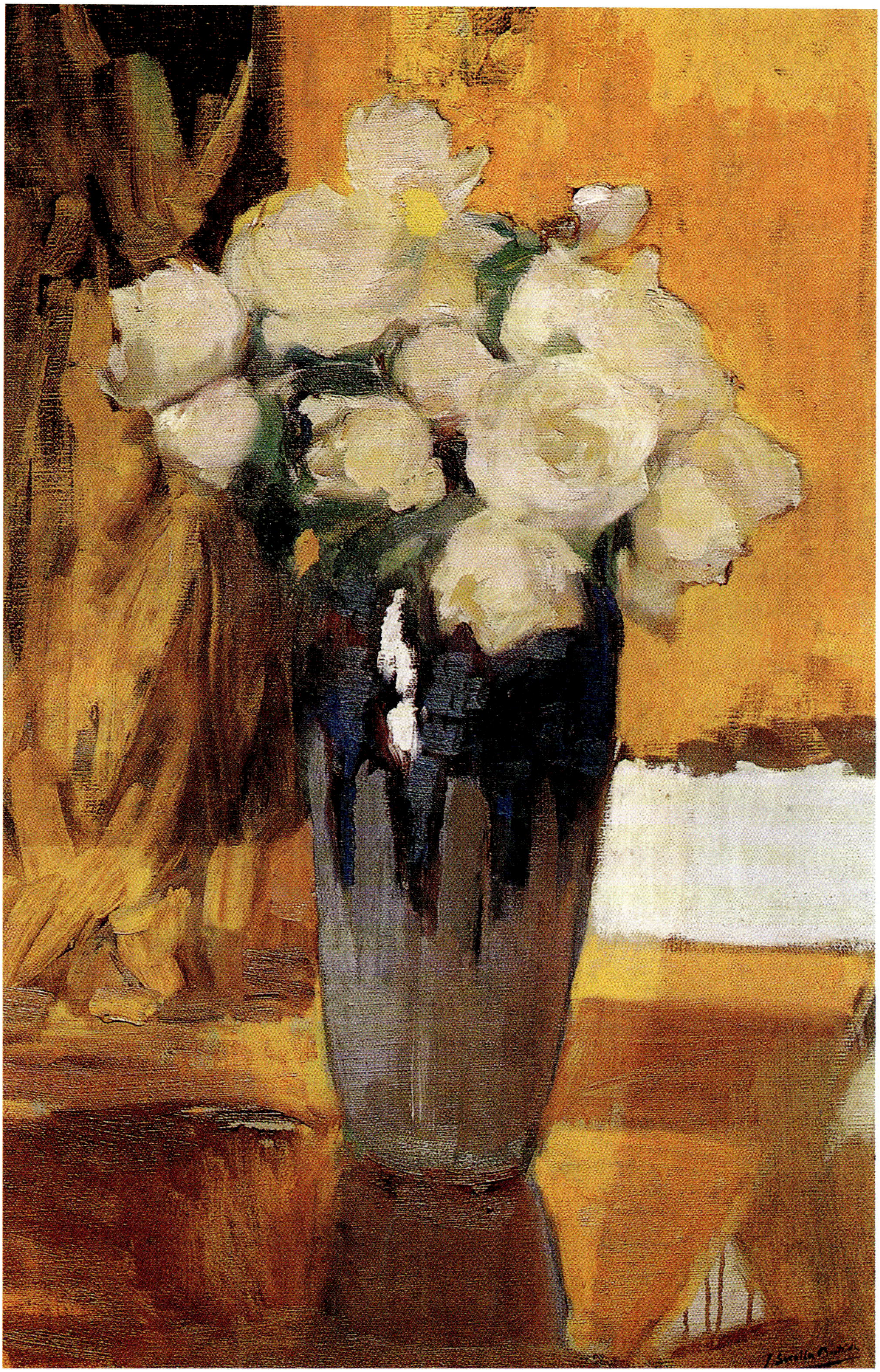

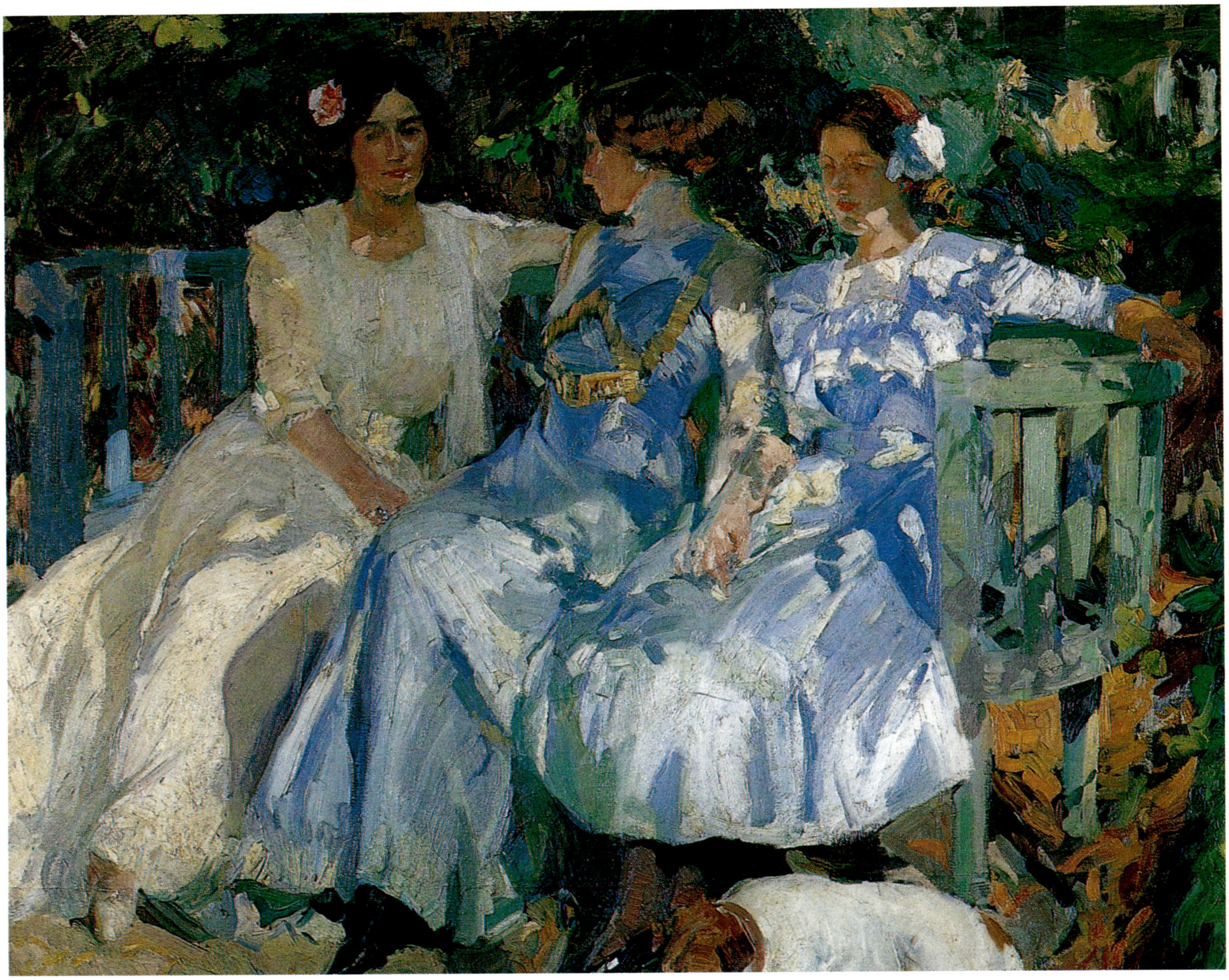

Mi mujer y mis hijas en el jardín
(My Wife & Daughters in the Garden)
1910, oil on canvas, 166 × 206 cm
Private collection

Like Edmund Peel says, "Sorolla's ideal was to depict nature just as it is." In comparison with the elitist elegance of Sargent, Sorolla compares the naturalness of this family portrait in which the protagonists blend in with their surroundings with the portrait of Louis Comfort Tiffany.

the worlds of politics, science, literature and art. All sorts of characters repeatedly posed for him, from the Spanish monarchs, members of the royal family and high society ladies and, of course, all the members of his family as well as nearly all his closest acquaintances, there being a total amount of more than 500 works corresponding to this genre.

Regarding the technique employed in such works, it would be logical to think that a paintbrush like Sorolla's, so quick in achieving what it proposed, would work in the same way as that applied to his composition paintings. The lack of interest for portrait painting on the part of the artist probably explains how this ended up becoming an almost mechanical activity for him. It would frequently occur that, in order to link those canvases more closely to the rest of his work, he would on occasions also paint them outdoors, always searching for problems of light and colour effects.

Examples of the latter are: *Esposa del escritor Pérez de Ayala*, *Alfonso XIII con uniforme de húsares*, *Antonio Carda en la playa de Valencia* and those of *Raimundo de Madrazo, Amalio Cimeno* and *Pérez de Ayala* with a garden background.

However, the artistic temperament of Sorolla, so fond of the luminous effects of natural light, was not the most appropriate for that genre. On one oc-

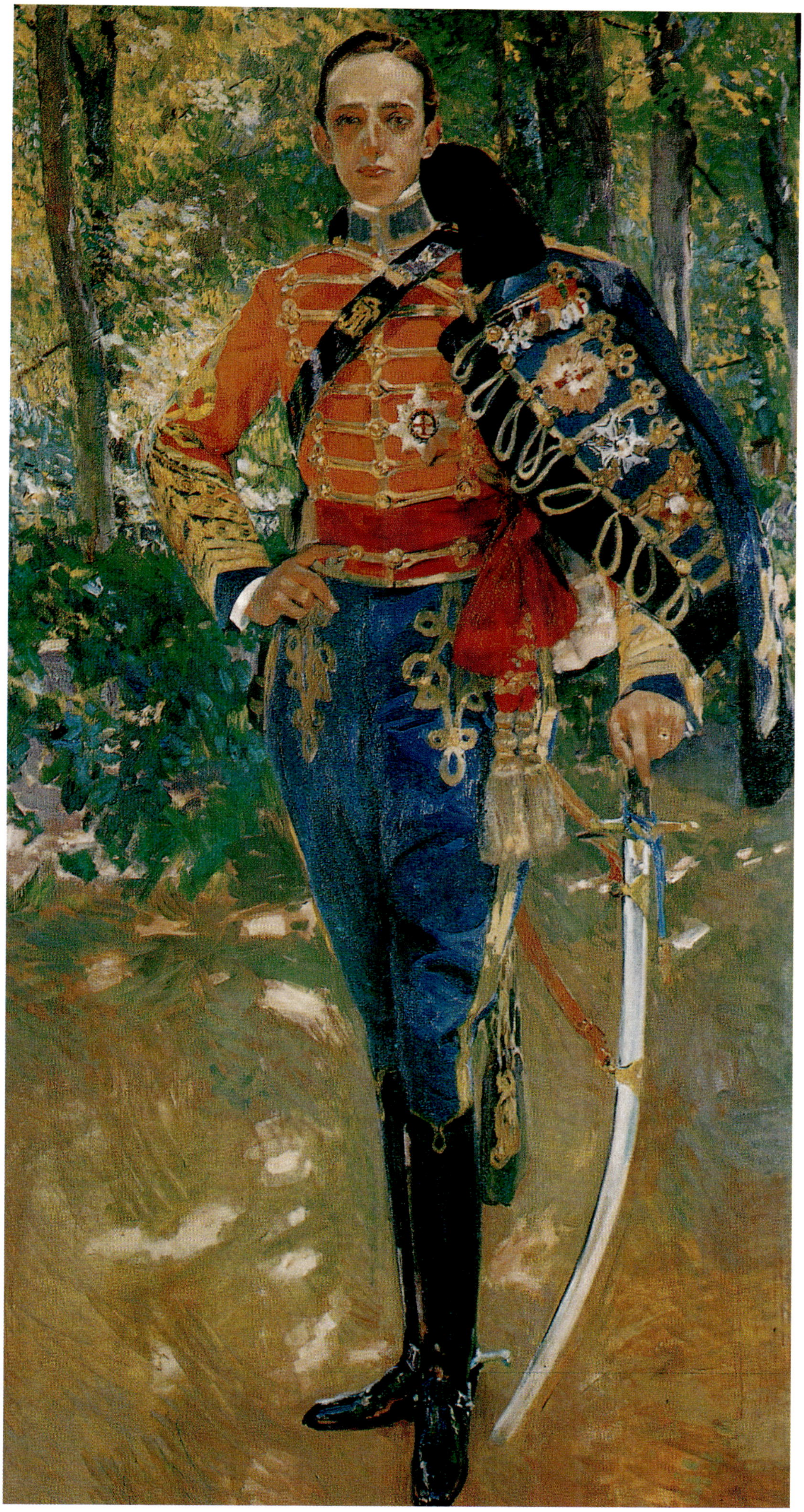

Alfonso XIII con uniforme de húsares
(Portrait of King Alfonso XIII Wearing the Uniform of the Hussars)
1907, oil on canvas, 208 × 108 cm
Madrid: Palacio Real

Although, like in the previous case, this canvas precedes the last period of the artist in time, it is a portrait of somebody who is not a member of the family, Sorolla approaches what we could call a plein-air portrait, in a very different way to that of the cosmopolitan North American portrait painter he admired so much, John Singer Sargent.

casion, he even exclaimed: "Me, a portrait painter ... and ladies' portraits! I can't believe it!" He managed to achieve a reasonable composition in many of them, but in most cases they are much surpassed by his famous vibrating beach scenes. The nervous swipes of his paintbrush didn't allow him to waste time making an analysis of the model, and the artist himself defended that procedure to an American journalist: "I find that portraits have to be painted quickly ... it doesn't matter how long it takes you to get ready, the trouble you take to study your model. But when you begin the work, you must finish it practically in one session, because otherwise your model will get tired and change their expression, and you also get tired. I hate my work getting cold. And, irrespective of the time spent on the canvas, the result must look as if it has been easily done in one go."

He also pointed out the difficult field of children's portraits, where, being able to use his children as models, he managed to learn how to depict the innocent grace and charm of childhood in some works.

Después del baño o La bata rosa
(After the Bath or The Pink Robe)
1916, oil on canvas, 208 × 126.5 cm
Madrid: Museo Sorolla

The effects of the rays of sunlight filtering through the cane screen produce a chiaroscuro that half lights the scene up. A girl is changing from her wet clothes into dry ones with the aid of a woman. In spite of being an interior composition, it is one of those works in which the true protagonist is Sorolla's sempiternal light.

Valencia beach scenes and landscapes

The most beautiful of all the works painted by Sorolla during what would be his last stage on Valencia beach, in the summer of 1916, is the one titled *Después del baño* ["After the Bath"] or *La bata rosa* ["The Pink Robe"], a prodigious study of light, where the softness and translucence of colour balance the sensation of flesh and clothes of the bodies of the two women in the shade of a cane screen through which a few rays of sunlight filter and behind which a portion of the blue sea can be seen. The artist himself admitted in a letter that this was the most important and one of the best works he had painted in his life, having a very high opinion of it.

That would be the last summer Sorolla painted in Valencia. Since the summer of 1894, the beach of his hometown had been the wonderful setting for someone who knew how to find an incomparable framework to let his inspiration run wild, capturing those suggestive scenes that made him famous on the canvas. With the same subjects and models seen every day on the beach, year after year Sorolla made his compositions, at the same time as the quality of his painting improved and his paintings took on a more concise and real expression. As he refined his vision of colour, his skill in drawing simplified the study of the outline, obtaining his greatest achievements during those cheerful summer days which would paradoxically be his last.

Sorolla's rich colourist palette allowed him to also become a landscape painter with extraordinary possibilities. Inspired by nature in all its infinite diversity, with its full possibilities of vibration and light, capturing everything that moved in that natural world, be it a tree branch swaying in the breeze or a cloud moving along in the sky, or children playing and fishermen working in the water. In his production we must highlight the groups comprising the beautiful views of Seville and Granada, but now as more schematic interpretations, although inspired by those carried out previously, and the numerous versions of the garden of his house. Most of them are colour impressions carried out very quickly in only one session, but are nonetheless virtuous. They represent, in short, an exquisite chromatic chord and an unforgettable display of pictorial diction. The loose and rapid brushstrokes of the second group, leaving out detail and using a palette of mainly pinks and mauves, he reveals the intimacy of his home, at the same time as he allows the spectator to see, carefully guided by the artist, how his garden unfolds before their eyes.

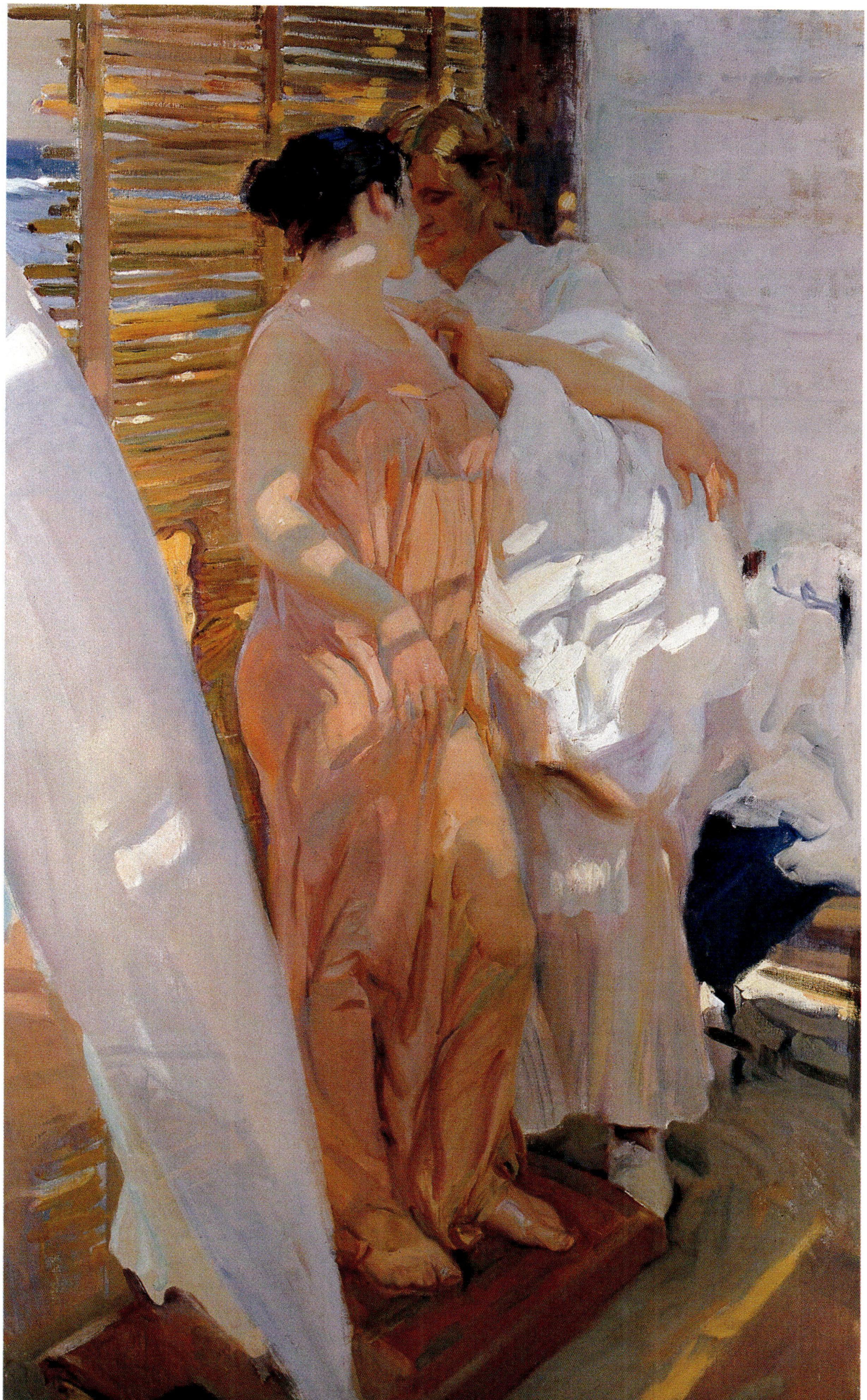

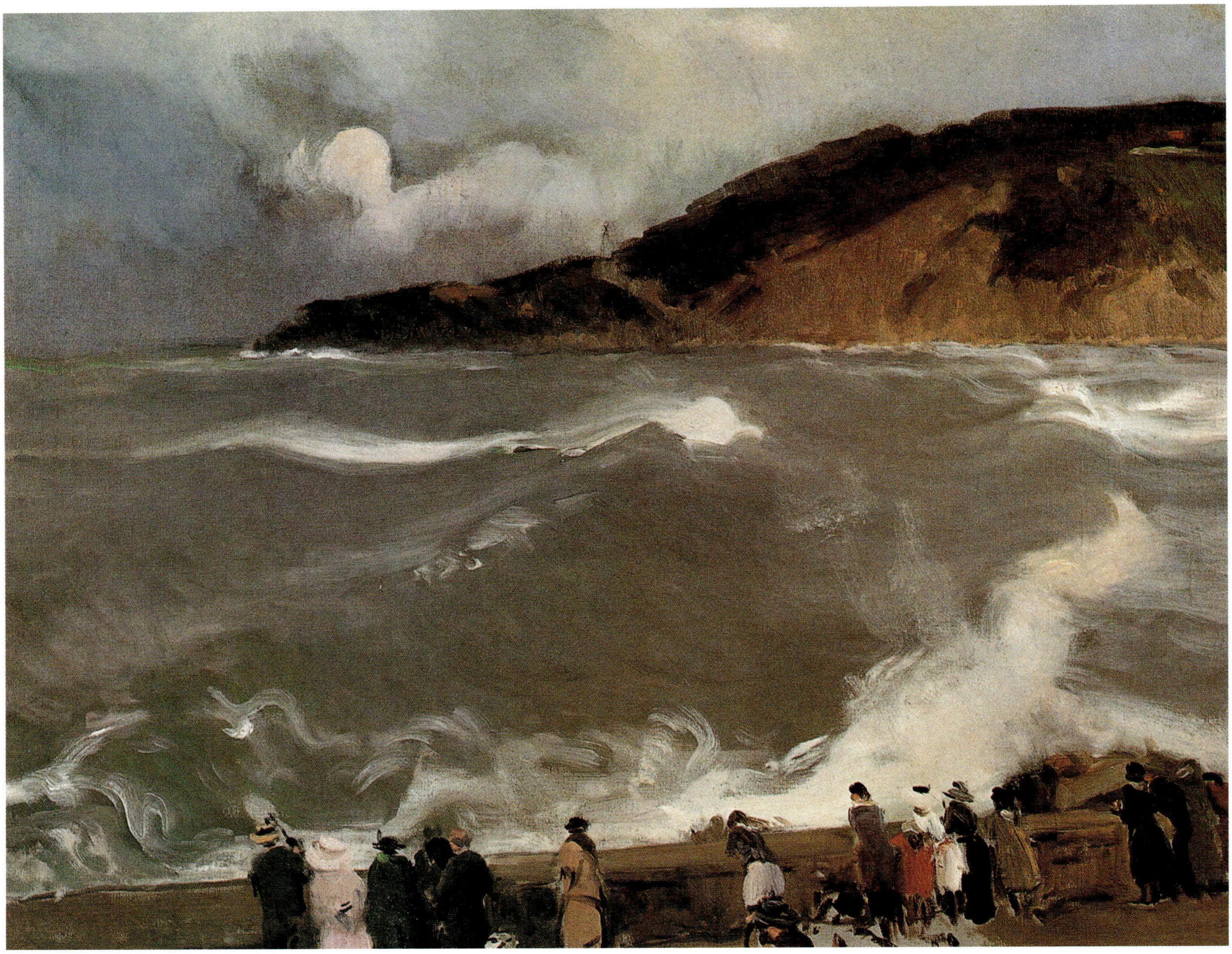

Rompeolas. San Sebastián
(Breakwater. San Sebastián)
C. 1917, oil on canvas, 81 × 104 cm
Madrid: Museo Sorolla

Although his sea was the Mediterranean, this didn't stop him from being ever-fascinated by the Cantabrian Sea. In comparison to the tranquil waters of the Valencian coast, the rough seas of northern Spain attracted him and were depicted on many an occasion. In this canvas the protagonist is the vastness of the sea; the human figures in the foreground being, like us, mere onlookers.

A frustrated hope

Happy but exhausted, once work had finished on the Hispanic Society project, Sorolla left Ayamonte with the intention of spending some time in his native Valencia. Later he went to Majorca with his wife and daughter Elena, his disciple Santiago Martínez and, for a few days, his friend Doctor Sandoval. From there they visited Ibiza, and although the artist should have spent his time resting, on both islands he painted several sea and rock studies, apart from the canvas commissioned to him by Ryan, the millionaire, some years earlier, on the subject of his tobacco business.

By mutual agreement, they decided to portray a scene somewhat different to what was habitual in that type of theme, the result being *Los contrabandistas* ["The Smugglers"], an oil painting inspired by the scenery on both islands. At the end of September, Sorolla returned to Valencia. He was planning to travel to New York in January the following year, since he wanted to personally hand over the 14 panels that he zealously kept in his studio to the Hispanic Society. Huntington, once informed that the work had been completed, having had the occasion to see some of the canvases on one of his almost annual trips to Madrid, eagerly awaited the moment of their arrival.

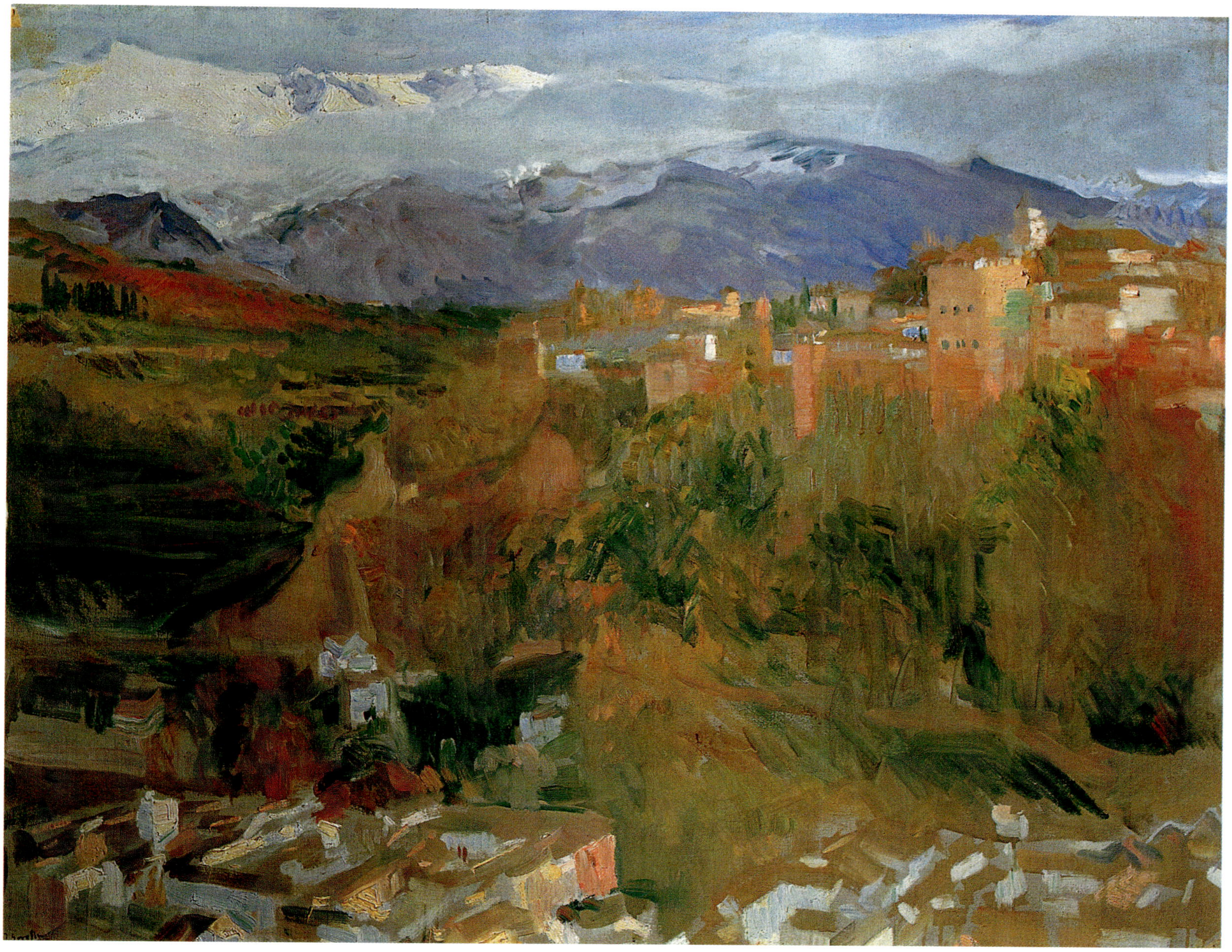

After returning to Valencia, his presence was sought again in Madrid, since he had to take up his post as professor of colour and composition at the Escuela de San Fernando, whose appointment by "Royal Order" had been extended until the end of that academic year. However, Sorolla could only carry out his academic obligations for one year, since he suffered a stroke in June 1920. Not only did this illness interrupt his teaching career, but it cut short his artistic career forever. During three cruel years he suffered in agony, leading his family to despair since they couldn't do anything to help him.

At the beginning of 1921, his family at least hoped that an exhibition could be held in the Prado Museum on the works painted for the Hispanic Society (upon agreement with Mr. Huntington to avoid breaching one of the clauses) before they were sent off to New York, but obscure interests thwarted the possibility of Sorolla seeing, although he could no longer understand, his splendid task and the magnitude of his last triumph. Finally, the panels were handed over by the painter's wife and children in December 1922, as well as 25 portraits of illustrious Spaniards also painted for the New York society and that had remained in the artist's studio. All the red tape related with the payment of the works, as well as the preparations required for their installation, meant that the exhibition room would not be opened until three years later, on 25th January 1926.

Granada
1917, oil on canvas
Madrid: Museo Sorolla

The compositions made by Sorolla in Granada were mainly based on the Moorish enclaves of The Alhambra and Generalife. Here his vision becomes wider, focusing on the Generalife, with the mountains of Sierra Nevada in the background.

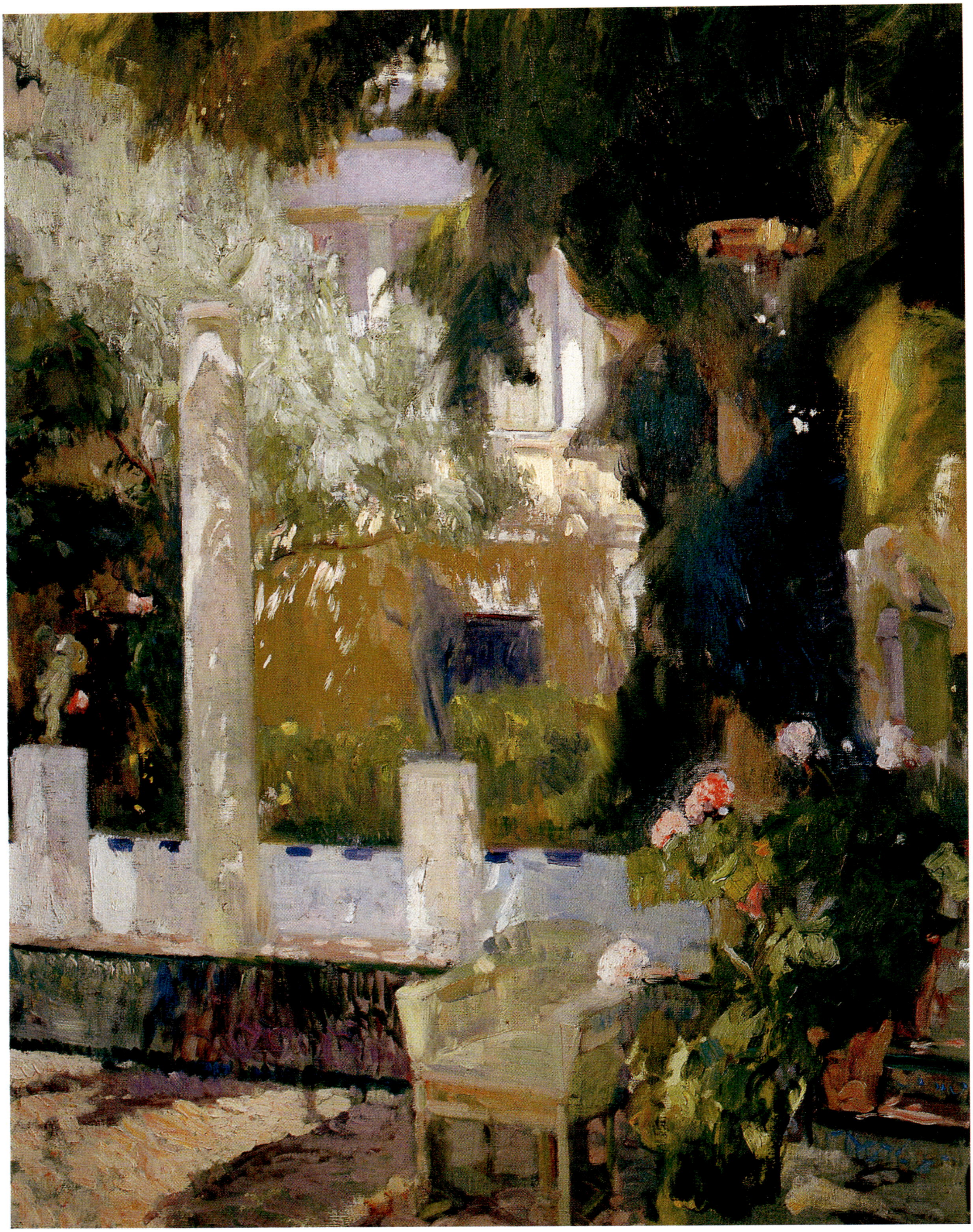

Jardín de la casa de Sorolla
(Garden of the Sorolla Family Home)
1920, oil on canvas, 104 × 87.5 cm
Madrid: Museo Sorolla

This is a fully impressionist work, showing us the corner of the third garden of the artist's house through broken columns which separate it from the second space. This canvas was painted merely for his own pleasure; it is an emotional view, without any intention of faithfully depicting this personal space.

Jardín de la casa de Sorolla
(Garden of the Sorolla Family Home)
Detail

Taken out of its context, this chair is completely undefined, almost abstract. The thick, bold brushstrokes, a palette full of lively colours, especially blues, mauves and pinks, the artist's personal gaze, all make this detail a small work of art, a worthy culmination of an artistic career which reached the dizzying heights of art.

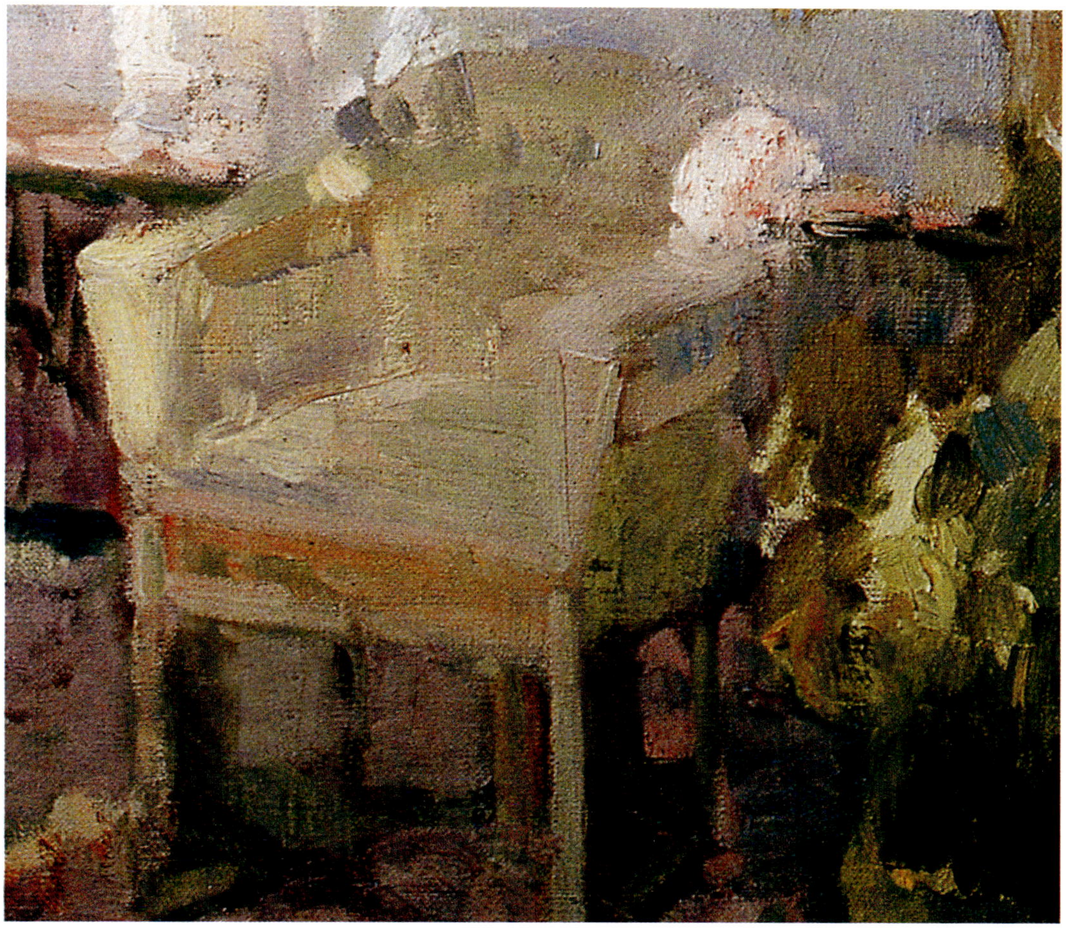

At the time, the only thing that could make up for the artist's absence was the fact that the Hispanic Society was opening up to the art world one of its brightest exhibition rooms in which the stamp of Sorolla's palette vibrated like never before.

During the first summer of his illness, and hoping that something could be done to help the artist, Sorolla's family took him to San Sebastián. But if there was any improvement in his state of health, it was very slight, since a second stroke put an end to any possible hope of recovery. However, he was taken to the same place the following summer and, in 1922, to his Malvarrosa beach in Valencia. It was an especially intense and dramatic moment when the painter, not aware of anything, was carried in an armchair onto the shore by his children who anxiously hoped that the sight of those waters he had painted so many times would cause some kind of reaction on the lifeless face of the artist who had not yet turned sixty. But nothing occurred. For the first time, the grandeur of the sea, the white surf and the gentle sound of the rolling waves caused no effect whatsoever on what used to be the painter's sharp and lively senses.

One year later, on 10th August 1923, he put away his easel and abandoned his paintbrushes forever, but the admiration that he had aroused among his contemporaries would not be forgotten. Although he died 10 years after the arrival of Cubism and Dadaism in New York, and his work was gradually absorbed from then on by the growing wave of the avant-garde movements and because of the consequences of Spain's isolation due to its civil war, Sorolla, with his death and personal style, knew how to elegantly close one of the most brilliant chapters of Spanish painting in which he was known as the master of colour and a very special interpreter of light.

BIBLIOGRAPHY

ABRIL, Marcelo: *Joaquín Sorolla, o la plena luz en nuestra pintura (Pintura Antigua y Moderna)*. Barcelona, 1944.
ACEBAL, Francisco: *Sorolla*, in *La Vanguardia*. Barcelona, 29th May 1944.
AGUILERA, Emiliano M.: *Nuevo Museo madrileño*: *La casa de Sorolla*, in *El Liberal*. Madrid, 7th August 1931.
AGUILERA, Vicente: *Sorolla y Benlliure en el Salón de Otoño*, in *Voz de Galicia*. La Coruña, 25th October 1932.
ALCAHALI, Barón: *Diccionario biográfico de artistas valencianos*. Valencia, 1897.
ALCÁNTARA, Francisco: *El arte español en América: Sorolla y Zuloaga en Nueva York*, in *El Imparcial*. Madrid, 23rd June 1909.
ALDANA, Salvador: *Joaquín Sorolla y su tiempo*, in *Archivo de Arte Valenciano*. Valencia, 1963.
BAROJA, Pío: *Joaquín Sorolla*, in *Informaciones*. Madrid, 25th May 1951.
BERUETE, Aureliano de: *Joaquín Sorolla y Bastida*, in *Ateneo*. Madrid, July 1906.
BERUETE, Aureliano de: *Sorolla*, in *Historia de la Pintura española en el siglo XIX*. Madrid, 1926.
BERUETE, Aureliano de; DOMÉNECH, Rafael, et alter: *Sorolla: Su obra en el arte español y su obra en la Argentina*. Buenos Aires, 1942.
BLASCO IBÁÑEZ, Vicente: *El gran Sorolla*, in *El Pueblo*. Valencia, 9th June 1900 and 31st December 1933.
BLOCH, Herman: *The Sorolla Exhibition of Paintings*, in *The Call*. New York, 25th February 1909.
CAMBA, Francisco: *Sorolla*, in *El Imparcial*. Madrid, 15th February 1918.
CARY, Elizabeth Luther: *Sorolla y Bastida: One of the Great Modern Masters*, in New York Times. New York, 14th February 1909.
DOMÉNECH, Rafael: *El arte de Sorolla y su triunfo en la América del Norte*, in *El Liberal*. Madrid, 3rd March 1909.
EZCURRA, Ángel: *El Mediterráneo, Valencia y Sorolla*, in *ABC*. Madrid, 28th April 1944.
FUSTER, Antonio F.: *J. Sorolla. La grandeza del pequeño formato*. Madrid, 1975.
GAYA NUÑO, Juan Antonio: *Autorretratos de artistas españoles (Esto es España)*. Barcelona, March 1950.
GUILLOT, José: *Joaquín Sorolla. El pincel deslumbrador*. Plasencia, no date.
HUTIN, Marie: *Ateliers d'artistes: Joaquín Sorolla*, in *Journal des Arts*. Paris, 7th April 1906.
LÓPEZ, Mauricio: *Impresiones de Arte*. Madrid, 1931.
MAEZTU, Ramiro de: *Sorolla en Londres*, in *La Prensa*. Buenos Aires, 24th June 1908.
MARTÍNEZ DE LA RIVA, Ramón: *El pintor que aprisionó el sol*, in *Blanco y Negro*. Madrid, 7th April 1918.
NAVASCUÉS, Pilar de: *Sorolla y Sargent. Una relación inédita*, in *Goya*, No. 189. Madrid, November-December 1985.
OSSORIO Y BERNARD, Manuel: *Galería biográfica de artistas españoles del siglo XIX*. Madrid, 1884.
PANTORBA, Bernardino de: *Historia y crítica de las Exposiciones Nacionales de Bellas Artes celebradas en España.*Madrid, 1948.
PANTORBA, Bernardino de: *La pintura de Sorolla*, in *Revista de Ideas Estéticas*. Madrid, October-December 1963.
PANTORBA, Bernardino de: *La vida y la obra de Joaquín Sorolla*. Madrid, 1970.
PEEL, Edmund (coord.): *Joaquín Sorolla y Bastida*. Barcelona, 1990.
ROMERO, José: *La casa en la que nunca se pone el sol*, in *Mundo Gráfico*. Madrid, 7th November 1934.
SÁNCHEZ CANTÓN, Francisco Javier, and PITA ANDRADE, José: *Los retratos de los reyes de España*. Barcelona, 1948.
SAPORI, Francesco: *Artisti stranieri contemporanei: La Spagna di Sorolla*, in *Giornale di Sicilia*. Palermo, 13th September 1934.
SCHARP, Arthur: *The Art of Joaquín Sorolla*. Chicago, 1910.
SIMÓ, Trinidad: *Joaquín Sorolla*. Valencia, 1980.
STEVENSON, Gordon: *Sorolla in Chicago and in Spain*, in *New York Times Book Review and Magazine*. New York, 19th August 1923.
TEIXIDOR, Juan: *Joaquín Sorolla*, in *Destino*. Barcelona, 7th February 1948.
TOWNSEND, James B.: *A Spanish Master's Works*, in *American Art News*. New York, 13th February 1909.
WEDMORE, Frederick: *Sorolla's Art*, in *Pall Mall Gazette*. London, May 1908.
ZABALA, Arturo: *Cuando el joven Sorolla estuvo en Roma*, in *Jornada*. Valencia, 27th May 1944.
ZULUETA, Luis de: *Sorolla en Berlín*, in *Forma*. Barcelona, May 1904.

SOROLLA AND THE CRITICS

"The first painter at this Exhibition, as at many others, has been our fellow countryman Joaquín Sorolla. One only needs to observe how fervently the public flock to see his works to understand that Sorolla is the star of the Exhibition, the artist who reigns over the rest of the exhibitors."

Vicente Blasco Ibáñez, *Crónica artística. Sorolla* (1887)

"Today Sorolla is the best all-round artist of all. He masters every genre, in all of them displaying his prodigious skills; and, as he is extraordinarily perseverant in his work, always spurred on by the incentive of emulation, it is he who has been chosen to command those young people who are so eager for glory, who, with their noble effort, are ready to raise Spanish art to the height it deserves, as Bastien-Lepage has done for French art, Herkommen, English art, Fierle, German art and Ettore Tito, Italian art."

Augusto Comas, *La Exposición Internacional de Bellas Artes de 1892* (1893)

"As usually occurs with everything that is a surprise, a natural wonder, abundance and overabundance, there aren't words to define the personality of Mr. Sorolla ... he is a painter 'who must be successful' in everything he embarks upon."

Arsène Alexandre, *La vie artistique. L'exposition Sorolla* (1906)

"Sorolla is one of the glories of Valencia... he is one of the glories of modern Spain. He is treading on a triumphal path that takes him to the heights of contemporary art and to universal fame ... he is one of the most beautiful painters of all times and the worthy continuer of the great masters of 16th century Spanish painting called Velázquez and Goya."

Max Nordau, *Notas de Arte. Joaquín Sorolla y Bastida. Su obra pictórica* (I906)

"At present Sorolla seems to be at the peak of his career. In the prime of his life, his ambition is stimulated by his success, and each problem overcome strengthens him and spurs him on to make an even greater effort."

Charles M. Kurtz, *A great Spanish artist. Joaquín Sorolla y Bastida* (1907)

"The colourist art of Sorolla y Bastida has the colour of life itself."

Max Ludwig, *Aus den Kunstsalons* (1907)

"Sorolla works like lightning. He first makes a charcoal drawing, and then spreads the colour with large, bold brushstrokes. At the beginning, his canvases look frightfully chaotic."

William E. B. Starkweather, *Joaquín Sorolla, the man and his work* (1909)

"With the exception of Goya, who revolutionised modern art, and to whom he owes a lot, many people think Sorolla y Bastida lies very close behind Velázquez on the list of Spanish great masters."

J. G. Mottet, *Sorolla y Bastida Exhibition* (1909)

"As a permanent memorial of the Sorolla exhibition, the Hispanic Society reprinted eight of the chief appreciations published on the work of this conquering painter of sunlight, adding also the tributes of the press ... This record is of an eminently documental value. The future may take it very seriously as a literary and psychological curiosity. To the present writer it was a disconcerting chorus of praise for a kind of work that he cannot believe has enduring stuff in it. One may agree with everything that is said about Sorolla's athleticism of the brush and ready command of the primary colors, one may accept his gusto without cavil, and yet question whether the zeal that took nearly 160,000 people to see his pictures had much to do with the more permanent qualities in the art ... The future historian of the psychology of the throng will marvel that a New York before whom Besnard and Zorn had been brought, which boasted, itself, an Alden Weir and a Childe Hassam, which knew the work of the consummate technician Tarbell, put itself to sheer physical discomfort to get a passing glimpse of the paintings of Sorolla."

Frank Jewett Mather, Jr., *The Painting of Sorolla* (1910)

"Archer Milton Huntington, the renowned Hispanophile who founded the Hispanic Society, has dedicated an unusual monument to Spain: this room of the provinces, the high altar of a people who engendered an entire world. And this wasn't all that Huntington did: he paid the well-deserved, final tribute to the memory of Joaquín Sorolla, something that hadn't been done in Spain, proclaiming him, with a sole exhibition of these, his final works, the greatest Spanish painter of our times. The greatest! Why not admit it? He can no longer hear us, nor can he thank us for it ... He no longer cares about our praises, and our criticism won't affect him either! Let's be generous with the 'dead who lives', even though the 'living' who die won't forgive us."

Miguel de Zárraga, *El grandioso monumento que acaba de erigirse a España en Nueva York* (1926)

"During these days of 1963 when Spain has celebrated (rather poorly, to be perfectly honest) the one hundredth anniversary of Sorolla's birth, France has also celebrated the anniversary of Delacroix' death with its customary splendour."

Bernardino de Pantorba, *La pintura de Sorolla* (1963)

"I'd invite an expert in Sorolla to carefully review the master's production... not everything has been said about Sorolla."

Enrique Lafuente Ferrari, *prologue to Trinidad Simó, Joaquín Sorolla* (1980)

"The reaction of the critics to Sorolla's painting was very diverse. This was probably due to the natural ideological confrontation among the different artistic trends existing in the late 19th and early 20th centuries [...] The position regarding those who were opposed to his way of painting shows that the effort he made to achieve his ideal was something of which Sorolla was fully aware and not just a casual and irreflexive determination."

Edmund Peel, *Joaquín Sorolla* (1989)

"Sorolla is the most characteristic representative of the national school, ratified by his tremendous triumph at the Exposición Nacional in 1901, with *Triste herencia.* He also presented his Whistlerian-style *La madre* (1855) at this exhibition, which went completely unnoticed, except for one of the most prestigious critics that scornfully described it as 'nothing but a monochromatic touch of colour'."

José Gutiérrez Burón, *Del Realismo al lmpresionismo* (1992)

ALPHABETICAL INDEX OF WORKS